Today, at one and the same time, scholarly publishing is drawn in two directions. On the one hand, this is a time of the most exciting theoretical, political and artistic projects that respond to and seek to move beyond global administered society. On the other hand, the publishing industries are vying for total control of the ever-lucrative arena of scholarly publication, creating a situation in which the means of distribution of books grounded in research and in radical interrogation of the present are increasingly restricted. In this context, MayFlyBooks has been established as an independent publishing house, publishing political, theoretical and aesthetic works on the question of organization. MayFlyBooks publications are published under Creative Commons license free online and in paperback. MayFlyBooks is a not-for-profit operation that publishes books that matter, not because they reinforce or reassure any existing market.

1. Herbert Marcuse, *Negations: Essays in Critical Theory*
2. Dag Aasland, *Ethics and Economy: After Levinas*
3. Gerald Raunig and Gene Ray (eds), *Art and Contemporary Critical Practice: Reinventing Institutional Critique*

ART AND CONTEMPORARY CRITICAL PRACTICE

Art and Contemporary Critical Practice:
Reinventing Institutional Critique

Gerald Raunig and Gene Ray (eds)

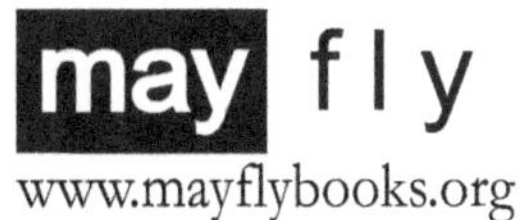

www.mayflybooks.org

First published by MayFlyBooks in paperback in London and free online at www.mayflybooks.org in 2009.

ISBN (Print) 978-1-906948-02-3
ISBN (PDF) 978-1-906948-03-0

This work has been published in conjunction with the European Institute for Progressive Cultural Policies (www.eipcp.net).

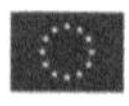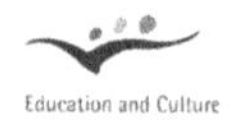

Culture 2000

The publication has been carried out within the framework of transform.eipcp.net and with the support of the Culture 2000 program of the European Union. It reflects the views only of the authors, and the Commission cannot be held responsible for any use which may be made of the information contained therein.

Contents

INSTITUTIONS OF EXODUS

INSTITUENT PRACTICES AND MONSTER INSTITUTIONS

Contributors

Boris Buden is a philosopher living in Berlin. In the 1990s he was editor of the magazine *Arkzin*, Zagreb. Among his translations into Serbocroatian are two books of Sigmund Freud. Buden is the author of *Barikade* (Zagreb 1996/1997), *Kaptolski Kolodvor* (Beograd 2001), *Der Schacht von Babel* (Berlin 2004; *Vavilonska jama*, Beograd 2007) and, together with Stefan Nowotny, *Übersetzung. Das Versprechen eines Begriffs* (Turia + Kant 2008).

Rosalyn Deutsche is a critic and art historian living in New York. She teaches modern and contemporary art, feminist theory and urban theory at Barnard College, Columbia University. Her publications include the influential book *Evictions: Art and Spatial Politics* (MIT Press, 1998).

Marcelo Expósito is an artist mostly based in Barcelona. He was co-founder and co-editor of *Brumaria* magazine (2002-2006). He teaches video theory and history at Facultad de Bellas Artes, Universidad de Castilla-La Mancha (Cuenca), art theory at Universitat Pompeu Fabra (Barcelona), and art and politics at Independent Studies Programm (PEI) at Macba (Barcelona).

Marina Garcés is professor for contemporary philosophy at the University Oberta de Catalunya and at the University of Zaragoza. She is author of the book *In the prisons of the possible* (Ediciones Bellaterra, Barcelona, 2002) and she collaborates with such magazines as *Archipiélago, Zehar* o *Le passant ordinaire* and with institutions such as Arteleku (San Sebastián) o Unia-Arte y pensamiento (Sevilla). Since

2003 she co-ordinates the activity of Espai en Blanc (http://www.espaienblanc.net).

Brian Holmes is a culture critic who works directly with artist and activist groups. He publishes in *Springerin, Brumaria* and *Multitudes*, and is the author of the books *Hieroglyphs of the Future* (Arkzin/WHW, 2002) and *Unleashing the Collective Phantoms* (Autonomedia, 2008).

Jens Kastner is a sociologist and art historian working at the Academy of Fine Arts in Vienna. He is editor of *Bildpunkt: Zeitschrift der IG Bildende Kunst*. His recent books are *Transnationale Guerilla: Aktivismus, Kunst und die kommende Gemeinschaft* (Unrast, 2007) and, together with Bettina Spörr, *nicht alles tun* (Unrast, 2008).

Maurizio Lazzarato is a sociologist, philosopher and independent researcher specializing in studies of relationships of work, economy and society. He is a member of the editorial team of *Multitudes*. His latest publications include *Les révolutions du capitalisme* (Les empêcheurs de penser en rond, 2004) and, together with Antonella Corsani, *Intermittents et Précaires* (éditions Amsterdam, 2008).

Isabell Lorey is a political scientist living in Berlin. From 2001 to 2007 she was assistant professor for Gender & Postcolonial Studies at the University of the Arts Berlin and lecturer at the Center for Transdisciplinary Gender Studies at the Humboldt University Berlin. She has published on feminist and political theory, with special focus on Michel Foucault, biopolitical governmentality and critical whiteness studies. She is currently working on a book about Roman struggles of order, concepts of community and immunization.

Nina Möntmann is Professor and Head of the Department of Art Theory and the History of Ideas at the Royal University College of Fine Arts in Stockholm. From 2003 to 2006 she was Curator at the Nordic Institute for Contemporary Art (NIFCA) in Helsinki. Currently she is curatorial advisor for Manifesta 7, 2008. She is a correspondent for *Artforum*, and contributes to *Le Monde Diplomatique, Parachute, metropolis m, Frieze* and others. Her recent publications include *Kunst als sozialer Raum*, Köln (Walther König, 2002); *Art and its Institutions* (Black Dog Publishing, 2006).

Stefan Nowotny is a philosopher living in Vienna. He works at the eipcp and has published various essays on philosophical and political topics, co-edited several anthologies, and translated texts from both French and English into German. His recent books include: *Instituierende Praxen. Bruchlinien der Institutionskritik* (together with Gerald Raunig, Turia + Kant 2008); *Übersetzung. Das Versprechen eines Begriffs* (together with Boris Buden, Turia + Kant 2008).

Gerald Raunig is a philosopher and art theorist living in Vienna. He works at the eipcp and is co-founder of the magazine *Kulturrisse* and the multilingual web journal *transversal*. Raunig is the author of *Art and Revolution: Transversal Activism in the Long Twentieth Century* (Semiotext(e)/MIT Press 2007) and *A Thousand Machines* (Semiotext(e)/MIT Press, 2009, forthcoming).

Gene Ray is a critic and theorist living in Berlin. A member of the Radical Culture Research Collective (RCRC), he writes frequently for the journals *Third Text* and *Left Curve*. He is the author of *Terror and the Sublime in Art and Critical Theory* (Palgrave Macmillan, 2005) and editor of *Joseph Beuys: Mapping the Legacy* (DAP, 2001). *Whither Tactical Media?*, a special issue of *Third Text* co-edited with Gregory Sholette, has been published in Fall 2008.

Raúl Sánchez Cedillo is a writer and translator living in Madrid. Since 1991 he has been collaborating with the post-operaist research and political networks, and has edited a number of works by Antonio Negri, Félix Guattari and others. Politically, he was active in the antimilitarist and Insumisión movement during the 1990s, later in the okupación and Centros Sociales Okupados movements and the first cyberactivism network in Spain, www.sindominio.net. Since 2000 he's been promoting new self-educational and political projects, mainly the Madrid based Universidad Nómada.

Simon Sheikh is a curator and critic living in Berlin and Copenhagen. He is an Assistant Professor of Art Theory and a Coordinator of the Critical Studies Program, Malmö Art Academy in Sweden. He was director of Overgaden – Institute for Contemporary Art in Copenhagen from 1999 to 2002, and was Curator at NIFCA, Helsinki, from 2003 to 2004. Editor of the magazine *Øjeblikket* (1996-2000), and a member of the project group GLOBE (1993-2000). His recent publications include the anthologies *We are all Normal* (with Katya Sander) (Black Dog Publishing, 2001), *In the Place of the Public Sphere?* (b_books, 2005) and *Capital (It Fails Us Now)*(b_books, 2006).

Hito Steyerl works as a filmmaker, video artist and author in the area of essayist documentary film and postcolonial criticism. A producer as well as theorist, her films have received international awards and are screened on TV in many countries. She is Visiting Professor for Experimental Media Creation at Universität der Künste, Berlin. Her recent book is *Die Farbe der Wahrheit* (Turia + Kant, 2008).

Universidad Nómada http://www.universidadnomada.net/

Paolo Virno is a philosopher who lives in Rome and teaches at the University of Calabria. He was politically active as a member of the Italian political group Potere Operaio during the 1970s, for which he was imprisoned for three years before being acquitted. He is the author of *Convenzione e materialismo* (1986), *Mondanità* (1994), *Parole con parole* (1995), *Il ricordo del presente: Saggio sul tempo storico* (1999), *Grammatica della moltitudine* (2001; in English as *A Grammar of the Multitude*, 2004), *Esercizi di esodo* (2002), *Quando il verbo si fa carne: Linguaggio e natura umana* (2003), *Motto di spirito e azione innovativa* (2005). He is contributor of the philosophical review *Forme di vita*.

Acknowledgments

Many warm thanks to the following friends, participants and supporters of the Transform project:

Andrea Hummer	Brian Holmes
Bernhard Hummer	Imre Szeman
Birgit Mennel	Charles Esche
Raimund Minichbauer	Solvita Krese
Stefan Nowotny	Jorge Ribalta
Boris Buden	Stella Rollig
Aileen Derieg	Ulf Wuggenig
Marcelo Expósito	Wolfie Christl
Therese Kaufmann	Ralf Traunsteiner
Isabell Lorey	MayFlyBooks
Monika Mokre	All partners in the project Transform
Andrea Salzmann	
Simon Sheikh	All *transversal* authors and translators
Hito Steyerl	

Preface

The essays collected in this volume were selected from Transform, a three-year (2005-8) research project of the European Institute for Progressive Cultural Policies (eipcp). Following up on the eipcp's previous Republicart project (2002-5), Transform supported a wide range of activities, research and exchanges focused on investigating political and artistic practices of 'institutional critique'. These included exhibitions, conferences and the publication of the web journal *transversal*, in which all of the following essays appeared.

For the Transform project, artists, activists, writers, theorists and researchers were encouraged to interrogate the history of the relations between 'institutions' and 'critique' and to consider the present and future possibilities for the theory and practice of institutional critique along three related but still distinct lines of inquiry. These lines were sketched as follows at the beginning of the project, in the summer of 2005:

1. The line of art production. The thesis here is that following the two phases of institutional critique in the 1970s and 1990s, now a new phase of critique is emerging, which goes beyond the two earlier phases, particularly as a combination of social critique, institutional critique and self-critique.

2. The line of art institutions. Here questions will be raised about the development of radical positions taken by critical art institutions, not only against the background that open, socially critical art associations, museums and initiatives are increasingly under pressure, partly from authoritarian repressive cultural policies, partly

from neo-liberal populist cultural policies. Beyond this defensive figure and the question of counter-strategies, new forms of the organization of critical art institutions are to be reflected on.

3. The line of the relationship of institution and critique as movement: at this most general level the question of the mutual interrelationship of institution and movement, machines and state apparatuses, is to be addressed, and how this relationship can be made productive in the sense of emancipatory policies and beyond the abrupt demarcation between the two poles.

From the beginning of the Transform project, it was clear that 'institutional critique' has long been an established stream of artistic practices with, now, well over three decades of history and development behind it. From its now almost mythical origins, this stream has given rise to transversal practices that cannot be classified as purely or exclusively 'artistic'. The institutional critique of the 1960s and 70s formed a loose, barely coherent nexus that can only be understood within the context of micro and macro-political developments before and around 1968. Accordingly, the Transform project has oscillated over the last three years between the three lines sketched at the outset and the fields and practices from which they can hardly be separated. At the same time, a movement became discernible – even if not a rigidly linear one – from the major concerns of the first to the second and finally the third line of inquiry.

I. What is Institutional Critique?

The timeliness of the project quickly became apparent. Although it was conceived in 2004, its concrete beginnings in September 2005 coincided with a wave of renewed interest in institutional critique within the field of art itself – an interest confirmed by a series of symposia, publications and themed issues of art journals and magazines. These debates, which included diverse perspectives on the genealogy of institutional critique and on the operations of its canonization, are fully reflected in the first of twelve Transform issues of the web journal *transversal*, under the title 'Do You Remember Institutional Critique?' (January 2006). What appears in retrospect as the 'first wave' of institutional critique was initiated in the 1960s and 70s by artists such as Michael Asher, Robert Smithson, Daniel Buren, Hans Haacke and Marcel Broodthaers, among others. They investigated the conditions of the museum and art field, aiming to oppose, subvert or break out of rigid institutional frameworks. In the late 1980s and 90s, in a changed context, these practices were developed into diverse artistic projects by new protagonists like Renee Green, Christian Philipp Müller, Fred Wilson and Andrea Fraser. To the economic and political discourse of their predecessors, the practices of this 'second generation' added a growing awareness of the forms of subjectivity and the modes of its formation. Second wave practices continued however to circulate under the name of institutional critique.

The process by which these first two waves of institutional critique have become a recognized part of art history was not without controversy and debate. Still, the canonization of these practices proceeds on a terrain that is quite orderly, operates by clear rules and borders, and is characterized by a certain amount of depoliticization and self-reference. However, our thesis concerning a 'third phase' of institutional critique provoked some very different interpretations among the participants of the Transform project. Some of the authors in this book focus on art institutions themselves, insofar as these are emerging as the new and paradoxical agents of institutional critique. Others seek to analyze the 'extradisciplinary investigations' undertaken by contemporary artist-activists and to reflect on what some see as a new artistic internationalism developing in conjunction with political activism. And while the attention of the mainstream art world has moved on from the debates about institutional critique, the question of the character of, what we have called, 'instituent practices' remains especially relevant for the actors in the overlapping fields of art and politics. Without over-determining the concept of 'instituent practices', we can say that it refers to strategies and initiated processes that in some respects take their bearings from traditions of institutional critique, even as in other respects they go beyond anything recognizable in the movement now canonized as part of art history. As the texts in this volume show, this tendency towards new activist and instituent practices is one direction in which practitioners and theorists are actively attempting to renew and reinvent institutional critique under difficult contemporary conditions.

II. Institutions of Exodus

The second line of inquiry inescapably had to pass through a reflection on the pressure of economic and administrative logics bearing down on all institutions in the cultural field, including those with which the eipcp has collaborated in realizing the Transform project. The eipcp's own position as 'project institution' within the paradoxes of a relative and critical autonomy created a self-reflexive debate on the future of critical institutions as such. In fact, the very idea of a 'project institution' is glaringly contradictory. For if the concept of 'institution' implies a desire for long-term duration, continuity and security, the concept of 'project' by contrast implies limited duration and the negative effects, such as precarization and insecurity, associated with it. Accordingly, one issue of *transversal* took on the tasks of reflecting on the conditions that make critical institutions possible and of seeking to specify the modes of action for politicizing these conditions, fractures and contradictions under the title 'Progressive Institutions' (April 2007).

The questions that begin to emerge at this point are of course not limited to institutions of the cultural field: they concern the conditions for critical and resistant institutions generally. Various recent approaches in philosophy and political theory, including those advanced by Gilles Deleuze, Michel Foucault, Judith Butler, Antonio Negri and Paolo Virno, among others, as well as by some authors in the present volume, have undertaken to develop a 'non-dialectical' concept of resistance and critique, one seeking above all to establish a different conceptualization of contradiction, negation and reaction. The proposals for this conceptual development extend from the various figures of 'flight' (nomadism, desertion, destitution, withdrawal and treason) to differing concepts of 'exodus'. As thought by the authors in this volume, exodus is not a naïve exit 'out of every kind of institution', but refers rather to the deliberations and actualizations of 'institutions of exodus'.

III. Instituent Practices and Monster Institutions

Over the course of the project, the third line of inquiry brought the relations between social movements and their institutions to the foreground. In play here are the marked degradation of representative democracy in Europe, the frustrations and processes of internal transformation to be seen in the alter-globalization movement following September 11 and the so-called 'war on terror', as well as increasing social marginalization and misery seen by many as an effect of national and transnational institutions. In any case, the third line helped to clarify as a concrete question the problem that became central to the debates generated by the project: which form of institutions and instituting do contemporary social movements need?

For answers to questions of this kind, two concepts became most important for the project: 'instituent practices' and 'monster institutions'. Deriving from Antonio Negri's concept of 'constituent power', understood as a permanent process of *con*stitution, *in*stituent practices thwart the logics of institutionalization; they invent new forms of instituting and continuously link these instituting events. Against this background, the concept of 'instituent practices' marks the site of a productive tension between a new articulation of critique and the attempt to arrive at a notion of 'instituting' after traditional understandings of institutions have begun to break down and mutate. When we speak of an 'instituent practice', this actualization of the future in a present becoming is not the opposite of institution in the way that utopia, for instance, is the opposite of bad reality. Nor is it to be understood simply in the way that Antonio Negri's concept pair 'constituent power/constituted power' is conceptualized, necessarily in relation to being instituted or constituted power. Rather, 'instituent practice' as a process and concatenation of instituent events means an absolute concept exceeding mere opposition to institutions: it does not oppose the institution, but it does flee from institutionalization and structuralization.

But while fleeing, 'instituent practice' searches for a weapon. Introducing monsters into existing institutions, it gives birth to new forms of institutions, monster institutions. Deliberations of such a kind led, by the end of the project, to a collaboration with the Spanish Universidad Nómada on an issue of *transversal* entitled 'Monster Institutions' (May 2008). The essays in it reflect on the possibilities for new forms of institutionality in conjunction with social movements and with a clear focus on the new generation of social centers in Europe. From this perspective it is also possible to reverse the movement described above: the transversal quality of artistic institutional critique does not only challenge and thwart the borders of the field of art; the strategies and specific competencies of art can also be deployed to spur on a general reflection on the problems of institutions, the predicaments of critique and the openings for new 'instituent practices'.

xviii

I

WHAT IS INSTITUTIONAL CRITIQUE?

1

Instituent Practices: Fleeing, Instituting, Transforming[*]

Gerald Raunig

(Translated by Aileen Derieg)

When we propose in the announcement of our Transform project the provisional thesis that a new 'phase' of institutional critique will now emerge,[1] following the two previous 'phases' – the first beginning in the late 1960s, the second in the late 1980s – this thesis is based less on empirical evidence than on a political and theoretical necessity to be found in the logic of institutional critique itself. Both 'phases' of this now-canonized practice developed their own strategies and methods within their respective contexts. The resemblances between them are deep – and go beyond even what the categories of art history and criticism would suggest. At the same time, there are clear divergences grounded in the differing social and political conditions within which each emerged. Things have changed tremendously since Michael Asher, Robert Smithson, Daniel Buren, Hans Haacke, Marcel Broodthaers and others initiated what appears in retrospect as the first wave of institutional critique. In the late 1980s and 90s, in a changed context, these practices developed into diverse artistic projects that continued to circulate under the same name. Now, if institutional critique is not to be fixed and paralyzed as something established in the field of art and remaining constrained by its rules, then it must continue to change and develop in a changing society. It must link up with other forms of critique both within and outside the art field – whether these forms emerged in opposition to existing conditions or were the resistance that provoked those conditions in the first place.[2] Against the background of this kind of transversal exchange among forms of critique – but also without naively imagining spaces somehow free from domination and

3

institutions – institutional critique needs to be rethought as a critical attitude and as what I call an 'instituent practice'.

In his 1978 lecture 'What is Critique?' Michel Foucault describes the spread and replication of governmentality in Western Europe in the sixteenth century, claiming that along with this governmentalization of all possible areas of life and finally of the self, critique also developed as the art not to be governed *like that*. Even without going into more depth here on the continuities and breaks between the historical forms of developing liberal governmentality and the current forms of neo-liberal governmentality (see Isabell Lorey's essay in the third section of this volume), it may be said that the relationship between *government* and *not to be governed like that* is still a prerequisite today for reflecting on the contemporary relationship between institution and critique. In Foucault's words:

> [T]his governmentalization, which seems to me to be rather characteristic of these societies in Western Europe in the sixteenth century, cannot apparently be dissociated from the question 'how not be governed?' I do not mean by that that governmentalization would be opposed in a kind of face-off by the opposite affirmation, 'we do not want to be governed, and we do not want to be governed *at all*'. I mean that, in this great preoccupation about the way to govern and the search for the ways to govern, we identify a perpetual question which could be: 'how not be governed *like that*, by that, in the name of those principles, with such and such an objective in mind and by means of such procedures, not like that, not for that, not by them'. (Foucault, 1997a: 28)

Here Foucault insists on the shift from a fundamental negation of government toward a maneuver to avoid this kind of dualism: from *not to be governed at all* to *not to be governed like that*, from a phantom battle for a *big other* to a constant struggle in the plane of immanence, which – as I would like to add – is not (solely) actualized as a fundamental critique of institutions, but rather as a permanent process of instituting. Foucault continues:

> And if we accord this movement of governmentalization of both society and individuals the historic dimension and breadth which I believe it has had, it seems that one could approximately locate therein what we could call the critical attitude. Facing them head on and as compensation, or rather, as both partner and adversary to the arts of

governing, as an act of defiance, as a challenge, as a way of limiting these arts of governing and sizing them up, transforming them, of finding a way to escape from them or, in any case, a way to displace them. (Foucault, 1997a: 28)

These latter categories are the ones I want to focus on in terms of the transformation and further development of the question of contemporary forms of institutional critique: transformations as ways of escaping from the arts of governing, lines of flight, which are not at all to be taken as harmless or individualistic or escapist and esoteric, even if they no longer allow dreaming of an entirely different exteriority. "Nothing is more active than a flight!" as Gilles Deleuze and Claire Parnet write (2002: 36) and as Paolo Virno echoes almost literally: "Nothing is less passive than the act of fleeing, of exiting" (2004a: 70).

If the 'arts of governing' mean an intertwining of governing and being governed, government and self-government, then *'transforming* the arts of governing' does not consist simply of any arbitrary transformation processes in the most general sense, because transformations are an essential aspect of the context of governmentality itself. It is more a matter of specifically *emancipatory* transformations, and this also rescinds a central aspect of the old institutional critique. Through their emancipatory character these transformations also assume a transversal quality, i.e. their effects extend beyond the bounds of particular fields.

In contrast to these kinds of emancipatory transversal transformations of the 'arts of governing', there is a recurring problem in art discourse: that of reducing and enclosing more general questions in one's own field. Even though (self-)canonizations, valorizations and depreciations in the art field – as well as in debates on institutional critique practices – are often adorned with an eclectic, disparate and contradictory selection of theory imports, these imports frequently only have the function of disposing of specific art positions or the art field. A contemporary variation of this functionalization consists of combining poststructuralist immanence theories with a simplification of Pierre Bourdieu's field theory. The theories that argue, on the one hand, against an outside in the sense of Christian or socialist transcendence, for instance, and, on the other, for the relative autonomy of the art field, are blurred here into the defeatist statement, "We are trapped in our field" (Fraser, 2005). Even the critical actors of the 'second generation' of institutional critique do not appear to be free from these kinds of closure phantasms. Fraser, for instance, conducts an offensive self-historicization in her essay 'From the Critique of Institutions to an Institution of Critique', published in *Artforum* in 2005. In her account, all possible forms of institutional critique are ultimately limited to a critique of the 'institution of art' (Bürger, 1984) and its sub-institutions. Invoking Bourdieu, she writes:

> [J]ust as art cannot exist outside the field of art, we cannot exist outside the field of art, at least not as artists, critics, curators, etc. And what we do outside the field, to the extent that it remains outside, can have no effect within it. So if there is no outside for us, it is not because the institution is perfectly closed, or exists as an apparatus in a 'totally administered society', or has grown all-encompassing in size and scope. It is because the institution is inside of us, and we can't get outside of ourselves. (Fraser, 2005: 282)

Although there seems to be an echo of Foucault's concept of self-government here, there is no indication of forms of escaping, shifting, transforming. Whereas for Foucault the critical attitude appears simultaneously as 'partner' and as 'adversary' of the arts of governing, the second part of this specific ambivalence vanishes in Fraser's account, yielding to a discursive self-limitation that barely permits reflection on one's own enclosure. Against all the evidence that art – and not only critical art – over the whole twentieth century produced effects that went beyond the restricted field of art, she plays a worn-out record: art is and remains autonomous, its function limited to its own field. "With each attempt to evade the limits of institutional determination, to embrace an outside, we expand our frame and bring more of the world into it. But we never escape it" (Fraser, 2005: 282).

Yet exactly this kind of constriction is refused in Foucault's concept of critique, the critical attitude: instead of inducing the closure of the field with theoretical arguments and promoting this practically, thus carrying out the art of governing, a different form of art should be pushed at the same time which leads to *escaping the arts of governing*. And Foucault is not the only one to introduce these new non-escapist terms of escape. Figures of flight, of dropping out, of betrayal, of desertion, of exodus: these are the figures that several authors advance as post-structuralist, non-dialectical forms of resistance in refusal of cynical or conservative invocations of inescapability and hopelessness. With these kinds of concepts Gilles Deleuze, Paolo Virno and others attempt to propose new models of non-representationist politics that can be turned equally against Leninist concepts of revolution aimed at taking over the state and against radical anarchist positions imagining an absolute outside of institutions, as well as against concepts of transformation and transition in the sense of a successive homogenization in the direction of neo-liberal globalization. In terms of their new concept of resistance, the aim is to thwart a dialectical idea of power and resistance: a positive form of dropping out, a flight that is simultaneously an 'instituent practice'. Instead of presupposing conditions of domination as an immutable horizon and yet fighting against them, this flight changes the conditions under which the presupposition takes place. As Paolo Virno writes in *The Grammar of the Multitude*, exodus transforms "the context within which a problem has arisen, rather than facing this problem by opting for one or the other of the provided alternatives" (Virno, 2004a: 70).

When figures of flight are imported into the art field, this often leads to the misunderstanding that it involves the subject's personal retreat from the noise and babble of the world. Protagonists such as Herman Melville's Bartleby in Deleuze and Giorgio Agamben or the 'virtuoso' pianist Glenn Gould in Virno are seen as personifications of individual resistance and – in the case of Bartleby – of individual withdrawal. In a conservative process of pilferage and reinterpretation, in critical art discourse these figures are displaced so far from their starting point that flight no longer implies, as it does with Deleuze, fleeing to look for a weapon. On the contrary, here the old images of retreat into an artist hermitage are rehashed, which are not only deployed by the new circles of cultural pessimism against participative and relational spectacle art, but also against collective interventionist, activist or other experimental strategies. For example, when *Texte zur Kunst* editor Isabelle Graw turns to "the model of the preoccupied painter working away in his studio, refusing to give any explanation, ostentatiously not networking, never travelling, hardly showing himself in public", it is allegedly to prevent the principle of the spectacle from "directly accessing his mental and emotional competencies" (Graw, 2005: 46).

Although Graw refers to Paolo Virno directly before the passage quoted, neither Virno's problematization of the culture industry nor his concept of exodus tends toward these kinds of bourgeois expectations of salvation by the artist-individual. With the image of the solitary painter, who eludes the "new tendency in capitalism to take over the whole person" (Graw, 2005: 47) by obstinately withdrawing his person, Graw links a contemporary analysis with an ultra-conservative result. Even after the countless spectacular utilizations of this stereotype, it appears that the same old artist image – contrary to Virno's ideas of virtuosity – can today still or once again be celebrated as anti-spectacular.

What the poststructuralist proposals for dropping out and withdrawal involve, however, is anything but this kind of relapse into the celebration of an individual turning away from society. The point is to thwart dichotomies such as that of the individual and the collective, to offensively theorize new forms of what is common and singular at the same time. Paolo Virno in particular has lucidly developed this idea in *A Grammar of the Multitude*. Alluding to Karl Marx's notion of the 'general intellect' from the *Grundrisse*, Virno posits the notion of a 'public intellect'. Following Marx, 'intellect' is not to be understood here as a competence of an individual, but rather as a shared link and constantly developing foundation for individuation. Thus Virno neither alludes to media intellectuals in the society of the spectacle, nor to the lofty ideas of the autonomous thinker or painter. That kind of individualized publicity corresponds more to Virno's negative concept of 'publicness without a public sphere': "The *general intellect*, or public intellect, if it does not become a *republic*, a public sphere, a political community, drastically increases forms of submission" (Virno, 2004a: 41).

Virno focuses, on the other hand, on the social quality of the intellect.[3] Whereas the alienated thinker (or even painter) is traditionally drawn as an individual withdrawing from idle talk, from the noise of the masses, for Virno the noise of the multitude is itself the site of a non-state, non-spectacular, non-representationist public sphere. This non-state public sphere is not to be understood as an anarchic place of absolute freedom, as an open field beyond the realm of the institution. Flight and exodus are nothing negative, not a reaction to something else, but are instead linked and intertwined with constituent power, re-organizing, re-inventing and instituting. The movement of flight also preserves these 'instituent practices' from structuralization and closure from the start, preventing them from becoming institutions in the sense of constituted power.

What does this mean in relation to the artistic practices of institutional critique? From a 'schematic perspective', the 'first generation' of institutional critique sought a *distance from* the institution; the 'second' addressed the inevitable *involvement in* the institution. I call this a schematic perspective, because these kinds of 'generation clusters' are naturally blurred in the relevant practices, and there were attempts – by Andrea Fraser, for instance – to describe the first wave as being constituted by the second (including herself) and also to attribute to the first phase a similar reflectedness on their own institutionality. Whether this is the case or not, an important and effective position can be attributed to both generations in the art field from the 1970s to the present, and in some cases relevance is evident that goes beyond the boundaries of the field. Yet the fundamental questions that Foucault already implicitly raised, which Deleuze certainly pursued in his book on Foucault, are not posed with the strategies of distanced and deconstructive intervention in the institution: do Foucault's considerations lead us to enclose ourselves more and more in power relations? And most of all, which lines of flight lead out of the dead end of this enclosure?

To make use of Foucault's treatments of this problem for the question of new 'instituent practices', I would like to conclude this article by returning to the later Foucault, specifically to his Berkeley lecture series 'Discourse and Truth', delivered in the autumn of 1983, and to the term *parrhesia* broadly explained there.[4]

In classical Greek, *parrhesia* means 'to say everything', freely speaking truth without rhetorical games and without ambiguity, even and especially when this is hazardous. Foucault describes the practice of *parrhesia* using numerous examples from ancient Greek literature as a movement from a political to a personal technique. The older form of *parrhesia* corresponds to publicly speaking truth as an institutional right. Depending on the form of the state, the subject addressed by the *parrhesiastes* is the assembly in the democratic agora, the tyrant in the monarchical court.[5] *Parrhesia* is generally understood as coming from below and directed upward, whether it is the philosopher's criticism of the tyrant or the citizen's criticism of the majority in the agora: the specific potentiality of *parrhesia* is found in the unequivocal gap between the one who takes a risk to express everything and the criticized sovereign who is impugned by this truth.

Over the course of time, a change takes place in the game of truth "which – in the classical Greek conception of *parrhesia* – was constituted by the fact that someone was courageous enough to tell the truth to *other people*… [T]here is a shift from that kind of *parrhesiastic* game to another truth game which now consists in being courageous enough to disclose the truth about *oneself*" (Foucault, 1997b: 150). This process from public criticism to personal (self-)criticism develops in parallel to the decrease in the significance of the democratic public sphere of the agora. At the same time, *parrhesia* comes up increasingly in conjunction with education. One of Foucault's relevant examples here is Plato's dialogue *Laches*, in which the question of the best teacher for the interlocutor's sons represents the starting point and foil. The teacher Socrates no longer assumes the function of the *parrhesiastes* in the sense of exercising dangerous contradiction in a political sense, but rather by moving his listeners to give account of themselves and leading them to a self-questioning that queries the relationship between their statements (*logos*) and their way of living (*bios*). However, this technique does not serve as an autobiographical confession or examination of conscience or as a prototype of Maoist self-criticism, but rather to establish a relationship between rational discourse and the lifestyle of the interlocutor or the self-questioning person. Contrary to any individualistic interpretation especially of later Foucault texts (imputing a 'return to subject philosophy', etc.), here *parrhesia* is not the competency of a subject, but rather a movement between the position that queries the concordance of *logos* and *bios*, and the position that exercises self-criticism in light of this query.

In keeping with a productive interpretation for contemporary institutional critique practices, my aim here is to link the two concepts of *parrhesia* described by Foucault as a genealogical development, to understand hazardous refutation in its relation to self-revelation. Critique, and especially institutional critique, is not exhausted in denouncing abuses nor in withdrawing into more or less radical self-questioning. In terms of the art field this means that neither the belligerent strategies of the institutional critique of the 1970s nor art as a service to the institution in the 1990s promise effective interventions in the governmentality of the present.

What is needed here and now is *parrhesia* as a double strategy: as an attempt of involvement and engagement in a process of hazardous refutation, and as self-questioning. What is needed, therefore, are practices that conduct radical social criticism, yet which do not fancy themselves in an imagined distance to institutions; at the same time, practices that are self-critical and yet do not cling to their own involvement, their complicity, their imprisoned existence in the art field, their fixation on institutions and the institution, their own being-institution. 'Instituent practices' that conjoin the advantages of both 'generations' of institutional critique, thus exercising both forms of *parrhesia*, will impel a linking of social criticism, institutional critique and self-criticism. This link will develop, most of all, from the direct and indirect concatenation with political practices and social movements, but without dispensing with artistic competences and strategies, without dispensing with resources of and effects in the art field. Here exodus would not mean relocating to a different country or a different field, but betraying the rules of the game through the act of flight: 'transforming the arts of governing' not only in relation to the institutions of the art field or the institution art as the art field, but rather as participation in processes of instituting and in political practices that traverse the fields, the structures, the institutions.

Notes

*   The author thanks Isabell Lorey and Stefan Nowotny for critical remarks and advice.

1. The project announcement, first published online in 2005, is reprinted – in revised format – in the preface to this volume.

2. On the temporal and ontological priority of critique-resistance, see Deleuze: "The final word of power is that resistance comes first" (1988: 89, trans. modified). See also Raunig (2007: 48-54).

3. Klaus Neundlinger and I discuss the social character of 'intellect' more fully in our introduction to the German edition of *A Grammar of the Multitude* (Virno, 2005: 9-21).

4. My ideas on Foucault and *parrhesia* were first developed for the eipcp conference 'Progressive Art Institutions in the Age of the Dissolving Welfare State', held in Vienna in 2004, and first published online (Raunig, 2004).

5. The oldest example of political *parrhesia* is the figure of Diogenes, who, precarious in his barrel, commands Alexander to move out of his light. Like the citizen expressing a minority opinion in the democratic setting of the agora, the cynic philosopher also practices a form of *parrhesia* with regard to the monarch in public.

2

The Institution of Critique

Hito Steyerl

In speaking about the critique of institutions, the problem we ought to consider is the opposite one: the institution of critique. Is there anything like an institution of critique and what does it mean? Isn't it pretty absurd to argue that something like this exists at a moment when critical cultural institutions are undoubtedly being dismantled, underfunded, subjected to the demands of a neo-liberal event economy and so on? However, I would like to pose the question on a much more fundamental level. The question is: what is the internal relationship between critique and institution? What sort of relation exists between the institution and its critique or on the other hand – the institutionalization of critique? And what is the historical and political background for this relationship?

To get a clearer picture of this relationship we must first consider the function of criticism in general. On a very general level, certain political, social or individual subjects are formed through the critique of institutions. Bourgeois subjectivity as such was formed through such a process of critique, and encouraged to leave behind 'self-incurred immaturity', to quote Immanuel Kant's famous definition of enlightenment (Kant, 2000: 54). This critical subjectivity was of course ambivalent, since it entailed the use of reason only in those situations we would consider as apolitical today, namely in the deliberation of abstract problems, but not the criticism of authority. Critique produces a subject who should make use of reason in public circumstances, but not in private ones. While this sounds emancipatory, the opposite is the case. The criticism of authority is according to Kant futile and private.

Freedom consists in accepting that authority should not be questioned. Thus, this form of criticism produces a very ambivalent and governable subject; it is as much a tool of governance as of that resistance with which it is often assumed to be aligned. But the bourgeois subjectivity formed thereby was very efficient. And in a certain sense, institutional criticism is integrated into that subjectivity, something which Karl Marx and Friedrich Engels explicitly refer to in their *Communist Manifesto*, namely as the capacity of the bourgeoisie to abolish and to melt down outdated institutions and everything else that is useless and petrified, as long as the general form of authority itself isn't threatened. The bourgeois class had formed through a limited, so to speak, institutionalized critique and also maintained and reproduced itself through its continuous application. And in this way critique had become an institution in itself, a governmental tool that produces streamlined subjects.

But there is also another form of subjectivity that is produced by criticism and also institutional criticism. An obvious example is the French citizen, a political subject of French formed through an institutional critique of the French monarchy. The latter institution was eventually abolished and even beheaded. In this process, an appeal was already realized that Marx was to launch much later: the weapons of critique should be replaced by the critique of weapons. In this vein one could say that the proletariat as a political subject was produced through the criticism of the bourgeoisie as an institution. This second form produces forms of subjectivity that probably are just as ambivalent, but with a crucial difference: it abolishes the institution that it criticizes instead of reforming or improving it.

So in this sense institutional critique serves as a tool of subjectivation of certain social groups or political subjects. And which sort of different subjects does it produce? Let's take a look at different modes of institutional critique within the artfield of the last decades.

To simplify a complex development: the first wave of institutional criticism in the art sphere in the 1970s questioned the authoritarian role of the cultural institution. It challenged the authority that had accumulated in cultural institutions within the framework of the nation state. Cultural institutions such as museums had taken on a complex governmental function. This role has been brilliantly described by Benedict Anderson in his seminal work *Imagined Communities*, where he analyzes the role of the museum in the formation of colonial nation states. In his view, the museum, in creating a national past, retroactively also created the origin and foundation of the nation, and that was its main function (Anderson, 1983). But this colonial situation, as in many other cases, points at the structure of the cultural institution within the nation state in general. And this situation, the authoritarian legitimation of the nation state by the cultural institution through the construction of a history, a patrimony, a heritage, a canon and so on, was the one that the first wave of institutional critique set out to criticize in the 1970s.

Their justification in doing so was ultimately a political one. Most nation states considered themselves to be democracies founded on the political mandate of the people or citizens. In that sense, it was easy to argue that any national cultural institution should reflect this self-definition and that any national cultural institution should thus be founded on similar mechanisms. If the political national sphere was – at least in theory – based on democratic participation, why should the cultural national sphere and its construction of histories and canons be any different? Why shouldn't the cultural institution be at least as representative as parliamentary democracy? Why shouldn't it include for example women in its canon, if women were at least in theory accepted in parliament? In that sense the claims that the first wave of institutional critique voiced were of course founded in contemporary theories of the public sphere, and based on an interpretation of the cultural institution as a potential public sphere. But implicitly they relied on two fundamental assumptions. First, this public sphere was implicitly a national one because it was modeled after the model of representative parliamentarism. Institutional critique justified itself precisely on this point. Since the political system of the nation state is at least in theory representative of its citizens, why shouldn't a national cultural institution be? And this analogy was more often than not grounded in material conditions, since most cultural institutions were funded by the state. Thus, this form of institutional critique relied on a model based on the structure of political participation within the nation state and a Fordist economy, in which taxes could be collected for such purposes.

Institutional critique of this period related to these phenomena in different ways. Either by radically negating institutions altogether, by trying to build alternative institutions or by trying to be included in mainstream ones. Just as in the political arena, the most effective strategy was a combination of the second and third model, which demanded for example that cultural institutions include minorities and disadvantaged majorities such as women. In this sense institutional critique functioned like the related paradigms of multiculturalism, reformist feminism, ecological movements and so on. It was a new social movement within the arts scene.

But during the next wave of institutional criticism in the 1990s, the situation was somewhat different. It wasn't much different from the point of view of the artists or those who tried to challenge and criticize institutions that, in their view, were still authoritarian. Rather, the main problem was that they had been overtaken by a right-wing form of bourgeois institutional criticism, precisely the process by which "all that is solid melts into air" (Marx and Engels, 1998: 38). Thus, the claim that the cultural institution ought to be a public sphere was no longer unchallenged. The bourgeoisie had de facto decreed that a cultural institution was primarily an economic one and as such had to be subjected to the laws of the market. The belief that cultural institutions ought to provide a representative public sphere broke down with Fordism, and it is not by chance that, in a sense, institutions which still adhere to the ideal of creating a public sphere have survived longer in places where Fordism is still hanging on. Thus, the second wave of institutional critique was in a sense unilateral since claims were made which at that time had at least partially lost their legitimative power.

The next factor was the relative transformation of the national cultural sphere that mirrored the transformation of the political cultural sphere. First of all, the nation state is no longer the only framework of cultural representation – there are also supranational bodies like the European Union. And secondly, their mode of political representation is very complicated and only partly representative. It represents its constituencies symbolically rather than materially. To play on the additional meanings in the German word for 'representation': *Sie stellen sie eher dar, als sie sie vertreten* ('They *portray* more than they *represent*'). Thus, why should a cultural institution materially represent its constituency? Isn't it somehow sufficient to symbolically represent it? And although the production of a national cultural identity and heritage is still important, it is not only important for the interior or social cohesion of the nation, but also very much to provide it with international selling points in an increasingly globalized cultural economy. Thus, in a sense, a process was initiated which is still going on today. That is the process of the cultural or symbolic integration of critique into the institution or rather only into the surface of the institution without materially altering the institution or its organization in any deeper sense. This mirrors a similar process on the political level: the symbolic integration of minorities, for example, while maintaining political and social inequality, the symbolic representation of constituencies into supranational political bodies and so on. In this sense the bond of material representation was broken and replaced with a more symbolic one.

This shift in representational techniques by the cultural institution also mirrored a trend in criticism itself, namely the shift from a critique of institution towards a critique of representation. This trend, which was informed by cultural studies, feminist and postcolonial epistemologies, somehow continued in the vein of the previous institutional critique by comprehending the whole sphere of representation as a public sphere, where material representation ought to be implemented, for example in form of the unbiased and proportional display of images of women or black people. This claim somehow mirrors the confusion about representation on the political plane, since the realm of visual representation is even less representative in the material sense than a supranational political body. It doesn't represent constituencies or subjectivities but creates them; it articulates bodies, affects and desires. But this is not exactly how it was comprehended, since it was rather taken for a sphere where one has to achieve hegemony – a majority on the level of symbolic representation, so to speak – in order to achieve an improvement of a diffuse area hovering between politics and economy, state and market, subject as citizen and subject as consumer, as well as between representation and representation. Since criticism could no longer establish clear antagonisms in this sphere, it started to fragment and to atomize it, and to support a politics of identity which led to the fragmentation of public spheres and their replacement by markets, to the culturalization of identity and so on.

This representational critique pointed at another aspect, namely the unmooring of the seemingly stable relation between the cultural institution and the nation state. Unfortunately for institutional critics of that period, a model of purely symbolic representation gained legitimacy in this field as well. Institutions no longer claimed to materially represent the nation state and its constituency, but only claimed to represent it symbolically. And thus, while one could say that the former institutional critics were either integrated into the institution or not, the second wave of institutional critique was integrated not into the institution but into representation as such. Thus, again, a Janus-faced subject was formed. This subject was interested in more diverse and less homogenous forms of representation than its predecessor. But in trying to create this diversity, it also created niche markets, specialized consumer profiles, and an overall spectacle of 'difference' – without effectuating much structural change.

But which conditions are prevailing today, during what might tentatively be called an extension of the second wave of institutional critique? Artistic strategies of institutional critique have become increasingly complex. They have fortunately developed far beyond the ethnographic urge to indiscriminately drag underprivileged or unusual constituencies into museums, even against their will – just for the sake of 'representation'. They include detailed investigations, such as for example Allan Sekula's *Fish Story*, which connects a phenomenology of new cultural industries, like the Bilbao Guggenheim, with documents of other institutional constraints, such as those imposed by the World Trade Organization or other global economic organizations. They have learned to walk the tightrope between the local and the global without becoming either indigenist and ethnographic, or else unspecific and snobbish. Unfortunately, this cannot be said of most cultural institutions that would have to react to the same challenge of having to perform both within a national cultural sphere and an increasingly globalizing market.

If you look at them from one side, then you will see that they are under pressure from indigenist, nationalist and nativist demands. If you look from the other side, then you will see that they are under pressure from neo-liberal institutional critique, that is to say, under the pressure of the market. Now the problem is – and this is indeed a very widespread attitude – that when a cultural institution comes under pressure from the market, it tries to retreat into a position which claims that it is the duty of the nation state to fund it and to keep it alive. The problem with that position is that it is an ultimately protectionist one, that it ultimately reinforces the construction of national public spheres and that under this perspective the cultural institution can only be defended in the framework of a New Left attitude seeking to retreat into the remnants of a demolished national welfare state and its cultural shells and to defend them against all intruders. In other words, it tends to defend itself ultimately from the perspective of its other enemies, namely the nativist and indigenist critics of institution, who want to transform it into a sort of sacralized ethnopark. But there is no going back to the old Fordist nation-state protectionism, with its cultural nationalism, at least not in any emancipatory perspective.

On the other hand, when the cultural institution is attacked from this nativist, indigenist perspective, it also tries to defend itself by appealing to universal values like freedom of speech or the cosmopolitanism of the arts, which are so utterly commodified as either shock effects or the display of enjoyable cultural difference that they hardly exist beyond this form of commodification. Or it might even earnestly try to reconstruct a public sphere within market conditions, for example with the massive temporary spectacles of criticism funded by the German *Bundeskulturstiftung* (National Foundation for Culture). But under reigning economic conditions, the main effect achieved is to integrate the critics into precarity, into flexibilized working structures within temporary project structures and freelance work within cultural industries. And in the worst cases, those spectacles of criticism are the decoration of large enterprises of economic colonialism such as in the colonization of Eastern Europe by the same institutions that are producing the conceptual art in these regions.

If in the first wave of institutional critique criticism produced integration into the institution, in the second one only integration into representation was achieved. But now in the third phase there seems to be only integration into precarity. And in this light we can now answer the question concerning the function of the institution of critique as follows: while critical institutions are being dismantled by neo-liberal institutional criticism, this produces an ambivalent subject which develops multiple strategies for dealing with its dislocation. It is on the one side being adapted to the needs of ever more precarious living conditions. On the other, the need seems never to have been greater for institutions that could cater to the new needs and desires that this constituency will create.

3

Anti-Canonization: The Differential Knowledge of Institutional Critique

Stefan Nowotny

(Translated by Aileen Derieg)

Wanting to canonize artistic practices of institutional critique is a rather paradoxical endeavor. The reason is quickly evident. Canonization itself belongs to the specifically institutional practices that institutional critique refers to – and indeed *critically* refers to. Tacitly ignoring one of these critical impulses is hence inscribed in every canonization attempt, even though a retrospective acknowledgement of the relevance of these impulses is intended. 'Relevance' itself is categorized in the framework of a historiography that is entangled in its own preconditions, clinging jealously to the notion that in the end it has to be the art whose history is to be written.

The results are well known, not only in terms of the art subsumed under the name 'institutional critique', but also in terms of what is called 'political art' in general. Bert Brecht is treated as a revolutionary of theater art who was eccentric enough to be a communist as well; the Situationists are seen as oddballs of fine art who no less eccentrically maintained that changing perceptions of the streets was more important than changing perceptions of painting. And the 'art' of 'institutional critique'? As a 'current' it has meanwhile also aged sufficiently to provide a welcome occasion for various historicizations, self-historicizations or even 'examinations of topicality', which – instead of examining it – regularly become entangled in the self-referentiality specific to the art field, and specifically examining it as *institutional practice*.

It is not particularly helpful when one established canon or another is itself declared – in a duplication of the retrospective gesture – the object of negotiation by contrasting it with a possible 'other' or expanded canon. This is naturally not intended to deny that a critical query and contestation of dominant canonizations, their complicity with social-political power relations, their legitimizing and stabilizing function in terms of these hegemonic relations were (and are) an important element of the insights of institutional critique. Nevertheless, guidelines for action are not to be seamlessly derived from theoretical insights in the sense that the *end* of changing criticized conditions is already to be reached with the *means* of an expanded or counter-canon. This circumvention suffers from the problem of all superficial theories of hegemony: an insufficient reflection on the level of the means themselves. Where the critical impulse is at least maintained as a social-political one, this is usually accompanied by a fetishization of the ends, which ultimately obscures a critical examination of the means altogether; where it withdraws into the self-contemplation of the contexts it started from (and this is of particular interest here), the result is the fetishization of a certain *form of ends*.

What is fetishized in the latter case is less the end itself, but rather the form in which it is sought, that is, more precisely, the form of aiming at something or the link binding means and ends together. And this link proves to be all the more deceptive, since an incautious consideration of the form of ends and means may depict one and the same thing. Pursuing an end according to a certain form and treating it solely within the confines of this form, however, does not at all signify a sufficient reflection on the means. Instead, it simply signifies fixing the means as such to a spectrum placed beyond the realm of critique, a spectrum that yet results from a specific, fundamentally contingent connection between means and ends in need of reflection. And it ultimately signifies constraining the possible ends themselves, to the extent that the only acceptable end is one that corresponds to a given spectrum of means.[1]

A flagrant example of fixing institutional critique art practices to art as the form of ends is found, for instance, in an issue of *Texte zur Kunst* devoted to institutional critique. There, Isabelle Graw proposes expanding the canon of 'the usual suspects' (Michael Asher, Daniel Buren, Hans Haacke, Andrea Fraser, etc.) with artists such as Jörg Immendorff or Martin Kippenberger. The concern that the existing canon could be 'at the expense' of certain artists, whose work "could be equally regarded as questioning the institution of art or as an attack on it" (Graw, 2005: 47) is just as characteristic as the 'expense' rhetoric that Graw utilizes, which appears at least ambiguous in the context of the magazine that conceptually addresses a match between art criticism and the art market (or more precisely: that is to be read against the background of the highly conflictual interweaving of symbolic and material valuation systems, which is characteristic of the art field throughout modernism).

No less characteristic is the specification of Graw's concern, which immediately follows: this relates to painting, the canonical neglect of which is deplored as a proven medium of institutional critique. Accordingly, the figure of the 'ostentatiously' solitary atelier painter, who withdraws his 'mental and emotional competences' from public access, is stylized into the carrier of an institutional critique revolt, into an anti-neo-liberal spectacle dissident. The genius in individual revolt need only withdraw and produce; all the others can devote themselves to the contemplative viewing of the fruits of his competences (Nowotny, 2005), specifically – why not? – in the form of 'institutional critical' painting. Meanwhile, the 'institution of art' carries on in its old familiar bourgeois variation undeterred – if it were not for the unfortunate battle against its neo-liberal adversaries, in which it is entangled.

The irony of all this is that Graw's concerns are not only due to the dissatisfaction that art fixed to "its presumed capability of critique" is "underestimated", but also that they claim to do justice to another concern, namely that an "inflationary assertion of critique" could ultimately lead to the "neutralization of every possibility of really achieving critique" (Graw, 2005: 41, 43). The latter concern indeed touches on a central problem that is inextricably linked with the *activity* of critique – as opposed to its mere assertion – and which has been widely discussed in the art field, not least of all since the publication of Luc Boltanski and Eve Chiapello's *The New Spirit of Capitalism*. How does critical activity relate to its effects? To what extent is it capable of keeping alive its differential deployment aimed at change beyond the respective self-assurance of a 'critical distance', in other words, feeding it into a social context and counteracting its own neutralization or the ways it is even inverted for uncritical purposes?

However, Graw does not let this concern leap any borders, but encloses it within the boundaries of the very field that art criticism routinely – *institutionally* – plows. For this reason, the questions remain obscured that would arise from the inversion of Graw's suspicion about 'fixing' art to its capability for critique: namely, whether the critique that is manifested in institutional critique practices is not underestimated when it is fixed to its character as art. In fact, in terms of canonization, this question can be traced even in the 'first generation' of institutional critique art practices, for it is an essential element of the critical impulses of these practices. It may be sufficient here to recall Robert Smithson's essay 'Cultural Confinement' from 1972, which sees the conditions for neutralizing the explosiveness of critique specifically in its fixation to being art (and not in the reverse fixation), that is in the confinement of the critical to a predetermined framework of representation:

> Museums, like asylums and jails, have yards and cells – in other words, neutral rooms called *galleries*. A work of art when placed in a gallery loses its charge, and becomes a portable object or surface disengaged from the outside world. A vacant white room with lights is still a submission to the neutral [...] The function of the warden-curator is to separate art from the rest of society. Next comes integration. Once the work of art is totally neutralized, ineffective, abstracted, safe, and politically lobotomized, it is ready to be consumed by society. (Smithson, 2001: 16)

It would be too simple to reduce the scope of Smithson's criticism to the museum-bound forms of representation and curatorship that it directly refers to. The operative structure that it describes, namely the 'political lobotomization' of the potential charge of artistic works that follows from isolation and neutralizing reintegration, can also be observed often enough where art works in public space, intended as political interventions, only provoke meager debates about art or occasionally about cultural policies, instead of really triggering the intended political discussions. The 'warden-curator' as functionary of this operative structure is abetted, in turn, by a whole series of further functionaries, including, not least of all, the professional discourse producers of the art field. This also applies to the artists themselves, whom Smithson is already far from locating in a naively asserted outside of the institutional field of power per se, which is evident, for instance, in his polemic against post-minimalist art practices:

> Also, I am not interested in art works that suggest *process* within the metaphysical limits of the neutral room. There is no freedom in that kind of behavioral game playing. The artist acting like a B. F. Skinner rat doing his *tough* little tricks is something to be avoided. Confined process is no process at all. It would be better to disclose the confinement rather than make illusions of freedom. (Smithson, 2001: 16)

The institutional critique impulse originating with artists like Smithson not only ties into the desire for a positively productive 're-socialization' of their own activities going beyond the boundaries of the art field, but also into the impulse to critically query one's own role as an artist and the forms of artistic self-confinement. Adrian Piper succinctly formulated the task of self-criticism that becomes apparent in this latter impulse (and which can be expanded to other functionaries within the art field) no less polemically than Smithson in a text written in 1983:

> [T]here is no biological necessity about a socially conditioned disinclination to perform the difficult and often thankless task of political self-analysis. It is not as though artists are congenitally incapacitated by having right cerebral hemispheres the size of a watermelon and left cerebral hemispheres the size of a peanut. (Piper, 2001: 50-1)

That not only the sharpness and decisiveness of these kinds of statements, but especially the multiple layers of the critical gesture inherent to them are marginalized in the discussion today, in favor of routine canonizations and counter-canonizations, may have something to do with the fact that the reason for current debates on art institutions and other public institutions is the impact of neo-liberal policies on these institutions. And as in other areas as well, the extent of political defensiveness and a lack of orientation in light of rampaging neo-liberal reforms is expressed, not least of all, in the defense of instruments and institutions that might well have been the subject of a critical examination yesterday. Instead of targeting what can generally be identified as 'art' and classified in 'currents', against this background it would seem advisable not to fall back behind the institutional critique of historical political analyses of modern art and exhibition institutions – or 'art' as an institutional field – like Carol Duncan's *Civilizing Rituals*

(1995) for instance, or Tony Bennett's *The Birth of the Museum* (1995). With Bennett's historically precise reconstruction of the modern museum and exhibition complex in mind, for example, carried out against the background of Foucault's analyses of governmentality (Nowotny, 2003a; 2005), it would be better to begin by considering the overlapping of various governmentality arrangements in which institutional critique has to orient itself today, both within the art field and beyond it. Given the growing divergence between political economy and nation-state frameworks, this overlapping must be seen as inherently contradictory.

Yet if every form of historiography must ultimately be regarded as an institutional practice itself and an 'outside the institution' cannot simply be presumed, but rather questions must be raised about the possibilities of a transformation of institutional practices, how can an alternative to canonization be imagined that is not a counter-canonization? One possibility certainly consists in a *political* analysis of the respective constellation, in which institutional critique is articulated. This means assuming a perspective which takes into account the specific functionality of the art field within the concrete social-political context, ranging beyond the self-referential structures of this field, and which also includes a view to the changes, to which this functionality and thus the conditions of critique are subjected. Here I would like to propose a somewhat different approach, however, which does not contradict the first at all, but should rather be appended to it: an approach that envisions 'critique' less in keeping with the model of a *judgement structure* (roughly speaking, in other words, a subject that *positions* itself *vis-à-vis* the criticized conditions), but rather with the model of a practice (meaning a subject that *is involved* and *involves itself* in a specific way *in* the criticized conditions).

Perhaps too little attention has previously been given to the fact that Foucault – where he talks about 'suppressed knowledges', the 'local discursivities' that are denigrated by the dominant discourse – describes these forms of knowledge as, among others, 'differential knowledge' (Foucault, 1999: 16). What does the notion of differentiality refer to here? On the one hand, certainly to the resistance of this knowledge, to the fact that "it owes its force to the sharpness with which it enters into opposition with everything around it". On the other hand, however, it also refers to this knowledge being differential *in itself* (also self-pluralizing for this reason), to the fact that it cannot be "transposed into unanimity" – even though the Foucauldian genealogy itself, as a tactic of its description, exposes it to a certain danger of uniformed coding and re-colonization (Foucault, 1999: 21). Not least of all, this knowledge is *differential* because it does not allow itself, being resistive, to be subjected to any authorized discursive field, to any authorization by a dominant discourse, but instead recognizes the power effects found in the separation of knowledge into fields and in furnishing these fields with discursive authorities, yet without composing itself into a new totality of knowledge. Hence as plural knowledge it also does not 'organize' itself under a unified form, but rather in an open, non-dialectical game of concurrence. For precisely this reason, the Foucauldian genealogy can be concerned with "preparing a historical knowledge of struggles and introducing this knowledge into current tactics" (Foucault, 1999: 17).

The struggles that Foucault was specifically thinking of in the mid-1970s – and through which "for ten, fifteen years now [...] it has become possible to criticize things, institutions, practices, discourses to a tremendous and overflowing extent" (Foucault, 1999: 13) – were particularly those of anti-psychiatry, attacks on gender hierarchies and sexual morals, and on the legal and penal apparatus. Why should we not append the battles of institutional critique practices to this list (it is not a coincidence that Robert Smithson compares the 'cells' of the museums with those of 'asylums and prisons' in the passage quoted above...)? What could come into view through this kind of perspective is not so much – or at least not solely – the question of the respective critical assessment of art institutions, and certainly not of a canon, but rather an open field of a knowledge of action, a practical knowledge that rejects reintegration into the form of ends specific to art and in which the difference of institutional critique is actualized. We find it in the most diverse tactics of context politicization, self-masking, alienation, parody, the situation-specific refraction of themes, research, discursive and material context production, in self-institutionalization, in production that starts with social interaction, or even simply in a more or less developed renegade position.

A historiography and investigation of institutional critique could be oriented to these practices, if the aim is to introduce this knowledge into current tactics.

Notes

1. An example from – at least at first glance – outside the art field that indicates the background of these reflections (namely Walter Benjamin's essay 'On the Critique of Violence'): Pursuing the end of justice under the form of law, in other words as a legal end, means nothing more than considering it (egally) capable of generalization, whereby the form of law is placed beyond dispute both at the level of the means (legal claims, laws, etc.) and at the level of the ends (e.g. the non-contradictory regulation of human affairs).

4

Notes on Institutional Critique

Simon Sheikh

The very term 'institutional critique' seems to indicate a direct connection between a method and an object: the method being the critique and the object the institution. In the first wave of institutional critique from the late 1960s and early 1970s – long since celebrated and relegated by art history – these terms could apparently be even more concretely and narrowly defined: the critical method was an artistic practice, and the institution in question was the art institution, mainly the art museum, but also galleries and collections. Institutional critique thus took on many forms, such as artistic works and interventions, critical writings or (art-)political activism. However, in the so-called second wave, from the 1980s, the institutional framework became somewhat expanded to include the artist's role (the subject performing the critique) as institutionalized, as well as an investigation into other institutional spaces (and practices) besides the art space.[1] Both waves are today themselves part of the art institution, in the form of art history and education as much as in the general de-materialized and post-conceptual art practice of contemporary art. It shall not be my purpose here, however, to discuss or access the meaning of institutional critique as an art historical canon, or to engage in the writing of such a canon (I shall respectfully leave that endeavor for the *Texte zur Kunst* and *October* magazines of this world). Instead, though, I would like to point out a convergence between the two waves, that seems to have drastically changed in the current 'return' of institutional critique that may or may not constitute a third wave. In either of its historical emergences, institutional critique was a practice mainly, if not exclusively, conducted by artists, and directed *against* the (art) institutions, as a critique of their ideological and representative social function(s). Art's institutions, which may or may not contain the artists' work, were seen, in the words of Robert Smithson, as spaces of 'cultural confinement' and circumscription, and thus as something to attack aesthetically, politically and theoretically. The institution was posed as a problem (for artists). In contrast, the current institutional-critical discussions seem predominantly propagated by curators and directors of the very same institutions, and they are usually opting *for* rather than against them. That is, they are not an effort to oppose or even destroy the institution, but rather to modify and solidify it. The institution is not only a problem, but also a solution!

There has been a shift, then, in the placement of institutional critique, not only in historical time, but also in terms of the subjects who direct and perform the critique – it has moved from an outside to an inside. Interestingly, Benjamin Buchloh (1990) has described the historical moment of conceptual art as a movement from institutional critique and 'the aesthetic of administration to the critique of institutions', in a controversial essay entitled, tellingly, 'Conceptual Art 1962–1969: From the Aesthetics of Administration to the Critique of Institutions'. While Buchloh focuses on the emergence of conceptualism, his suggestive distinction is perhaps even more pertinent now that institutional critique is literally being performed by administrative aestheticians, i.e. museum directors, curators etc. (Buchloh, 1990). Taking her cue from Buchloh, Andrea Fraser goes a step further in her recent essay 'From the Critique of Institutions to an Institution of Critique', where she claims that a movement between an inside and an outside of the institution is no longer possible, since the structures of the institution have become totally internalized. "We are the institution", Fraser (2005: 282) writes, and thus concludes that it is rather a question of creating critical institutions – what she terms 'an institution *of* critique', established through self-questioning and self-reflection (Fraser, 2005). Fraser also writes that the institutions of art should not be seen as an autonomous field, separate from the rest of the world, the same way that 'we' are not separate from the institution. While I would certainly agree with any attempt to view art institutions as part of a larger ensemble of socio-economic and disciplinary spaces, I am nonetheless confused by the simultaneous attempt to integrate the art world into the current (politico-economic) world system *and* the upholding of a 'we' of the art world itself. Who exactly is this 'we'? If the art world is seen as part of a generalized institutionalization of social subjects (that in turn internalizes the institutionalization), what and where are the demarcation lines for entry, for visibility and representation? If one of the criteria for institutions is given in the exclusions performed by them (as inherent in any collection), the question which subjects fall outside institutionalization, not due to a willful act or exodus as certain artistic movements thought and desired, but through the expulsions at the very center of institutions that allow them to institutionalize? Obviously, this would require a very expanded notion of institutional critique – one that lies somewhat outside the history of institutional critique as discussed here.

So, to return to the object at hand, institutional critique as an art practice: what does it mean when the practice of institutional critique and analysis has shifted from artists to curators and critics, and when the institution has become internalized in artists and curators alike (through education, through art historical canon, through daily praxis)? Analyzed in terms of negative dialectics, this would seem to indicate the total co-optation of institutional critique by the institutions (and by implication and extension, the co-optation of resistance by power), and thus make institutional critique as a *critical* method completely obsolete. Institutional critique, as co-opted, would be like bacteria that may have temporarily weakened the patient – the institution – but only in order to strengthen the immune system of that patient in the long run. However, such a conclusion would hinge around notions of subjectivities, agencies and spatialities that institutional critique, arguably, tried to deconstruct. It would imply that the historical institutional critique was somehow 'original' and 'pure', thus confirming the authenticity of the artist-subjects performing it (as opposed to the current 'institutional' subjects), and consequently reaffirming one of the ideas that institutional critique set out to circumvent, namely the notion of authentic subjects per se (as represented by the artist, reified by the institution). If institutional critique was indeed a discourse of disclosure and demystification of how the artistic subject as well as object was staged and reified by the institution, then any narrative that (again) posits certain voices and subjects as authentic, as possible incarnations of certain politics and criticalities, must be said to be not only counter to the very project of institutional critique, but perhaps also the ultimate co-optation, or more accurately, hostile take-over of it. Institutional critique is, after all, not primarily about the intentionalities and identities of subjects, but rather about the politics and inscriptions of institutions (and, thus, about how subjects are always already threaded through specific and specifiable institutional spaces).

Rather, one must try to historicize the moments of institutional critique and look at how it has been successful, in terms of being integrated into the education of artists and curators, that is of what Julia Bryan-Wilson has termed 'the curriculum of institutional critique' (Bryan-Wilson, 2003). One can then see institutional critique not as a historical period and/or genre within art history, but rather as an analytical tool, a method of spatial and political criticism and articulation that can be applied not only to the art world, but to disciplinary spaces and institutions in general. An institutional critique of institutional critique, what can be termed 'institutionalized critique', has then to question the role of education, historicization and how institutional auto-critique not only leads to a questioning of the institution and what it institutes, but also becomes a mechanism of control within new modes of governmentality, precisely through its very act of internalization. And this is the expanded notion of institutional critique that I briefly mentioned above, and which could become the legacy of the historical movements as much as an orientation for what so-called 'critical art institutions' claim to be.

Notes

1. James Meyer (1993) has tried to establish a genealogy rather than a mere art history of institutional critique.

5

Criticism without Crisis:
Crisis without Criticism

Boris Buden

Why do we talk today about institutional critique in the field of art? The answer is very simple: Because we (still) believe that art is intrinsically equipped with the power of criticism. Of course, we don't simply mean art criticism here but something more than that, the ability of art to criticize the world and life beyond its own realm, and even, by doing that, to change both. This includes, however, some sort of self-criticism, or more precisely, the practice of critical self-reflexivity, which means that we also expect of art – or at least used to expect – to be critically aware of the conditions of its possibility, which usually means, the conditions of its production.

These two notions – to be aware of the conditions of possibility and production – point at two major realms of modern criticism: the theoretical and the practical-political realm. It was Immanuel Kant who first posed the question about the conditions of possibility of our knowledge and who understood this question explicitly as an act of criticism. From that point on we may say that modern reflection is either critical – in this self-reflexive way – or it is not modern.

But we are not going to follow this theoretical line of modern criticism here. We will concentrate instead on its practical and political meaning, which can be simply described as a will for radical change, in short, the demand for revolution, which is the ultimate form of practical and political criticism. The French Revolution was not only prepared through the bourgeois criticism of the absolutist state. It was nothing but this criticism *in actu*, its last word turned into political action. The idea of revolution as an ultimate act of criticism has found its most

33

radical expression in Marxist theoretical and political concepts. Remember that the young Karl Marx explicitly characterized his own revolutionary philosophy as "the ruthless critique of everything existing". He meant this in the most radical sense as a criticism that 'operates' in the very basement of social life, that is, in the realm of its material production and reproduction, something we understand today, perhaps oversimplifying, as the realm of economy.

In this way criticism has become one of the essential qualities of modernity. For almost two centuries to be modern meant simply to be critical – in philosophy as much as in moral questions, in politics and social life as much as in art.

But there is also another concept, which – as a sort of its complement – has long accompanied the idea and practice of modern criticism, and that is the concept of crisis. A belief that the two – crisis and criticism – have something in common, that there is an authentic relation, or better, an interaction between them, equally belongs to the modern experience. Therefore, an act of criticism almost necessarily implies the awareness of a crisis and vice versa; a diagnosis of crisis implies the necessity of criticism.

Actually, criticism and crisis didn't enter the historical scene at the same time. Criticism is the child of the eighteenth century Enlightenment. It was born and developed out of the separation between politics and morality, a separation that criticism has deepened and kept alive throughout the modern age. It was only through the process of criticism – the criticism of all forms of traditional knowledge, religious beliefs and aesthetic values, the criticism of existing juridical and political reality and finally the criticism of the mind itself – that the growing bourgeois class could impose its own interests and values as the highest instance of judgement and in that way develop the self-confidence and self-conscience it needed for the decisive political struggles to come. In this context one shouldn't underestimate the role of art and literary criticism especially in the development of the modern philosophy of history. It was precisely art and literary criticism that produced at that time among the intelligentsia the awareness of a contradiction between the 'old' and the 'modern' and in that way shaped a new understanding of time capable of differentiating the future from the past. But at the end of this period arises also the awareness of the approaching crisis: "We are approaching the state of crisis and the century of revolutions", writes Jean-Jacques Rousseau (1966: 252). Whereas for Enlightenment thinkers revolution was a synonym for an inevitable historical progress, which occurs necessarily as a kind of natural phenomenon, Rousseau by contrast understood it as the ultimate expression of crisis, which brings about the state of insecurity, dissolution, chaos, new contradictions, etc. In connection with the crisis – which it has prepared and initiated – criticism loses its original naïvety and its alleged innocence. From now on criticism and crisis go together shaping the modern age of civil wars and revolutions, which instead of bringing about the expected historical progress, cause chaotic dissolutions and obscure regressive processes, often completely beyond rational control. The interaction between criticism and crisis is one of the major qualities of what later was conceptualized as the 'dialectics of enlightenment'.

In the meantime the interplay of both notions became a sort of *terminus technicus* of modernist progress introducing a difference – and simultaneously a relation – between 'old' and 'new'. To say that something has gone into crisis meant above all to say that it has become old; that is, that it has lost its right to exist and therefore should be replaced by something new. Criticism is nothing but the act of this judgement, which helps the old to die quickly and the new to be born easily.

This also applies to the development of modern art, which also follows the dialectics of criticism and crisis of its forms. So we understand for instance realism as a critical reaction to the crisis of Romanticism, or the idea of abstract art as a critique of figurative art, which has exhausted its potential and therefore went into crisis. Also the tension between art and 'prosaic reality' was interpreted through the dialectics of crisis and criticism. So was modern art – especially in Romanticism – often understood as a criticism of ordinary life, of ordinariness as such, or in other words of a life that had lost its authenticity or its meaning – in short, a life that had also gone into some kind of crisis.

Let us now go back to the question, whether this dialectics of criticism and crisis still makes some sense to us today. A few months ago in Austria I had an opportunity to pose this question directly. I moderated a discussion on the legacy of the artistic avant-garde today in the post-communist Eastern Europe. I hoped everybody would agree when I said that the avant-garde is still the most radical case of modernist art criticism – both in terms of a criticism of traditional art of its time and in terms of a criticism of existing reality, precisely in the moment of its – widely recognized and acknowledged – crisis. After five hours of debate, the conclusion was that the critical experience of avant-garde art is of no value at all today, at least not in Eastern Europe.

The participants in the discussion were mostly younger artists from central and southern regions of Eastern Europe, the Czech Republic, Slovakia, Hungary, Serbia, Romania and also Turkey. Actually, only the representative of Turkey was prepared to take the topic seriously and believed that the critical stance of the avant-garde still makes some sense to us today. The most open and most radical in his refusal of the avant-garde question was the representative of the Czech Republic. He argued that the avant-garde experience is actually a problem of generations. For him, it is an older generation of artists and art historians that still sees some challenge in the avant-garde and is bothered by this question. The younger generation, he believes, is already beyond the problem of the political meaning of art, or relations between politics and aesthetics. He gave this example: the old generation still discusses vehemently whether or not we need to consider the political meaning of Leni Riefenstahl's work. For the young generation, on the contrary, this simply doesn't matter any more. They have so to speak a direct insight into her art without any political connotations. They see it as what it really is – a pure art in its pure aesthetic value and meaning.

In fact I was not interested at all in this topic, since I know these people and their interests, so I didn't actually expect them to be really interested in the avant-garde. However, there was another issue I found much more interesting there. The participants were actually all members of the so-called Transit-Project. This is a project that was launched a few years ago by an Austrian bank with the aim of supporting art in Eastern Europe. The participants were representatives of the project in their countries. Since I know that this particular bank has earned an enormous amount of money in Eastern Europe, I was curious whether they would have any opinion on that fact – that is, on the way they are paid for their artistic work, or on the role of art and art funding under these circumstances.

I was also motivated by an article that appeared around then in the Viennese daily *Der Standard*. It reported on the profits of Austrian banks and insurance companies in Eastern Europe. In it, one could read that the result of the so-called business activity of the Generali Holding Vienna (an insurance company) had tripled the year before. The annual net profit had doubled in the same year. One can only wonder how this had been possible. The answer was to be found in the subtitle of the same article: 'The growth engine Eastern Europe'. It is due to the eastern expansion of the holding – and Austrian banks too – that they can make such profits. I hoped that the participants would somehow tackle this issue. To speak more openly, I wanted to provoke some sort of criticism. Unfortunately, it didn't work. Nobody found the economic, material conditions of their art making worth mentioning.

It seems that the critical legacy of the avant-garde in post-communist Europe is finally dead. Moreover, it also seems that there is no authentic interest among young artists in institutional criticism, in what we have called above self-criticism: critical awareness of the conditions of the possibility of their art and the conditions of its production.

The reason for this is obvious: our perception of avant-garde criticism is essentially framed by the historical experience of communism. This means that the experience of the avant-garde, as much as the experience of radical criticism, appears to us today only from our post-communist (post-totalitarian, or post-ideological) perspective. It appears as a phenomenon of our past, as a phenomenon, to use Francis Fukuyama's (1992: xi) notion, of a lower level of humanity's ideological evolution. In short it appears that, as a problem, it belongs to the concerns of an older generation, to use words of the Czech colleague, and thus by implication is sooner or later going to die out.

But let me, at this point, pose an 'impossible' question: is communism really dead? As far as I know, it is not only still alive, but also proves, in some fields, its superiority over capitalism. Yes, I really mean today's China. (Please don't tell me that this is not the real communism. There has never been a real communism. I can remember very well that from the perspective of Yugoslavian communism – also often dismissed, due to the market economy, as not being an authentic, real one – the Soviet and whole East-block communism was defined as a form of state-capitalism). Why don't we then learn about radical criticism and self-criticism from Chinese communists who obviously seem to have been more successful than their Western comrades? But before we ask the highest theoretical authority of the Chinese communism about the true meaning of criticism and self-criticism, let me remind you of a historical fact: In the historical reality of the nineteenth and twentieth centuries the idea of communist revolution itself became an institution – in the form of the communist movement and the Communist Party in its various national forms. As an institution, the communist movement also developed its own institution of criticism, the institution of so-called self-criticism, which played the extremely important function of informing the self-conscious subject of revolutionary action and later of a socialist community.

For Chairman Mao, conscientious practice of self-criticism was one of the most important hallmarks distinguishing a Communist Party from all other political parties. Let me quote him: "As we say, dust will accumulate if a room is not cleaned regularly, our faces will get dirty if they are not washed regularly. Our comrades' minds and our Party's work may also collect dust, and also need sweeping and washing". Therefore, self-criticism is for Mao "the only effective way to prevent all kinds of political dust and germs from contaminating the minds of our comrades and the body of our Party".

This sounds very funny to us today, like an infantile ideological fairy tale. But let me point to a crucial contradiction in Mao's concept of self-criticism: it has nothing to do whatsoever with the crisis of capitalism or with any sort of crisis. Although Mao describes communist self-criticism as the most effective weapon of Marxism-Leninism, he doesn't justify it with the ideological principals of Marxism-Leninism. On the contrary, his definition of self-criticism seems to be completely non-ideological, simply a matter of trivial common sense: a clean face is better than a dirty one, a clean room better than one full of dust, germs are bad for health.

Why this trivialization? And, what is even more important, what happened to the crisis, where has it gone, why has it suddenly disappeared? Why this particular form of communist criticism – a self-criticism that is not related to any sort of crisis? In the guise of the communist political movement both the crisis of capitalism and its criticism have merged into one single institution in which there is no possibility to differentiate between them. In other words, precisely in merging together they have become each other's outside. For the communist movement the crisis of capitalism was suddenly out there, in the outside of its own institution. But for capitalism, too, the criticism of its crisis can now be perceived only as coming from its own outside. The result is that communists couldn't see themselves as being part of the capitalist crisis and therefore, instead of resolving it, through their criticism, they have finally succeeded in making it stronger, more efficient, finally more sustainable or simply permanent. The problem was that communism and capitalism – or if you want, capitalism as crisis and its communist criticism – have never reached the point of a radical mutual exclusion, but on the contrary, were helping each other in moments of crises.

Why should we forget that it was precisely American capital which helped Bolshevik Russia to recover from the destructions of the civil war? And why forget the role of art in this story? The Soviets, as it is well known, were exchanging some of the most precious and also most expensive art works, mostly French paintings from the nineteen century, for new industrial technology from the United States. In our liberal jargon we today would call it a perfect win-win situation. The one side could get rid of what it considered at that time meaningless and historically obsolete (i.e., bourgeois art). And the other side could expand its markets, push forward employment and consequently stabilize the social situation and pacify its working class (i.e., escape its crisis). It didn't work, but not, as many believe today, because the Bolsheviks were primitives who couldn't recognize the real value of the artworks they possessed. Far from it: they knew all about the market value of those artworks, and this according to the pure capitalist logic. They treated them exclusively as commodities. But this became possible only after these artworks were artistically devaluated, after they had lost their artistic value as a consequence of an authentic art-criticism. It was actually the avant-garde art that stated the crisis of traditional art and – within what we today understand as pure history of art – radically criticized all these French paintings and destroyed their artistic value.

Moreover, it was now the artistic avant-garde itself that needed factories and working masses in order to articulate its artistic principles and produce its own artistic values. The avant-garde did not need museums and depots to collect its works and present them to an audience they didn't care about and were actually disgusted with. And who could provide the needed factories and working class? American industrial technology. Capitalism, in short. This is a wonderful example of how crisis and criticism of both capitalism and art can successfully work together, of course within an overall capitalist context, in order to produce – normality!

Another example of how capitalism and communism can function in harmony is of course today's China. To translate the reality into the dialectics of crisis and its criticism, it is precisely the rule of an institutionalized criticism of capitalism (i.e., the rule of the Chinese Communist Party) that today helps capitalism to survive its crises and persist. Not only by opening the world's largest market to global corporate capital, but also by providing it with cheap and highly disciplined labour. This doesn't happen, as so many believe, because today's Chinese communists have betrayed the very principles of the communist idea, and because, ceasing to criticize capitalism, they have started to improve it. They have not betrayed Mao. On the contrary, they stick faithfully to his true legacy.

Let me quote the Chairman once more. Discussing the necessity for self-criticism, he calls for personal sacrifice:

> As we Chinese Communists, who… never balk at any personal sacrifice and are ready at all times to give our lives for the cause, can we be reluctant to discard any idea, viewpoint, opinion or method which is not suited to the needs of the people? Can we be willing to allow political dust and germs to dirty our clean faces or eat into our healthy organisms? [C]an there be any personal interest… that we would not sacrifice or any error that we would not discard?

And let's remember that the famous Stalinist show trials would have never been possible without the institution of self-criticism and personal sacrifice. As is well known today, they were introduced at the beginning of the 1930s, precisely at the moment when collectivization started to produce catastrophic results, plunging Soviet society into deep crisis. It was self-criticism that then helped to project this crisis into an outside, to present it as an effect of the subversion from the outside, a work of imperialist spies and agents. It was therefore completely understandable that the institution had to be cleaned up from all those 'germs and parasites' which had eaten into the healthy organism of Soviet society. Criticism – in the guise of communist self-criticism – was used (or if you like misused), not to disclose the real crisis and its antagonisms and intervene in it (which would have been a classical Marxist approach), but on the contrary to hide it and in this way to make it permanent, that is, to transform or translate crisis in some sort of normality.

This is typical for today's situation: neither are we able to experience our time as crisis nor do we try to become subjects through an act of criticism. In the period of classical modernism, crisis was always experienced as an actual possibility of a break and criticism as this break itself. Obviously, such an experience is no longer possible for us today. There is no experience whatsoever of an interaction between crisis and critique. One cannot simply ignore Giorgio Agamben's warning, that one of the most important experiences of our times is the fact that we are unable to have any experience of it. The result is a permanent criticism that is blind to the crisis, and a permanent crisis that is deaf to criticism. In short, a perfect harmony!

6

Artistic Internationalism and Institutional Critique

Jens Kastner

(Translated by Aileen Derieg)

In 1970 a group called the Guerilla Art Collective Project placed military uniforms filled with meat and labeled 'SHIP TO…' in the main square in front of the university in San Diego. The action – at the same time a protest against the war in Vietnam and an art production (Breitwieser, 2003: 16) – was carried out on the borderline between installation and sculpture, as well as between art and politics. The group member who initiated the project was Allan Sekula, a student of the social philosopher Herbert Marcuse.

Marcuse was one of the most important advocates of social movements in the 1960s. His *One-Dimensional Man* (1964), influential for many students in Western Europe and North America during that period, saw in the protest movements new possibilities for the realization of alternative, non-alienated ways of living, an approach that later became conventional in research dealing with social movements. However, it was not only these possibilities that united the various upheavals since the mid-1960s and partly enabled the conjoining of very different concerns – feminist, anti-colonialist, anti-racist, anti-authoritarian, anti-imperialist and anti-militarist. Similar in some ways to Dada fifty years earlier, in terms of what the actors had in common, 1968 as an international or transnational upheaval, as 'a world revolution' (*il manifesto*), in which widespread artistic mobilization was also involved, was based primarily on negative internationalist motivations: the war against Vietnam conducted by the USA was the outstanding negatively uniting element. "The military intervention of the USA in the Vietnam conflict gave the protests of the various national student avant-garde groups an international dimension, an idea that united them, and a common strategy" (Gilcher-Holtey, 2003: 49). Just as social criticism was linked at the political level in the urban centers through this negative bracket with liberation movements in developing countries, at the cultural level agitation by politicized students joined forces with artists expanding their methods. Countless artistic actions took place in the most diverse countries in the course of the protest movements, linking anti-war ideas with local social, cultural and political concerns, and especially joined them with the actions of the social movements. In his history of conceptual art Tony Godfrey (2005: 190) wonders about "how little the political situation was directly addressed by art" in light of the vehement student unrest, but he considers the importance of the Vietnam war in the development of art in the late 1960s and early 1970s so great that he begins every chapter of his book by elaborating on it.

My thesis is that the internationalist orientation functions both as the potential link between artistic and social movements and as a possible means for overcoming the structural obstacles between both. This conjunction is by no means to be taken for granted, nor is it generally the case. It is blocked, according to Pierre Bourdieu, by the complete difference and incompatibility of the respective fields. Although there exists a "structural affinity between literary avant-garde and the political avant-garde" (Bourdieu, 1996: 251), the reconciliation of the two "in a sort of summation of all revolutions – social, sexual, artistic" (Bourdieu, 1996: 387) repeatedly runs into the rifts or hurdles that exist between the two areas. It was not unusual for these hurdles to appear even in the context of 1968. They were evident, for example, in the repeatedly occurring, mutual vituperation between political activists and activist artists. In 1971 Henryk M. Broder, for instance, contended that the Vienna Actionist Otto Muehl was "no leftist, but an anal-fascist", whereas Muehl criticized the bourgeois mentality of all revolutionaries, who "put on their comfy slippers" again when they are finished revolting (Raunig, 2007: 290). The controversies surrounding Muehl and the other actors from Vienna Actionism were ultimately so heated because the art scene in Austria had a certain dominance within the situation in 1968, which was generally marked, according to Robert Foltin (2004: 74) by "a lack of theory and by a low degree of militancy."[1]

The thesis that social and artistic movements come together and/or mutually permeate one another in artistic internationalism also contradicts two narrow readings of Bourdieu, which have been formulated in discussions about institutional critique. Andrea Fraser's reading (2005), for example, which picks up from Bourdieu, regards the art field as being so closed that everything done outside it can have no effects at all towards the inside – and vice versa. In the essay that opens this volume, Gerald Raunig rightly criticizes Fraser's position, and Stefan Nowotny in his text on 'anti-canonization' criticizes a similar position on the part of Isabelle Graw. Nowotny maintains that in Graw's essay 'Beyond Institutional Critique' is a "flagrant example of fixing institutional critique art practices to art" (this volume). However, Graw's position also stands for a second curtailment of Bourdieu's art field theory. In light of the sales-oriented clientele of a New York art fair, completely uninterested in content, she wrote in a *Tageszeitung* article in 2004 that "under these circumstances... the notion of art as an autonomous special sphere... can no longer be maintained" (Graw, 2005: 15). However, since the autonomization of the art field, the economy of symbolic goods, which Bourdieu speaks of, does not take place between the poles of total commercialization and 'pure production'.[2] Hence the existence and expansion of influential art fairs does not at all contradict the autonomy of the field.[3] Objections must therefore be raised against both of these constrictions: talking about the autonomy of the art field means neither asserting a social area incapable of achieving effects towards the outside, nor that a terrain exists here, which is untouched by economic, social and other influences. Instead, it is a matter of pointing out specific functionalities that differ from those in other social fields.[4]

The artist, photographer and art theoretician Allan Sekula also formulated the protest against the Vietnam War in another action, one that was photographically documented. In this six-part photo series an activist, barefooted and equipped with a Vietnamese peasant's straw hat and plastic machine gun, crawls through the wealthy suburbs of a large US city. The title of the 1972 action, *Two, three, many ... (terrorism)*, directly refers to Ernesto Che Guevara's anti-imperialist *foco* theory. In this context Guevara called for the creation of 'two, three, many' Vietnams to expand the so-called people's war against imperialism by creating multiple revolutionary hot spots. Sekula thus puts Che Guevara's internationalist appeal into an artistic form, indicating the justification for the appeal on the one hand, but on the other also representing a symbolic alternative to the non-artistic implementation of guerrilla concepts in the major urban centers. The *foco* theory was not only one of the foundations for the development of the 'urban guerrilla concept' by the Red Army Fraction (RAF) in 1971. Following a first wave of guerrilla movements limited to Latin America, a 'second wave' (Kaller-Dietrich and Mayer, undated) arose in Western cities based on the practices of the Tupamaros, the leftist urban guerrillas in Uruguay. The Weather Underground in the USA and other radical leftist groups in various western countries also referred directly or indirectly to this dictum from Che Guevara as they went underground (Jacobs, 1997).

The collage series *Bringing the War Home* (1967 – 1972) by the US artist and art theoretician Martha Rosler[5] is also to be seen in the context of *foco* theory. The collages show various motifs from the Vietnam War mounted in pictures from contemporary US American brochures for furnishings. By calling everyday furnishings into question as the furnishings of everyday life, Rosler builds here on an effect similar to that of the Berlin group Kommune 1 with their flyer about a fire in a Brussels department store in 1967. In this flyer, Kommune 1 satirically calls the fire an advertising gag for the USA, invoking the 'crackling Viet Nam feeling (of being there and burning too)', that everyone should be able to share (Enzensberger, 2004). This satire strategy also serves the idea of making injustice in developing countries directly comprehensible to people in major cities, making it palpable, in fact 'bringing the war home'.

If institutional critique is taken not merely as a label for works by the four or five protagonists that are always named (Michael Asher, Marcel Broodthaers, Daniel Buren, Hans Haacke, John Knight), but rather, as Hito Steyerl sees it in her essay in this volume, as 'a new social movement within the art field', then this would certainly include Martha Rosler and Allan Sekula. Questioning one's own role within the art system, linking this with concrete socio-political themes such as the criticism of US foreign policy and the criticism of the ideology of the idyllic private sphere of the family, suggests a version of institutional critique that goes beyond the constraints of art institutions like galleries and museums. It also covers more than Isabelle Graw (2005: 50) includes with the differentiated, expanded concept of institution, of corporate culture and celebrity culture. It is more to be understood as a criticism of the institutions of capitalist society altogether, in the sense of Marcuse's utopian idea that the aim is to work towards a society in which people are no longer enslaved by institutions. To this extent, Steyerl's analysis also needs to be expanded: institutional critique should not only be understood as a movement within the art field, but also as one that would hardly be imaginable without the social movements outside the art field.

Artistic internationalism – in other words a certain orientation of the subject matter of artistic work that nevertheless first develops in the confrontation with the viewers – proves to be the link between art movement and social movement. With regard to this functional link, works like those described above are to be defended against both their proponents and their opponents.

One of these opponents, for example, is Jacques Rancière (2006), who lists Rosler's aforementioned work as an example of art that too strongly disambiguates the relation between illusion and reality. In works like *Bringing the War Home*, according to Rancière, "the sense of fiction is lost" (Rancière, 2006: 91), which should, however, be central to the real politics of art. Rancière (2006: 87) argues for a "politics of art that is proper to the aesthetic regime of art" and which precedes the political action of the artist.[6] He maintains that the confrontation between two heterogeneous elements, as demonstrated in Rosler's collages, is characteristic of critical art. However, it tends to turn itself into a mere inventory of things. In turn, this taking inventory leads to the exact opposite of what was intended: the politics of art is reduced to "welfare and ethical imprecision" (Rancière, 2006: 96), or it dissolves into "the indeterminacy[...] that is called ethics today" (Rancière, 2006: 99). According to Rancière, art is political neither because of its message nor in the way that it represents social structures, ethnic and sexual identity or political struggles. "Art is primarily political in creating a space-time sensorium, in certain modes of being together or apart, of defining being inside or outside, opposite to or in the middle of" (Rancière, 2006: 77).

Yet Rosler and Sekula's works are by no means situated exclusively in the tradition of explicitly political agitation art like that of John Heartfield or Diego Rivera. However, even their works – denigrated by Rancière as 'directly' political art – could prove to be suitable for creating a sensorium, if, for example, the indeterminate specification of being together and apart, etc. is interpreted as a relationship, as it exists and is thematized in the relationship between work and viewer. For only very few 'political' works are limited solely to conveying messages and representing social/political conflicts. Michelangelo Pistoletto, for instance, in his mirror painting (*Vietnam*, 1962/1965) linked the art historical issue of the work-viewer relationship with political explicitness. Two persons, painted on tissue paper and cut out along their contours, are glued to a reflecting metal panel, a woman in a red trench coat and a man in a black suit with a tie, each of them holding a stick with a demo banner attached to the upper ends, on which the letters '...NAM' can be read. Looking at this life-sized picture, viewers are immediately drawn into the depiction of the scene, obviously an anti-Vietnam War demonstration. Here Pistoletto positions the viewers both opposite the picture as such and also in front of a political statement, directly involving them in both. According to Tony Godfrey (2005: 114), this artistic stance, which places the viewer in a direct relationship to the image, is "a crucial characteristic of Conceptual Art."

In the case of Sekula's *Two, three, many ... (terrorism)* and Rosler's *Bringing the War Home*, this kind of context is established through the internationalism of 1968. This internationalism involves more of a political stance than a (for example, Trotskyist) program, an awareness of the ways in which social battles in different regions of the world are mutually conditioned. Due not least of all to the anti-colonial liberation movements, with the student movements of the 1960s an anti-authoritarian internationalism – in contrast to the proletarian internationalism of the early twentieth century – gained "more significance theoretically as well[...] In fact, this was one of its central components. Internationalism and '68' formed a unit and must therefore also be treated as such" (Hierlmeier, 2002: 23). This internationalist perspective was realized in the social movements in this way perhaps even more than in the art field, within which it was criticized as obscuring western hegemony.[7]

The artistic internationalism is all the more to be emphasized also in response to proponents of Rosler's *Bringing the War Home*, such as Beatrice von Bismarck (2006). Martha Rosler continued her series in 2004 under the same title, but instead of motifs from the Vietnam War she used motifs from the US invasion of Iraq. Although there is no dismissing that Rosler's Iraq series is a 'self-quotation', as Bismarck (2006: 239) puts it, a comparable point of reference in terms of subject matter is certainly the rhetoric of freedom used by the US government both then and now. Nor is the observation false that the more garish choice of colors in comparison with the original series enhances the impression of uncanniness, understood in Freud's sense as a return of the repressed. "Especially in Rosler's photographic collages, in which the images of war break into the familiar homeyness, the home sweet home, as what is only seemingly alien, this return of the repressed finds a striking visual form" (Bismarck, 2006: 240).

Yet one crucial criterion still remains unmentioned in this account, specifically the integration of artistic work in the strategies and practices of the social movements. Although the US invasion of Iraq was accompanied by worldwide protests, this movement has for the most part long since ceased to operate in the context of a Guevara-like anti-imperialism. The tactic of 'bringing the war home' in any way was completely absent. And there is a reason for this: filling this slogan with emancipatory significance seems to be entirely unthinkable for social movements at a time when al-Qaida-style Islamic terror has struck Western capitals on many levels, on the one hand, and on the other is installed as a scenario of general threat. The war, or a war, has long since 'come home', has arrived in the Western urban centers, into which it first had to be brought in the 1960s and 1970s, although its effects are not those intended by movement actors in the 1960s. On the contrary, instead of enlightenment, awareness, empathy, emancipatory radicalization, an institutional and psychological insulation is taking place. The boom in security technologies and policies had already signaled the end of the urban guerrillas in the 1970s. Failing to reflect on this end and merely attempting to pick up from where it stopped thirty years earlier must give rise to perplexity in the case of an artist like Rosler. For she herself had emphasized how relatively "the measures of aesthetic coherence are applied to photographic practice" (Rosler, 1999: 122), and lamented a contemporary tendency to detach art works from their context. Although a link is made in the continuation of the series to an ethical issue, and the standpoint of the viewer in relation to the depicted situation is questioned, the political context of the emancipatory social movement and its strategies remains omitted – both in the work and in the criticism formulated by Bismarck.

With respect to the first phase of institutional critique, Sabeth Buchmann (2006) states that, in terms of the call for cultural and social relevance, it diverged from the historical avant-garde in that a different way of dealing with these issues was cultivated: the "radius of action was and is no longer society", according to Buchmann (2006: 22), "but rather specific public, institutional and/or media fields."

Neither the depreciation of the aesthetic value of artistic works like *Two, three, many ... (terrorism)* or *Bringing the War Home* nor their political de-contextualization does justice to their specific criticism. The works discussed here do indeed thematize central issues that are immanent to the art field, which are linked to the questions and concerns of social movements – with the normative turn, so to speak, of being embroiled in the production of the social world: if I am part of the historical process, then – according to one of the central ideas of *foco* theory, which has been criticized as being voluntaristic – it ultimately only depends on my determination (and that of a few others) to reverse the conditions. Both Rancière and Bismarck are building on a false focus: Rancière with his criticism of the unambiguousness that he claims exists in the confrontation with social conditions and destroys or does not enable the alleged 'politics of aesthetics'; and Bismarck (and even Rosler herself with her continuation) by overlooking this tie with the social context. It would be better to build instead on the hinge function between artistic issues and political forms of social movements. Tying into the art historical question of the relationship between artist, work and viewer would make it possible to draw from what Bourdieu called the 'space of possibilities', which "defines and delimits the universe of both what is thinkable and what is unthinkable" (Bourdieu, 2001: 373). In this sense, the development of artistic internationalism that is based on and rooted in the battles of the social movements and their practices of solidarity represents a potential expansion of this space.

Notes

1. On the connection between Vienna Actionism and the student movement, see Foltin (2004: 58) and Raunig (2007: 187-202).

2. Nina Tessa Zahner (2005) has analyzed the emergence of a third field, a 'sub-field of expanded production' in the context of the Pop Art of the 1960s. This conjoins elements from both poles in the figure of the artist as entrepreneur. The lasting transformations of the field that go back to these developments would have to be discussed separately.

3. The 'autonomy of the art field' that Bourdieu speaks of is thus not to be confused with the 'autonomy of the art work' that is asserted by modernist art theory. Bourdieu's whole theory ultimately aims to unmask the

'autonomy of the art work' as an ideology. Both Graw's slightly disgusted statement about the dominance of money on the one hand and Zahner's (2005: 290) recognition of Pop Art on the other, which credits Warhol for, among other things, "having pointed out the ideological content of the art that claims to be autonomous", are based on this misunderstanding.

4. Bourdieu (2003: 141) speaks of a "space with two dimensions and two forms of struggle and history": between the 'pure' and the 'commercial' pole there is the question of the legitimacy and the status of art; at another level the recognition of the works and the conflicts between young/new and old/established artists is at stake.

5. The first pictures of the series were published about 1970 as contributions to a magazine called *Goodbuy to all that* (No. 10), placed next to an article by the 'Angela Davis Committee in Defense of Women Prisoners'.

6. Rancière also decisively rejects the social conditions of judgments of taste and their integration in the symbolic struggles of a society that Bourdieu developed in *Distinction* (1982). He describes Bourdieu's demystification of the pure aesthetic gaze as a "cheap alliance between scientific and political progressive thinking", yet he has nothing to counter this with but the assertion of a singular "form of freedom and indifference[...], which joined aesthetics with the identification of what art is at all" (Rancière, 2006: 79). It would be interesting to discuss whether this is the reason why Rancière, as Christian Höller (2006: 180) stresses, is to be regarded "currently in the context of left-wing cultural circles as 'most wanted'."

7. For example, Rasheed Araeen's (1997: 100) criticism in 1978: "The myth of the internationalism of western art must be destroyed now[...] Western art expresses exclusively the characteristics of the west[...] Western art is not international. It is only a transatlantic art. It only reflects the culture of Europe and North America. The current 'internationalism' of western art is no more than a function of the political and economic power of the west, which imposes its values on other people. In an international context it would therefore be more appropriate to speak of an imperialistic art."

7

Extradisciplinary Investigations: Towards a New Critique of Institutions

Brian Holmes

What is the logic, the need or the desire that pushes more and more artists to work outside the limits of their own discipline, defined by the notions of free reflexivity and pure aesthetics, incarnated by the gallery-magazine-museum-collection circuit, and haunted by the memory of the normative genres, painting and sculpture?

Pop art, conceptual art, body art, performance and video each marked a rupture of the disciplinary frame, already in the 1960s and 70s. But one could argue that these dramatized outbursts merely *imported* themes, media or expressive techniques back into what Yves Klein had termed the 'specialized' ambiance of the gallery or the museum, qualified by the primacy of the aesthetic and managed by the functionaries of art. Exactly such arguments were launched by Robert Smithson in 1972 in his text on cultural confinement (Smithson, 1996), then restated by Brian O'Doherty in his theses on the ideology of the white cube (O'Doherty, 1986). They still have a lot of validity. Yet now we are confronted with a new series of outbursts, under such names as net.art, bio art, visual geography, space art and database art – to which one could add an archi-art, or art of architecture, which curiously enough has never been baptized as such, as well as a machine art that reaches all the way back to 1920s constructivism, or even a 'finance art' whose birth was announced in the Casa Encendida of Madrid just last summer.

The heterogeneous character of the list immediately suggests its application to all the domains where theory and practice meet. In the artistic forms that result, one will always find remains of the old

53

modernist tropism whereby art designates itself first of all, drawing the attention back to its own operations of expression, representation, metaphorization or deconstruction. Independently of whatever 'subject' it treats, art tends to make this self-reflexivity its distinctive or identifying trait, even its *raison d'être*, in a gesture whose philosophical legitimacy was established by Immanuel Kant. But in the kind of work I want to discuss, there is something more at stake.

We can approach it through the word that the Nettime project used to define its collective ambitions. For the artists, theorists, media activists and programmers who inhabited that mailing list – one of the important vectors of net.art in the late 1990s – it was a matter of proposing an 'immanent critique' of the Internet, that is, of the techno-scientific infrastructure then in the course of construction. This critique was to be carried out inside the network itself, using its languages and its technical tools and focusing on its characteristic objects, with the goal of influencing or even of directly shaping its development – but without refusing the possibilities of distribution outside this circuit.[1] What's sketched out is a two-way movement, which consists in occupying a field with a potential for shaking up society (telematics) and then radiating outward from that specialized domain, with the explicitly formulated aim of effecting change in the discipline of art (considered too formalist and narcissistic to escape its own charmed circle), in the discipline of cultural critique (considered too academic and historicist to confront the current transformations) and even in the 'discipline' – if you can call it that – of leftist activism (considered too doctrinaire, too ideological to seize the occasions of the present).

At work here is a new tropism and a new sort of reflexivity, involving artists as well as theorists and activists in a passage beyond the limits traditionally assigned to their practice. The word tropism conveys the desire or need to turn towards something else, towards an exterior field or discipline; while the notion of reflexivity now indicates a critical return to the departure point, an attempt to transform the initial discipline, to end its isolation, to open up new possibilities of expression, analysis, cooperation and commitment. This back-and-forth movement, or rather, this transformative spiral, is the operative principle of what I will be calling extradisciplinary investigations.

The concept was forged in an attempt to go beyond a kind of double aimlessness that affects contemporary signifying practices, even a double drift, but without the revolutionary qualities that the Situationists were looking for. I'm thinking first of the inflation of interdisciplinary discourses on the academic and cultural circuits: a virtuoso combinatory system that feeds the symbolic mill of cognitive capital, acting as a kind of supplement to the endless pinwheels of finance itself (the curator Hans-Ulrich Obrist is a specialist of these combinatories). Second is the state of indiscipline that is an unsought effect of the anti-authoritarian revolts of the 1960s, where the subject simply gives into the aesthetic solicitations of the market (in the neo-Pop vein, indiscipline means endlessly repeating and remixing the flux of prefabricated commercial images). Though they aren't the same, interdisciplinarity and indiscipline have become the two most common excuses for the neutralization of significant inquiry (Holmes, 2001). But there is no reason to accept them.

The extradisciplinary ambition is to carry out rigorous investigations on terrains as far away from art as finance, biotech, geography, urbanism, psychiatry, the electromagnetic spectrum, etc., to bring forth on those terrains the 'free play of the faculties' and the intersubjective experimentation that are characteristic of modern art, but also to try to identify, inside those same domains, the spectacular or instrumental uses so often made of the subversive liberty of aesthetic play – as the architect Eyal Weizman does in exemplary fashion, when he investigates the appropriation by the Israeli and US military of what were initially conceived as subversive architectural strategies. Weizman challenges the military on its own terrain, with his maps of security infrastructures in Israel; but what he brings back are elements for a critical examination of what used to be his exclusive discipline (Weizman, 2007). This complex movement, which never neglects the existence of the different disciplines, but never lets itself be trapped by them either, can provide a new departure point for what used to be called *institutional critique*.

Histories in the Present

What has been established, retrospectively, as the 'first generation' of institutional critique includes figures like Michael Asher, Robert Smithson, Daniel Buren, Hans Haacke and Marcel Broodthaers. They examined the conditioning of their own activity by the ideological and economic frames of the museum, with the goal of breaking out. As Stefan Nowotny and Jens Kastner show in their essays in this section of this volume, these artists had a strong relation to the anti-institutional revolts of the 1960s and 70s, and to the accompanying philosophical critiques. The best way to take their specific focus on the museum is not as a self-assigned limit or a fetishization of the institution, but instead as part of a materialist praxis, lucidly aware of its context, but with wider transformatory intentions. To find out where their story leads, however, we have to look at the writing of Benjamin Buchloh and see how he framed the emergence of institutional critique.

In a text entitled 'Conceptual Art 1962-1969', Buchloh (1990) quotes two key propositions by Lawrence Weiner. The first is *A Square Removed from a Rug in Use*, and the second, *A 36"x 36" Removal to the Lathing or Support Wall of Plaster or Wallboard from a Wall* (both 1968). In each it is a matter of taking the most self-referential and tautological form possible – the square, whose sides each repeat and reiterate the others – and inserting it in an environment marked by the determinisms of the social world. As Buchloh writes:

> Both interventions – while maintaining their structural and morphological links with formal traditions by respecting classical geometry... – inscribe themselves in the support surfaces of the institutions and/or the home which that tradition had always disavowed... On the one hand, it dissipates the expectation of encountering the work of art only in a 'specialized' or 'qualified' location... On the other, neither one of these surfaces could ever be considered to be independent from their institutional location, since the physical inscription into each particular surface inevitably generates contextual readings. (Buchloh, 1990)

Weiner's propositions are clearly a version of immanent critique, operating flush with the discursive and material structures of the art institutions; but they are cast as a purely logical deduction from minimal and conceptual premises. They just as clearly prefigure the symbolic activism of Gordon Matta-Clark's 'anarchitecture' works, like *Splitting* (1973) or *Window Blow-Out* (1976), which confronted the gallery space with urban inequality and racial discrimination. From that departure point, a history of artistic critique could have led to contemporary forms of activism and technopolitical research, via the mobilization of artists around the AIDS epidemic in late 1980s. But the most widespread versions of 1960s and 70s cultural history never took that turn. According to the subtitle of Buchloh's famous text, the teleological movement of late-modernist art in the 1970s was heading 'from the aesthetics of administration to the critique of institutions'. This would mean a strictly Frankfurtian vision of the museum as an idealizing Enlightenment institution, damaged by both the bureaucratic state and the market spectacle.

Other histories could be written. At stake is the tense double-bind between the desire to transform the specialized 'cell' (as Brian O'Doherty described the modernist gallery) into a mobile potential of living knowledge that can reach out into the world, and the counter-realization that everything about this specialized aesthetic space is a trap, that it has been instituted as a form of enclosure. That tension produced the incisive interventions of Michal Asher, the sledgehammer denunciations of Hans Haacke, the paradoxical displacements of Robert Smithson, or the melancholic humor and poetic fantasy of Marcel Broodthaers, whose hidden mainspring was a youthful engagement with revolutionary surrealism. The first thing is never to reduce the diversity and complexity of artists who never voluntarily joined into a movement. Another reduction comes from the obsessive focus on a specific site of presentation, the museum, whether it is mourned as a fading relic of the 'bourgeois public sphere', or exalted with a fetishizing discourse of 'site specificity'. These two pitfalls lay in wait for the discourse of institutional critique, when it took explicit form in the United States in the late 1980s and early 90s.

It was the period of the so-called 'second generation'. Among the names most often cited are Renee Green, Christian Philipp Müller, Fred Wilson and Andrea Fraser. They pursued the systematic exploration of museological representation, examining its links to economic power and its epistemological roots in a colonial science that treats the Other like an object to be shown in a vitrine. But they added a subjectivizing turn, unimaginable without the influence of feminism and postcolonial historiography, which allowed them to recast external power hierarchies as ambivalences within the self, opening up a conflicted sensibility to the coexistence of multiple modes and vectors of representation. There is a compelling negotiation here, particularly in the work of Renee Green, between specialized discourse analysis and embodied experimentation with the human sensorium. Yet most of this work was also carried out in the form of meta-reflections on the limits of the artistic practices themselves (mock museum displays or scripted video performances), staged within institutions that were ever-more blatantly corporate – to the point where it became increasingly hard to shield the critical investigations from their own accusations, and their own often devastating conclusions.

This situation of a critical process taking itself for its object recently led Andrea Fraser to consider the artistic institution as an unsurpassable, all-defining frame, sustained through its own inwardly directed critique (Fraser, 2005). Bourdieu's deterministic analysis of the closure of the socio-professional fields, mingled with a deep confusion between Weber's iron cage and Foucault's desire 'to get free of oneself', is internalized here in a governmentality of failure, where the subject can do no more than contemplate his or her own psychic prison, with a few aesthetic luxuries in compensation. Unfortunately, it all adds very little to Broodthaers' lucid testament (1987), formulated on a single page in 1975. For Broodthaers, the only alternative to a guilty conscience was self-imposed blindness – not exactly a solution! Yet Fraser accepts it, by posing her argument as an attempt to "defend the very institution for which the institution of the avant-garde's 'self-criticism' had created the potential: the institution of critique" (Fraser, 2005: 282).

Without any antagonistic or even agonistic relation to the status quo, and above all, without any aim to change it, what's defended becomes little more than a masochistic variation on the self-serving 'institutional theory of art' promoted by Arthur Danto, George Dickie and their followers (a theory of mutual and circular recognition among members of an object-oriented milieu, misleadingly called a 'world'). The loop is looped, and what had been a large-scale, complex, searching and transformational project of 1960s and 70s art seems to reach a dead end, with institutional consequences of complacency, immobility, loss of autonomy, capitulation before various forms of instrumentalization.

Phase Change

The end may be logical, but some desire to go much further. The first thing is to redefine the means, the media and the aims of a possible third phase of institutional critique. The notion of transversality, developed by the practitioners of institutional analysis, helps to theorize the assemblages that link actors and resources from the art circuit to projects and experiments that don't exhaust themselves inside it, but rather, extend elsewhere (Guattari, 2003). These projects can no longer be unambiguously defined as art. They are based instead on a circulation between disciplines, often involving the real critical reserve of marginal or counter-cultural positions – social movements, political associations, squats, autonomous universities – which can't be reduced to an all-embracing institution.

The projects tend to be collective, even if they also tend to flee the difficulties that collectivity involves, by operating as networks. Their inventors, who came of age in the universe of cognitive capitalism, are drawn toward complex social functions which they seize upon in all their technical detail, and in full awareness that the second nature of the world is now shaped by technology and organizational form. In almost every case it is a political engagement that gives them the desire to pursue their exacting investigations beyond the limits of an artistic or academic discipline. But their analytic processes are at the same time expressive, and for them, every complex machine is awash in affect and subjectivity. It is when these subjective and analytic sides mesh closely together, in the new productive and political contexts of communicational labor (and not just in meta-reflections staged uniquely for the museum), that one can speak of a 'third phase' of institutional critique – or better, of a 'phase change' in what was formerly known as the public sphere, a change which has extensively transformed the contexts and modes of cultural and intellectual production in the twenty-first century.

An issue of *Multitudes*, co-edited with the *Transform* web-journal, gives examples of this approach.[2] The aim is to sketch the problematic field of an exploratory practice that is not new, but is definitely rising in urgency. Rather than offering a curatorial recipe, we wanted to cast new light on the old problems of the closure of specialized disciplines, the intellectual and affective paralysis to which it gives rise, and the alienation of any capacity for democratic decision-making that inevitably follows, particularly in a highly complex technological society. The forms of expression, public intervention and critical reflexivity that have been developed in response to such conditions can be characterized as extradisciplinary – but without fetishizing the word at the expense of the horizon it seeks to indicate.

On considering the work, and particularly the articles dealing with technopolitical issues, some will probably wonder if it might not have been interesting to evoke the name of Bruno Latour. His ambition is that of 'making things public', or more precisely, elucidating the specific encounters between complex technical objects and specific processes of decision-making (whether these are *de jure* or *de facto* political). For that, he says, one must proceed in the form of 'proofs', established as rigorously as possible, but at the same time necessarily 'messy', like the things of the world themselves (Latour and Weibel, 2005).

There is something interesting in Latour's proving machine (even if it does tend, unmistakably, toward the academic productivism of 'interdisciplinarity'). A concern for how things are shaped in the present, and a desire for constructive interference in the processes and decisions that shape them, is characteristic of those who no longer dream of an absolute outside and a total, year-zero revolution. However, it's enough to consider the artists whom we invited to the *Multitudes* issue, in order to see the differences. Hard as one may try, the 1750 km Baku-Tiblisi-Ceyhan pipeline cannot be reduced to the 'proof' of anything, even if Ursula Biemann did compress it into the ten distinct sections of the *Black Sea Files*.[3] Traversing Azerbaijan, Georgia and Turkey before it debouches in the Mediterranean, the pipeline forms the object of political decisions even while it sprawls beyond reason and imagination, engaging the whole planet in the geopolitical and ecological uncertainty of the present.

Similarly, the Paneuropean transport and communication corridors running through the former Yugoslavia, Greece and Turkey, filmed by the participants of the Timescapes group initiated by Angela Melitopoulos, result from the one of the most complex infrastructure-planning processes of our epoch, carried out at the transnational and transcontinental levels. Yet these precisely designed economic projects are at once inextricable from the conflicted memories of their historical precedents, and immediately delivered over to the multiplicity of their uses, which include the staging of massive, self-organized protests in conscious resistance to the manipulation of daily life by the corridor-planning process. Human beings do not necessarily want to be the living 'proof' of an economic thesis, carried out from above with powerful and sophisticated instruments – including media devices that distort their images and their most intimate affects. An anonymous protester's insistent sign, brandished in the face of the TV cameras at the demonstrations surrounding the 2003 EU summit in Thessalonica, says it all: ANY SIMILARITY TO ACTUAL PERSONS OR EVENTS IS UNINTENTIONAL.[4]

Art history has emerged into the present, and the critique of the conditions of representation has spilled out onto the streets. But in the same movement, the streets have taken up their place in our critiques. In the philosophical essays that we included in the *Multitudes* project, *institution* and *constitution* always rhyme with *destitution*.[5] The specific focus on extradisciplinary artistic practices does not mean radical politics has been forgotten, far from it. Today more than ever, any constructive investigation has to raise the standards of resistance.

Notes

1. See the introduction to the anthology *ReadMe!* (Bosma, 1999). One of the best examples of immanent critique is the project 'Name Space' by Paul Garrin, which aimed to rework the domain name system (DNS), which constitutes the web as a navigable space (Bosma, 1999: 224-9).

2. See 'Extradisciplinaire', online at http://transform.eipcp.net/transversal/0507.

3. The video installation *Black Sea Files* by Ursula Biemann, done in the context of the Transcultural Geographies project, has been exhibited with the other works of that project at Kunst-Werke in Berlin, December 2005 – February 2006, then at Tapies Foundation in Barcelona, March – May 2007; published in Franke (2005).

4. The video installation *Corridor X* by Angela Melitopoulos, with the work of the other members of Timescapes, has been exhibited and published in Franke (2005).

5. See Stefan Nowotny's essay on destitution in the last section of this volume, as well as Pechriggl (2007).

8

Louise Lawler's Rude Museum[*]

Rosalyn Deutsche

On the brink of World War II, Virginia Woolf advised women to remember, learn from and use derision, of which they had long been objects (Woolf, 1938: 6). *Three Guineas*, Woolf's classic essay of ethico-political thought, counts derision among the great 'un-paid teachers' of women, educating them about the behavior and motives of human beings, that is, about psychology, a field that Woolf, unlike many leftist critics today, did not separate from that of the political.[1] Before writing the essay, Woolf had received requests for contributions from three organizations, each promoting a different cause: women's education, the advancement of women in the professions, and the prevention of war. At least that is the book's conceit. She responded by linking the three movements, making clear that for her the goal of feminism was not just equality for women but a better, less war-like, society. Since, she argued, the professions as currently practiced encourage qualities that lead to war – grandiosity, vanity, egoism, patriotism, possessiveness, combativeness – women must not simply become educated professionals but do so differently: "How can we enter the professions and yet remain civilized human beings; human beings, that is, who wish to prevent war" (Woolf, 1938: 75)? Women can help, she suggested, by refusing to be deferential to the esteemed professions and instead considering it their duty to express the opinion that professional customs and rituals are contemptible. And what better way to accomplish this task than through humor, which, as Mignon Nixon notes, following Freud, discharges psychic energy, has pleasurable effects, and "promotes the defiance of deference"? (Nixon, 2005: 67).

Woolf's humor was of the type that Freud called 'tendentious'. It served the purpose of criticizing authority and, like hostile jokes, exploited "something ridiculous in our enemy" (Freud, 1960: 123-5). Here is a sample from her observations on professional dress:

> How many, how splendid, how extremely ornate they are – the clothes worn by the educated man in his public capacity! Now you dress in violet; a jeweled crucifix swings on your breast; now your shoulders are covered with lace; now furred with ermine; now slung with many linked chains set with precious stones. Now you wear wigs on your heads; rows of graduated curls descend to your necks. Now your hats are boat shaped, or cocked; now they mount in cones of black fur. (Woolf, 1938: 19)

Woolf derided men's professional trappings because of the hierarchical distinctions of rank and the will to power they signified: "Every button, rosette and stripe seems to have some symbolical meaning. Some have the right to wear plain buttons only; others rosettes; some may wear a single stripe; others three, four or five. And each curl or stripe is sewn on at precisely the right distance apart – it may be one inch for one man, one inch and a quarter for another" (Woolf, 1938: 19). Distinctions of dress, like adding titles before or letters after names, were designed to show superiority and to arouse competition and jealousy. Therefore the professional fashion system encouraged "a disposition towards war" (Woolf, 1938: 19).

Today, some critics find Woolf's hope that women, by virtue of their earlier exclusion, might change the professions outdated, irrelevant to a historical period in which women have to a considerable extent entered public life. Yet latent in Woolf's plea – what necessitates it – is, I think, the thoroughly timely recognition that the opposite is just as likely to occur: women can identify with the masculinist position. "It would be perfectly possible for a woman to occupy the role of a representative man", as Homi Bhabha puts it, explaining why he uses the term *masculinism* not to designate the power of actual male persons but to denote a position of power authorized by the claim that one comprehends and represents the social totality (Bhabha, 1992: 242). Masculinism understood in this sense is a relationship that can be sustained only by declaring war on otherness, by subjugating that which cannot be fully known. Woolf believed that cultural institutions cultivate the triumphalist relationship. Alert, like her anti-fascist contemporary

Walter Benjamin, to the barbarism underlying every 'document of civilization' (Benjamin, 1969: 256), she approached such documents warily. No venerated institution was safe from her derision. She even listed the British Royal Academy of Art, the institution that safeguarded standards of professional competence in art, among the great 'battlegrounds', whose members, she said, "seem to be as bloodthirsty as the profession of arms itself" (Woolf, 1938: 63).

Woolf was referring to combative behavior between the male academicians, but the Academy inflicted another kind of violence, one that can be discerned in Johann Zoffany's portrait of the academicians, *Life Class at the Royal Academy* (1772), a painting that has been an icon of feminist art history since Linda Nochlin used it to illustrate her landmark essay, 'Why Have There Been No Great Women Artists?' (Nochlin, 1971).[2] Nochlin treats Zoffany's conversation piece as a document of sexism, a work that shows an aspect of historical discrimination against women in the arts. Zoffany presented the academicians gathered around a nude male model at a time when women were excluded from access to the male nude and therefore from history painting, the most prestigious genre in the Academy's hierarchy. He solved the problem of including the Academy's two female founding members, Angelica Kauffmann and Mary Moser, by portraying them as painted portraits hanging on the wall. Directly facing the nude model, lit by a chandelier, stands Sir Joshua Reynolds, president of the Academy and author of the *Discourses on Art*, which he addressed as lectures to the 'Gentlemen' of the Royal Academy between 1769 and 1790. But, according to the critic Naomi Schor, 'Reynolds' does not just name a historical person; it is also "the proper name for the idealist aesthetics he promotes" (Schor, 1987: 17). The classical busts and figures strewn around Zoffany's life class allude to this aesthetic. Schor concludes that Reynolds' classical discourse, in which genius consists of the ability to comprehend a unity – what Reynolds enthusiastically called 'A WHOLE' – and in which the feminine is associated with the detail, which endangers masculine wholeness, cannot be separated from the discourse of misogyny (Schor, 1987: 5).

Idealist approaches to art are hardly limited to eighteenth-century classicism; they have remained alive for centuries in the widespread notion that the work of art is a complete, autonomous entity that elevates viewers above the contingencies of material life. Zoffany's *Academicians*, then, is not just a period piece that documents women's historical exclusion from art education. It also records the transformation of the female figure from artist to image, from viewing subject to visual object, to what feminists two hundred years later theorized as a signifier of 'to-be-looked-at-ness' (Mulvey, 1989: 14-26). That is, it documents the representational economy that Freud called fetishism, a perversion originating in the phallocentric attempt to triumph over the female body and its supposed threat to wholeness. Zoffany unwittingly shows us that the aesthetic institution is a masculinist battleground – an authoritarian rather than democratically agonistic realm – in a somewhat different sense than Woolf had in mind.

So far I have argued that Woolf's feminist challenge to cultural institutions is not gender-exclusive. Just as women can identify with masculine positions, men, who historically have occupied actual positions of power, can dis-identify with them. That is, there can be a non-phallic masculinity. Still, it is interesting to note that when, in the 1970s and 80s, a group of mostly female artists, including Louise Lawler, entered art institutions in order to explore them as, precisely, battlegrounds, they did so differently than the first wave of institution-critical artists.[3] For whereas Marcel Broodthaers, Hans Haacke, Daniel Buren, and Michael Asher had drawn attention to the presence of economic and political power in the seemingly pure and neutral space of the museum and to the way the museum embodies dominant ideology and so exercises discursive power, and whereas works like Broodthaer's *Décor: A Conquest* (1975) and Haacke's *MoMA Poll* (1970) had, in different ways, specifically connected museums to war, the second wave – such diverse artists as Lawler, Victor Burgin, Andrea Fraser, Judith Barry, Silvia Kolbowski, Barbara Kruger, Sherrie Levine, Fred Wilson, and Mary Kelly, among others – at once extended and questioned the critique. Art historians have proposed a number of ways to distinguish between the work of the so-called first 'generation' of institutional critics and the second, postmodern generation, Lawler in particular: the second questions the authority of its own voice rather than simply challenging the authoritarian voice of museums, corporations, and governments (Foster, et al., 2004: 624); Lawler locates institutional power in a "systematized set of presentational procedures, whereas Asher, Buren, Haacke, and Broodthears situated power in a centralized building or elite" (Fraser, 1985: 123); Lawler explores not only the contextual production of meaning but, in deconstructive fashion, the boundlessness of context (Linker, 1986: 99). Still another difference is that, unlike the first generation, feminist postmodernists were influenced by psychoanalysis and recognized to varying degrees the political importance of articulating relationships between psychical and social realms. Following in Woolf's footsteps, they approached institutions of aesthetic display not only as producers of bourgeois ideology but as spaces where dangerous, masculinist fantasies are solidified.

Lawler may not have been an exponent of psychoanalytic feminism, but many of her photographs lead us into the heart of such 'solid wishes'. And they do so with what Birgit Pelzer aptly calls a 'dose of derision' (Pelzer, 2004: 32). Literary theorist Kenneth Gross uses the term 'solid wishes' in *The Dream of the Moving Statue*, a book about relationships between figural statues and fantasy, about statues *as* fantasies. "Works of sculpture", writes Gross, are "solid wishes, or vehicles of a wish for things that *are* solid" (Gross, 1992: 198). It seems fitting, then, that some of the works in which Lawler most astutely exposes the art institution's fantasy life are a group of photographs, taken in the late 1970s and early 80s, that depict figural sculpture, and, in particular, classical and neoclassical statues, in museum settings. *Statue before Painting, 'Perseus with the Head of Medusa' by Canova* (1982) is exemplary. It served as the introductory image in Lawler's first published portfolio of the photographs she calls 'arrangements of pictures'. The black-and-white portfolio, itself an arrangement of pictures, appeared in the Fall 1983 issue of the journal *October*. Lawler's 'arrangements' depict art objects in their contexts of display, calling attention to the presentational apparatus of specific arts institutions and, at the same time, to 'art as institution', a phrase coined by Peter Bürger to refer to a more dispersed aesthetic apparatus: "The concept 'art as an institution'… refers to the productive and distributive apparatus and also to ideas about art that prevail at a given time and that determine the reception of works" (Bürger, 1984: 22). In such works as *Statue before Painting*, Lawler puts existing museological arrangements of artworks on display and makes visible the elements of the presentational apparatus, which, though authoritative, generally lie on the margins of the museum-goer's visual and cognitive field – architecture, labels, vitrines, pedestals, guards, installation shots, catalogues, security systems, and so on. Lawler appropriates the museum's arrangements and re-arranges them in a manner that recalls Freud's approach to dream interpretation, an approach that re-arranges the space of the dream, bringing its peripheral elements, its details, into focus (and *vice versa*) in order to analyze the dream-work that distorts the wish at the dream's core. While it is tempting to see Lawler's arrangements, with their fragmented objects, exaggerated details, and enigmatic juxtapositions, as dream scenarios, they might more accurately be regarded as analyses of the museum's 'dreams', of the desire embodied in its arrangements.

Lawler shot *Statue before Painting, 'Perseus with the Head of Medusa', by Canova* in New York's Metropolitan Museum of Art, from the vantage point of the museum's Great Hall Balcony, where Antonio Canova's marble statue was then located. The statue occupied a position on the neoclassical museum building's processional axis, which begins at the steps leading to the main entrance, continues through the Great Hall and central staircase – both are overlooked by the balcony – and culminates at the arched entrance to the galleries of European paintings. *Perseus* stood across from the entrance, beneath an echoing arch on the balcony. The museum's official guidebook describes it as a second, more refined version of a sculpture that, when first executed and exhibited in Canova's studio between 1770 and 1800, "was acclaimed as the last word in the continuing purification of the Neoclassical style" (Howard, 1994: 265). Like 'Reynolds', 'Canova', too, is a proper name for idealist aesthetics, whose patriarchal relations of sexual difference, observed in Zoffany's *Life Class*, are concretized in the roughly contemporaneous *Perseus*. Seen in Lawler's photograph from a low, oblique angle and radically cropped so that it is cut by the upper edge of the photograph, Canova's statue, its phallus, and its pedestal – architectural equivalent of the phallus – occupy the forefront of the viewer's vision. At the same time, pushed to the right edge of the image, the statue is dislodged from its central position, disrupting the Museum's symmetrical arrangement. Behind Perseus, beyond the balcony's balustrade, the staircase, flanked by colonnades of Corinthian columns, rises from the Great Hall below and leads to the double arches through which visitors, after ascending the stairs, enter the collection of paintings. Framed by the arches hangs Giovanni Battista Tiepolo's *The Triumph of Marius* (1729), the opening exhibit in the anteroom to the Museum's history of Western painting. Its upper portion is sliced by the lower edge of the sign inscribed with the word 'paintings', a mutilation that corresponds to that of the Perseus statue, which Lawler brings into visual alignment with the Tiepolo. In a second correspondence, the colossal painting dwarfs its spectators, who look up at it in an attitude that rhymes with our own angle of vision of statue and phallus in Lawler's photograph. Lawler accentuates this point of view, placing her viewers in a position that mimics not only that of the depicted viewers of Tiepolo but that of a small child catching sight of its parents' genitals. She thus suggests, perhaps unwittingly, that the psychic life of the museum bears a relation to infantile fantasies. The juxtaposition of the spectators' stance in front of the Tiepolo and Lawler's upward glance at Perseus literalizes both the deference with which art as institution treats works of art and the veneration with which classical antiquity regarded the phallus, defined as the figurative representation of the male organ. Drawing attention to the way the museum's arrangement includes a prescribed position for viewers, one that enforces a certain mode of spectatorship, Lawler simultaneously, as we shall see, makes Perseus the butt of derision and consequently re-positions her audience, inviting them to defy deference.

First, however, note one more similarity between the Tiepolo and the Canova, this one on the level of thematic content: each depicts a violent conquest in which a male protagonist establishes his authority by mastering difference – racial and sexual, respectively. Each glorifies war. In the Museum's words, *The Triumph of Marius* "shows the Roman general Gaius Marius in the victor's chariot while the conquered African king Jugurtha walks before him, bound in chains... The Latin inscription on the cartouche at the top translates, 'The Roman people behold Jugurtha laden with chains'" (Howard, 1994: 186). For his part, Canova portrays the classical hero Perseus holding aloft the head of Medusa, which he has just severed. Medusa, of course, is the female monster of classical mythology, who had snakes instead of hair and whose look turned men to stone.

At the time, Medusa's head had considerable currency among psychoanalytic feminists working in the visual arts, largely because in 1922 Freud had written a short essay about it and because in 1973, in an equally short text, 'You Don't Know What Is Happening, Do You Mr. Jones?', precursor to her famous 'Visual Pleasure and Narrative Cinema', Laura Mulvey had used Freud's interpretation as the basis of a theory of phallocentric investments in looking at images (Freud, 1968; and Mulvey, 1989: 6-13 and 14-26). Additionally, Medusa had become a symbol of feminist subversion of phallocentric mastery in such writing as Hélène Cixous's 'The Laugh of the Medusa' of 1975 (Cixous, 1981:

245-64). Freud, as is well known, analyzed Medusa's head as a fetish: an object – visual, in this case – of masculine fixation that originates in fear of the female body, which is (mis)perceived as castrated, as missing the penis and, more importantly, the phallus, signifier of the presence that makes the subject whole. For Freud, Medusa's horrifying, decapitated head, surrounded by hair, symbolizes the female genitals and therefore the horror of castration. At the same time, it serves as a 'token of triumph' over castration anxiety, an object that disavows and conquers the threat of sexual difference. Visually, it contains multiple penis replacements in the form of Medusa's snake-hair, and on the narrative level, it turns men to stone, thus stiffening them and reassuring them of the presence of the penis. Mulvey argued that just as Medusa's head is an image not of a woman but, rather, of the threatened masculine subject restored to wholeness, so in a culture ordered by phallocentric categorizations of human beings, in which the feminine is equated with absence and loss, images of women have served, in various ways, as self-images of men, or, more importantly, of the narcissistic masculine ego. The feminist discourse about fetishism was concerned with the nature of masculine subjectivity, especially as it is reinforced by vision.

When *October* published Lawler's 'Arrangement of Pictures', it mis-captioned *Statue before Painting*, calling it *Statue before a Painting*. The editorial 'correction' – the insertion of the indefinite article *a* – stemmed from a failure to get the title's joke, to understand that it is a joke. For the real title mimics the phrase *ladies before gentlemen*, which is part of and here stands for an idealizing patriarchal discourse that supposedly places women on pedestals. In conjunction with the photograph, the title links patriarchal ideals and idealist aesthetics, which the neoclassical statue represents, suggesting that there is an alignment of sexual and aesthetic hierarchies in the museum. The image reverses the order of genders in the original phrase, for here it is a male statue – a phallic figure – that stands before a painting and occupies a pedestal. But the reversal only reveals the true gender relations behind idealizing arrangements, showing that in the patriarchal visual field "the true exhibit is always the phallus", as Mulvey puts it (Mulvey, 1989: 13).

To an extent, Lawler retrieves the artistic practice, prevalent among certain sculptors in the mid-1950s to late 60s, of what Mignon Nixon, in her superb study of Louise Bourgeois, calls 'posing the phallus'. This practice, Nixon (2005: 66, 236) argues, targeted the phallus with humor, which has the political effect of undermining it as a patriarchal symbol, and inverts the seriousness of fetishism.[4] Yet Lawler's work differs from that of the earlier artists since, instead of sculpting a phallus, she uses her customary techniques of appropriation and montage – of "making meaning by juxtaposition and alignment" (Lawler, 2000) – to pose a found phallus, one of the many 'readymade' phalluses that proliferate in art museums, like snakes on Medusa's head. Posing the phallus in the context of an institution-critical work, in which Perseus takes up a position as guardian of the Museum's painting collection, *Statue before Painting* exhibits the role played by art as institution in reproducing sexual norms and maintaining the patriarchal overvaluation of the phallus.[5] For one thing, the photograph comments on the historical exclusion of female artists from the museum and, for another, it alludes to the male-dominated revival of traditional painting that was legitimated by art institutions in the 1970s and 1980s. But Lawler's photograph plays a bigger joke on the Metropolitan. It hints that what underlies, what precedes or comes before the museum's aesthetic arrangements is the desire solidified in both the form and subject matter of Canova's statue of Perseus. The idealized, neoclassical sculpture, substitute for an ideal body, materializes the phallocentric fantasy of the self, a self that in its dream of autonomy disavows its constitutive exclusion of and relation to others. In fact, Jacques Lacan, writing about the mirror stage as the matrix of narcissistic ego-formation, described the mirror image – external reflection of an idealized self – as "the *statue* in which man projects himself" (Lacan, 1977: 1-7). And the iconography of Perseus and Medusa foregrounds, as does the story told in Tiepolo's painting, the subordination and conquest of otherness – the warlike disposition – necessary to maintain the narcissistic fiction. The phallic statue metonymically alludes to the triumphalist subject positioned by the museum's idealist aesthetic.

Statue before Painting deprives Perseus of his token of triumph; Medusa's head is pushed outside the frame, Perseus is decapitated, and it would seem that Medusa, herself a kind of sculptor, has turned him to stone. Of course, this also fulfills his wish, soothing as well as testifying to his castration anxiety. Still, the most striking feature of the photograph is its attack on the integrity of the male body. The photographic cut challenges the sculpture's closure, exposing it to its outside. According to Christian Metz, the cut, which produces "the off-frame effect in photography", is a figure of castration because "it marks the place of an irreversible absence, a place from which the look has been diverted forever" (Metz, 1999: 217). Lawler's cut directs the diverted look to three objects that remain in the frame and that, as fetishes, represent attempts to establish integrity and disavow vulnerability – pedestal, phallus, and museum label, an element that visually echoes the phallus and no doubt bears the artist's proper name, the 'Name-of-the-Father', Lacan's name for the patriarchal order of sexual difference.[6] Precisely by giving prominence to these elements, Lawler takes away their authority,[7] as she does that of the grand staircase, itself an elevating structure that symbolically lifts visitors, just as the pedestal lifts the work of art, above the contingencies of everyday social life, encouraging them to take up the self-regarding position that Georges Bataille described in his definition of the museum as, precisely, a mirror:

> It is not just that the museums of the world as a whole today represent a colossal accumulation of riches but, more important, that all those who visit these museums represent without a doubt the most grandiose spectacle of a humanity liberated from material concerns and devoted to contemplation. We need to recognize that the galleries and the objects of art form only the container, the content of which is constituted by the visitors….The museum is the colossal mirror in which man finally contemplates himself in every respect, finds himself literally admirable, and abandons himself to the ecstasy expressed in all the art magazines. (Bataille, 1971: 239)

Statue before Painting reveals and refuses the museum's positioning of the spectator, and it does so with supreme economy. Like a really good tendentious joke that, according to Freud, allows the teller and the recipient or, in our case, artist and viewer, to enjoy the pleasure of being impolite to "the great, the dignified and the mighty" (Freud, 1960: 125). Indeed, Lawler calls one of her later arrangements of pictures, really an arrangement of statues, *The Rude Museum* (1987). 'Rude' refers to the photograph's subject matter – a museum devoted to the work of nineteenth-century French sculptor François Rude – but it can also be read as a pun that alludes to the barbaric fantasies fostered in art institutions and, more, to the acts of impropriety with which Lawler herself, in this and other photographs, re-arranges museums and, as I have argued, exposes their fantasies. That is, it alludes to Lawler's own rude museums.

The actual Rude Museum, located in the transept of St. Etienne church in Dijon, consists of casts of works by Rude, a great patriot and admirer of the antique, though given in his sculpture to romantic gestures. Dominating the upper portion of Lawler's photograph is a plaster cast of Rude's most famous work, the high stone relief on the Arc de Triomphe in Paris, *Departure of the Volunteers in 1792*, popularly known as *La Marseillaise* (1833-36). Near the center of the relief, which is severed by the frame of Lawler's picture so that the enormous figure of an especially militaristic Liberty hovering above cannot be seen, is a classically inspired male nude marching off to war. Like Canova's *Perseus*, Rude's soldier is beheaded by Lawler's cropping of the photograph, a cut that foreshadows the fate of later victims of the French Revolution. In the foreground, its foreshortened backside turned to the viewer, crouches a large hippopotamus sculpted by François Pompon (1855-1933). Stretching up its head and opening its mouth, it gawks at the hero's exposed phallus. The hippo could be regarded as yet another target of Lawler's humor, but I prefer to think of it as her ally, a *repoussoir* element that not only pushes back the principle scene but functions, by virtue of its comical deference (and open jaws), as a formidable threat to the phallic figure – as a rude viewer in the Rude Museum, like Lawler and those willing to listen to her tendentious joke.

For derisive impropriety, also made possible with the help of wild animals, nothing surpasses *Birdcalls* (1972/1981), an audiotape on which Lawler squeals, squawks, chirps, twitters, croaks, squeaks, and occasionally warbles the names – primarily the surnames – of twenty-eight contemporary male artists, from Vito Acconci to Lawrence Weiner.[8] Recorded by Terry Wilson, the tape sounds as though different species of birds are calling out to one another in some natural setting, say, a forest or garden. In 1984, Andrea Miller-Keller, a curator at the Wadsworth Atheneum, one venue where the work has been played, nicknamed it *Patriarchal Roll Call*.[9]

When Lawler made the tape she was unaware of the precise difference between the two types of sound signals made by birds: calls and songs. For the title, she selected 'calls' because she thought that 'song' connoted pleasure for the bird whereas 'call' seemed more strident.[10] Her choice turned out to be highly accurate, in keeping with the intention and execution of the work, since it is typically male birds that burst into songs, which are complex patterns of notes used to attract mates or establish territory. Calls, by contrast, consist of one or more short, repeated notes that convey messages about specific situations. If, for instance, a predator enters the immediate environment, birds give distress, alarm, and rally calls to signal the presence of a threat and to coordinate group activity against it (Kress, 1991: 80). Similarly, Lawler's *Birdcalls* originated in an act of self-defense. "In the early 1970s", she tells Douglas Crimp,

> my friend Martha Kite and I were helping some artists on one of the Hudson River pier projects. The women involved were doing tons of work, but the work being shown was only by male artists. Walking home at night in New York, one way to feel safe is to pretend you're crazy or at least be really loud. Martha and I called ourselves the 'due chanteusies', and we'd sing off-key and make other noises. Willoughby Sharp was the impresario of the project, so we'd make a 'Willoughby Willoughby' sound, trying to sound like birds. This developed into a series of bird calls based on artists' names. So, in fact, it was antagonistic. (Lawler, 2000)

The birdcalls started out as a humorous anti-predator response to the presence of two dangers in Kite and Lawler's habitat: physical attack in the streets of the city and discrimination in the alternative art world. Drawing a perhaps inadvertent parallel with real birds, Lawler describes the first birdcalls as 'instinctual' (Lawler, 2000). Interestingly, however, bird calls, including alarm calls, are not just involuntary, impulsive emotional displays but systems of communication that can be controlled (Marler and Evans, 1995: 138). Their frequency is affected by the presence or absence of companions, a phenomenon that ornithologists call the 'audience effect'. Some bird sounds are learned (Nottebohn, 2005: 146); some sentinel birds even give 'false alarms'. The birds' capacity for control and subversion accords with Lawler's tactics in *Birdcalls*, for while she situates herself in nature, which patriarchal systems of representation and sexual difference have traditionally opposed to culture and associated with the feminine, she treats it not as a place of confinement but, rather, of retreat and concealment, a refuge where she can escape Mulvey's 'to-be-looked-at-ness' and what Michel Foucault called the 'trap' or 'cage' of visibility (Foucault, 1979: 200). Occupying the place prescribed for women (and in this regard it should be noted that *bird* is slang for a young woman), but only in jest – literally *playing* nature – she appropriates it as a base from which to make forays, using sound as ammunition, into the territory of culture and to introduce tension into its hierarchical, gendered dichotomies, destroying their seeming naturalness. Heard but not seen, she challenges the proper name, the narcissistic ego, the Name-of-the-Father, and therefore the art world's relations of sexual difference, commenting on the fact that at the time she made *Birdcalls* "artists with name recognition were predominantly male" (Lawler, 2000).

Lawler produced the first publicly presented tape of *Birdcalls* in 1981, when, as Crimp has pointed out, the upcoming *Documenta 7* (1982) was an object of much art-world discussion (Crimp, 1993: 238). Rudi Fuchs, the international exhibition's director, planned to reaffirm the phallocentric, aestheticist notion of the work of art as a complete totality transcending its conditions of existence, and he therefore gave pride of place to neo-expressionism, a male-dominated trend of the 1970s and 1980s, which to a considerable extent represented a regression to aestheticism.[11] In preparatory versions of *Birdcalls*, Lawler had included only minimalist, post-minimalist, conceptual, and pop artists. Now, she added neo-expressionist painters Sandro Chia, Francesco Clemente, Enzo Cucchi, Anselm Kiefer, and Julian Schnabel, targeting the new upsurge in masculine name-recognition with feminist name-calling.

Birdcalls is an anomaly in Lawler's production, her only sound piece, unless one counts the two versions of *A Movie Will Be Shown Without the Picture* (1979 and 1983). Yet its derisive tactics are quintessential Lawler. When she plays *Birdcalls* during presentations of her work, Lawler simultaneously projects an arrangement of slides. Some bear the names of the artists who are being called. These are interspersed with slides of both her own and the male artists' works. Following the title slide, the first, introductory image is always *Statue before Painting, 'Perseus with the Head of Medusa', by Canova*, and this arrangement indicates that there is a commonality between tape and photograph. Both, for example, use mimicry. In 1982, Lawler wanted to produce a record of *Birdcalls* and planned to decorate the jacket with a photograph of a parrot – that excellent mimic – looking suspiciously over its shoulder and set against a brilliant red background.[12] The record was never made, but, subsequently, Lawler used the parrot photograph in other contexts, titling it *Portrait* (1982). Given its initial connection to *Birdcalls*, it might be regarded as a self-portrait, in camouflage. Except that Lawler's mimicry is far from mechanical. It is, rather, one of the skills she has honed to warn audiences away from the danger of 'a position of passive agreement'[13] with the art institution's grandiose fantasies, whose war-like effects, as Virginia Woolf knew, are no laughing matter.[14]

Notes

*   First published in Louise Lawler, *Twice Untitled and Other Pictures (looking back)*, Wexner Center for the Arts and MIT Press, 2006.

1. As Silvia Kolbowski asks about the rejection of psychoanalysis in current criticism: "Is psychoanalysis too feminine? i.e. too 'weak' to serve political analysis?" (2005: 18).

2. Zoffany's painting is alternatively titled *Academicians of the Royal Academy*.

3. It could also be argued that Lawler entered the artistic profession differently insofar as she has been reticent "about taking on the conventional role of the artist". See Lawler (2000).

4. Nixon's thesis differs from mine insofar as, using Melanie Klein, she argues that Bourgeois, Jasper Johns, Yayoi Kusama and Eva Hesse posed the phallus as, specifically, a part-object – a literal body part.

5. Nixon (2005: 71) suggests that Bourgeois did something similar when, in 1982, she posed with her sculpture *Fillette* (1968) for a portrait produced by Robert Mapplethorpe for her retrospective exhibition at the Museum of Modern Art.

6. To the list of fetishes that Lawler highlights, we could add Perseus's feet in the winged sandals that Athena and Hermes lent him to aid in the conquest of Medusa. Recall that Freud speculated that the foot fetish originates in the fact that the woman's feet are the last thing the child sees before he catches sight of her genitals. The foot fetish represents the male subject's denial of the traumatic sight.

7. Lawler (2000) has used the phrase 'Prominence given, authority taken', which is the title of an important interview she did with Douglas Crimp. The phrase can be read as a description of the way the museum positions the artists, or, conversely, of Lawler's resistance to that positioning.

8. The twenty-artists are Vito Acconci, Carl Andre, Richard Artschwager, John Baldessari, Robert Barry, Joseph Beuys, Daniel Buren, Sandro Chia, Francesco Clemente, Enzo Cucchi, Gilbert & George, Dan Graham, Hans Haacke, Neil Jenney, Donald Judd, Anselm Kiefer, Joseph Kosuth, Sol Lewitt, Richard Long, Gordon Matta-Clark, Mario Merz, Sigmar Polke, Gerhard Richter, Ed Ruscha, Julian Schnabel, Cy Twombly, Andy Warhol, and Lawrence Weiner.

9. This information comes from an email from the artist, 22 April 2005.

10. From a conversation with Lawler, 26 February 2005.

11. Lawler was not invited to participate in *Documenta 7*, but Jenny Holzer and the alternative gallery Fashion Moda asked her to contribute to their collaborative work: a trailer stationed at the entrance to the show, which would sell objects and souvenirs. For an account of the stationary that Lawler ended up selling at Fashion Moda's installation, see Crimp (1993).

12. Lawler wanted to sell the record at Jenny Holzer and Fashion Moda's trailer, which was installed at the entrance to Documenta 7.

13. From an artist's brochure distributed at 'Projects: Louise Lawler', *Enough*, New York, The Museum of Modern Art, September 19-November 10, 1987.

14. A recent photographic work by Lawler repeats the warning, which has become especially urgent at a time when the Bush administration has banned media images of coffins returning from the Iraq War and has treated certain, particularly Arab, deaths as un-grievable. Lawler's image, depicting the detached wings of a classical statue of Nike, goddess of victory, is titled *Grieving Mothers*.

9

Toward a Critical Art Theory

Gene Ray

Critical theory rejects the given world and looks beyond it. In reflection on art, too, we need to distinguish between uncritical, or affirmative, theory and a *critical* theory that rejects the *given art* and looks beyond it. Critical *art* theory cannot limit itself to the reception and interpretation of art, as that now exists under capitalism. Because it will recognize that art as it is currently institutionalized and practiced – business as usual in the current 'art world' – is in the deepest and most unavoidable sense 'art under capitalism', art under the domination of capitalism, critical art theory will rather be oriented toward a clear break or rupture with the art that capitalism has brought to dominance.

Critical art theory's first task is to understand how the given art supports the given order. It must expose and analyze art's actual social functions under capitalism. What is it *doing*, this whole sphere of activity called art? Any critical theory of art must begin by grasping that the activity of art in its current forms is contradictory. The 'art world' is the site of an enormous mobilization of creativity and inventiveness, channelled into the production, reception, and circulation of artworks. The art institutions practice various kinds of direction over this production as a whole, but this direction is not usually *directly* coercive. Certainly the art market exerts pressures of selection that no artist can ignore, if she or he hopes to make a career. But individual artists are *relatively* free to make the art they choose, according to their own conceptions. It may not sell or make them famous, but they are free to do their thing. Art, then, has not relinquished its historical claim to autonomy within capitalist society, and today the operations of this relative autonomy remain empirically observable.

On the other hand, a critical theorist is bound to see that art as whole is a stabilizing factor in social life. The existence of an art seemingly produced freely and in great abundance is a credit to the given order. As a luxurious surplus, art remains a jewel in power's crown, and the richer, more splendid and exuberant art is, the more it affirms the social status quo. The material reality of capitalist society may be a war of all against all, but in art the utopian impulses that are blocked from actualization in everyday life find an orderly social outlet. The art institutions organize a great variety of activities and agents into a complex systemic unity; the capitalist art system functions as a sub-system of the capitalist world system. Without doubt, some of these activities and artistic products are openly critical and politically committed. But taken *as a whole*, the art system is affirmative (Marcuse, 1968), in the sense that it converts the totality of art works and artistic practices – the sum of what flows through these circuits of production and reception – into 'symbolic legitimation' (to borrow Pierre Bourdieu's apt expression for it) of class society (Bourdieu, 1993: 128). It does so by *simultaneously* encouraging art's autonomous impulses and politically neutralizing what those impulses produce. Art *simulates* experiences of freedom, reconciliation, joy, solidarity and uninhibited communication and expression that are blocked in class society. Art is a form of compensation for the injustices, repressions and self-repressions, and impoverishments of experience that characterize everyday life under capitalist modernity. *As compensation*, art captures and renders harmless rebellious energies and dissipates pressures for change. In this way art is an *ideological support* for the social status quo and contributes to the reproduction of class society.

Frankfurt Modernism

The Frankfurt theorists pioneered and elaborated this dialectical understanding of art. Herbert Marcuse, Max Horkheimer and Theodor Adorno – working in close relation to others, including Walter Benjamin, Ernst Bloch and Siegfried Kracauer, and certainly stimulated by the different Marxist approaches of Bertolt Brecht and Georg Lukács – have shown us how art under capitalism can, at the very same time, be both relatively autonomous and instrumentalized into a support for existing society. Every work of art, in Adorno's famous formulation, is both autonomous and *fait social* (Adorno, 1997: 5). Every artwork is autonomous insofar as it asserts itself as an end-in-itself and pursues the logic of its own development without regard to the dominant logic of society; but every work is also a 'social fact' in that it is a cipher that manifests and confirms the reality of society, understood as the total nexus of social relations and processes. In the autonomous aspect of art's 'double character', the Frankfurt theorists saw an equivalent to the intransigence of critical theory. Free autonomous creation is a form of that reach for an un-alienated humanity described luminously by the young Karl Marx. As such, it always contains a force of resistance to the powers that be, albeit a very fragile one.

Their attempts to rescue and protect this autonomous aspect led the Frankfurt theorists to an absolute investment in the forms of artistic modernism. For them, and above all for Adorno, the modernist artwork or opus was a sensuous manifestation of truth as a social process straining toward human emancipation. The modernist work – and to be sure, what is meant here are the masterworks, the zenith of advanced formal experimentation – is an "enactment of antagonisms", an unreconciled synthesis of "un-unifiable, non-identical elements that grind away at each other" (Adorno, 1997: 176). A force-field of elements that are both artistic and social, the artwork indirectly or even unconsciously reproduces the conflicts, blockages and revolutionary aspirations of alienated everyday life. They saw this practice of autonomy threatened from two directions. First, from the increasing encroachments of capitalist rationality into the sphere of culture – processes to which Horkheimer and Adorno famously gave the name 'culture industry' (Horkheimer and Adorno, 2002). Second, from political instrumentalization by the Communist Parties and other established powers claiming to be anti-capitalist.

It was in response to his perceptions of this second threat that Adorno issued his notorious condemnation of politicized art (Adorno, 1992). Ostensibly responding to Jean-Paul Sartre's 1948 call for a *littérature engagée*, Adorno's position in fact had already been formed by the interwar context: the liquidation of the artistic avant-gardes in the USSR under Stalin and the Comintern's adoption of socialist realism as the official and only acceptable form of anti-capitalist art. Art that subordinates itself to the direction of a Party was for Adorno a betrayal of art's force of resistance. He took the position that art cannot instrumentalize itself on the basis of political commitments without undermining the autonomy on which it depends and thereby undoing itself as art. Autonomous (modernist) art is political, but only indirectly and only by restricting itself to the practice of its proper autonomy. In short, art must bear its contradiction and not attempt to overcome it. As the culture industry expanded and consolidated its hold over everyday consciousness and, indeed, as struggles of national liberation and urban uprisings politicized campuses over the course of the 1960s, Adorno responded by hardening his position.

There can be little doubt that the given artistic autonomy is threatened by the two tendencies Adorno pointed to. But there is little doubt either that his conception of the problem forecloses its possible solution. Culture industry and official socialist realism were not the only alternatives to the production of autonomist artworks. But Adorno in effect couldn't see these other alternatives because he had no category for them. The most convincing of these alternatives constituted itself by terminating its ties of dependency on the art institutions, abandoning the production of traditional art objects, and relocating its practices to the streets and public spaces. The formation of the Situationist International (SI) in 1957 was an announcement that this alternative had reached a basic theoretical and practical coherence. Adorno remained blind to it as he continued to polish the *Aesthetic Theory* until his death in 1969. So did his heir, Peter Bürger, who would publish *Theory of the Avant-Garde* in 1974.

An English translation of Bürger's book appeared in 1984. Since then, it has functioned mainly as a theoretical support for modernist positions within Anglophone (i.e., globalized) art and cultural discourse. It still tends to be cited by those happy to counter-sign any possible death certificate of the avant-gardes, and by those dismissive of attempts to develop practices in opposition to dominant institutions. In the present context, as the essays in the first section of this volume make clear, we would only need to read Andrea Fraser (2005) to see how Bürger is still brought in as an authority purportedly demonstrating the futility, infantilism and bad faith of all practices aimed directly against or seeking radically to break with established institutional power. For Fraser, Bürger, together with Pierre Bourdieu, becomes a resource for the justification of an ostensibly more mature and effective position within the institutions. However, even when it is called 'criticality', resignation remains resignation. It is not my purpose here to engage with specific readings of Bürger or even to represent fairly the development of Bürger's own positions since 1974. What follows is a critique of the arguments advanced in *Theory of the Avant-Garde*, since it is this text, in its English edition, that is operative today in support of a resigned and melancholic modernism. And in this regard, it is crucial to see Adorno standing behind Bürger. While in other respects, Adorno remains a key critical thinker for me, his rigid investments in artistic modernism are a political problem and, as such, are to be critically resisted.

Toward a Different Autonomy

With both Adorno and Bürger, the problem can be traced to a theoretically unjustified overinvestment in the work-form of modernist art. Bürger basically rewrites the history of the artistic avant-gardes as the development of the work-as-force-field so dear to Adorno. For Adorno, the avant-garde *is* modernist art, identity pure and simple. Bürger makes an important advance beyond this identification by grasping that the 'historical' avant-gardes had repudiated artistic autonomy in their efforts to re-link art and life – and that their specificity is to be located in this repudiation. But although Bürger works hard to differentiate his analysis from Adorno's, he returns to the fold, so to speak, by judging this avant-garde attack on the institution of autonomous art to be failure, a 'false supersession' (*falsche Aufhebung*) of art into life.

> The avant-garde intended the supersession (*Aufhebung*) of autonomous art by leading art over into a practice of life (*Lebenspraxis*). This has not taken place and presumably cannot take place within bourgeois society unless it be in the form of a false supersession (*falschen Aufhebung*) of autonomous art. (Bürger, 1984: 53-4, trans. modified)

The only successful result was an unintended one: after the historical avant-gardes, according to Bürger, a transformation takes place in the work-form of art. The organic, harmonized work of traditional art gives way to the (non-organic, allegorical) work-form in which disarticulated elements are held together in a fragmentary unity that refuses the semblance of reconciliation:

> Paradoxically, the avant-gardiste intention to destroy art as an institution is thus realized in the work of art itself. The intention to

> revolutionize life by returning art to its praxis turns into a
> revolutionizing of art. (Bürger, 1984: 72)

In other words, art cannot repudiate its autonomy, but it can go on endlessly repudiating its own traditions, so long as it does so in the form of modernist works. This pronouncement of failure and 'false supersession' is far too hasty. I will return to this point later. Here I want to question this investment in the institutionalized autonomy of art by contrasting it to the autonomy constituted through a conscious break with institutionalized art.

The Situationist alternative to art under capitalism was a more advanced and theoretically conscious breakout than the often partial and hesitant revolts of the early avant-gardes. Founded in 1957 but continuing in many respects the project of the Lettrist International (LI) from which many of its founding members came, the SI was a Paris-based network of mostly-European national 'sections' active until its self-dissolution in 1972. Formally combining the LI group around core members Guy Debord, Michèle Bernstein and Gil Wolman and the Imaginist Bauhaus around Asger Jorn, Constant and Giuseppe Pino-Gallizio, and soon assimilating the Munich-based Spur group around Hans-Peter Zimmer, Heimrad Prem and Dieter Kunzelmann, the SI undertook a radical collective critique of post-war commodity capitalism and the art system flourishing around a restored modernism. Drawing the practical conclusions, they transformed the SI within four years from a grouping of artists into a revolutionary organization of cultural guerrillas. The SI's critical process of progressive detachment from the art institutions culminated in an internal prohibition on the pursuit of an art career by any of its members. Situationist practice was radically politicized, but is not reducible to a simple or total instrumentalization. We can agree with Adorno that artists who paint what the Party says to paint have given up their autonomy; as apologists for the Central Committee's monopoly on autonomy, they are no more than instruments for producing compromised works. But the SI was a group founded on the principle of autonomy – an autonomy not restricted as privilege or specialization, but one that is radicalized through a revolutionary process openly aiming to extend autonomy to all. The SI did not recognize any Party or other absolute authority on questions pertaining to the aims and forms of revolutionary social struggle. Their autonomy was critically to study reality and the theories that would explain it, draw their own conclusions and act accordingly. In its own group process, the SI accepted nothing less than a continuous demonstration of autonomy by its members, who were expected to contribute as full participants in a collective practice. This process didn't always unfold smoothly (what process does?). But the much-criticized exclusions carried out by the group by and large reflect the painful attainment of theoretical coherence and are hardly proof of a lack of autonomy. 'Instrumentalization' is the wrong category for a conscious and freely self-generating (i.e., autonomous) practice.

Moreover, the Situationists were even more hostile than Adorno to official Communist parties and would-be vanguards. Their experiments in collective autonomy were far removed – and openly critical of – the servility of party militants. Alienation can't be overcome, as they put it, "by means of alienated forms of struggle" (Debord, 1994: 89). Their critical processing of revolutionary theory and practice was plainly much deeper than Adorno's – and was lived, as it must be, as a real urgency. They carried out an autonomous appropriation of critical theory, developed in a close dialectic with their own radical cultural practices and innovations. As a result, true enough, they ceased to produce modernist artworks. But they never claimed to have gone on with modernism; they claimed rather to have surpassed this dominant conception of art (Debord, 1994: 129-47). My point is that Situationist practice – however you categorize or evaluate it – was certainly no less autonomous than the institutionalized production of modernist artworks favored by Adorno. If anything, it was far more autonomous and intransigently critical. In comparison to Situationist practice, which continues to function as a real factor of resistance and emancipation, Adorno's claims for Franz Kafka and Samuel Beckett seem laughably inflated.

On the Supersession of Art

Situationist art theory, then, does not suffer from the categorical and conceptual impasses that led Frankfurt art theory to draw the wagons around the modernist artwork. For the Situationists, art oriented toward radical social change could no longer be about the production of objects for exhibition and passive spectatorship. Given the decomposition of contemporary culture – and in passing let's at least note that there is much overlap in the analyses of culture industry and the theory of spectacular society – attempts to maintain or rejuvenate modernism are a losing and illusory enterprise. With regard to the content and meaning of early avant-garde practice, the critical art theory developed by the SI in the late 1950s and early 60s and concisely summarized by Guy Debord in *The Society of the Spectacle* in 1967 is basically consistent with Bürger's later theorization. But the two theories diverge irreconcilably in their interpretation of the consequences.

The rise of capitalism – the tendency to reduce everything and everyone to commodity status and exchange value – was the material condition for the relative autonomy of culture; the bourgeois revolution was the political last act of a material process that had pulverized traditional bases of authority and released art from its old function of ritual unification. For the Situationists, as art became conscious of itself as a distinct sphere of activity in the new order, it logically began to press for the autonomy of its sphere. But self-consciousness also brought awareness of the impotence of this autonomy as a form of social *separation* and insights into its new functions in support of bourgeois power. The avant-gardes of the early twentieth century responded with a practical demand that separation be abolished and autonomy be generalized through revolution. This far Bürger is in agreement. But for him, the defeat of the revolutionary attempt to abolish capitalism makes the avant-garde breakout a failure that must be re-inscribed in the work-form of art, while for the Situationists this defeat is only one moment in a struggle that continues. For the SI, the logic of art – necessarily first *for* and then *against* autonomous separation – remains unchanged, and art can make its peace with separation only by deceiving itself. Resigned returns to institutionalized art and to the empty, repetitive formalist experiments of work-based modernism can only represent a process of decomposition: the "end of the history of culture" (Debord, 1994: 131).

In political terms, there are at this point just two irreconcilable options: either to be enlisted in culture's affirmative function – "to justify a society with no justification" (Debord, 1994: 138) – or to press forward with the revolutionary process. The institutions will organize the prolongation of art "as a dead thing for spectacular contemplation" (Debord, 1994: 131-2, trans. modified). The radical alternative is the supersession (*dépassement*; that is, *Aufhebung*) of art. The first aligns itself with the defense of class power; the second, with the radical critique of society. Surpassing art means removing it from institutional management and transforming it into a practice for expanding life here and now, for overcoming passivity and separation, in short for 'revolutionizing everyday life'. There are of course possibilities for modest critical practices within the art institutions, but these can always be managed and kept within tolerable limits. Maximum pressure on the given develops from a refusal of the art system *as a whole*, openly linked to a refusal of the social totality. The history of the real avant-gardes, then, is not the history of artistic modernism, but the attainment of consciousness about the stakes and the need for this overcoming

The main defect of Bürger's theorization can be located in his historical judgment on the early avant-gardes, because this judgment becomes a categorical foreclosure or blindness. For Bürger, the conclusion that the early avant-gardes failed in their attempts to supersede art follows necessarily from the obvious fact that the institution of art continues. There can be no dialectical overcoming without the negating moment of an abolition:

> [I]t is a historical fact that the avant-garde movements did not put an end to the production of works of art, and that the social institution that is art proved resistant to the avant-gardiste attack. (Bürger, 1984: 56-7)

Art is not abolished; therefore, no supersession. This leads Bürger to declare that the early avant-gardes are now to be seen as 'historical'. Henceforth, attempts to repeat the project of overcoming art can only be *repetitions of failure*; such attempts by the 'neo-avant-garde', as Bürger now names it, only serve to consolidate the institutionalization of the historical avant-gardes *as art*:

> In a changed context, the resumption of avant-gardiste intentions with the means of avant-gardism can no longer even have the limited effectiveness the historical avant-gardes achieved.... To formulate more pointedly: the neo-avant-garde institutionalizes the *avant-garde as art* and thus negates genuinely avant-garde intentions. (Bürger, 1984: 58).

Marcel Duchamp's gesture of signing a urinal or bottle drier was a failed attack on the category of individual production, but repetitions of this gesture merely institutionalized the ready-made as a legitimate art object (Bürger, 1984: 52-7).

The problem here is that Bürger restricts his analysis to *artworks* and to gestures that conform to this category. That he comes close to perceiving that this may be a problem is hinted in those places where he uses the term 'manifestation' (*Manifestation*) to refer to avant-garde practice:

> Instead of speaking of the avant-gardiste work (*Werk*), we will speak of avant-gardiste manifestation (*Manifestation*). A Dadaist manifestation does not have work character but is nonetheless an authentic manifestation of the artistic avant-garde. (Bürger, 1984: 50)

But soon it is clear that *all forms of practice* will in the end either be reduced to that category or else not recognized at all: "The efforts to supersede art become artistic manifestations (*Veranstaltungen*) that, independently of their producers' intentions, take on the character of works" (Bürger, 1984: 58). Bürger's limited examples show that what he has in mind by 'manifestation' are gestures that already fit the work-form, such as Duchamp's ready-mades or Surrealist automatic poems – or at most provocations performed before an audience at organized artistic events (*Veranstaltungen*).

Happenings and Situations

Bürger is aware of the 'happening' form developed by Allan Kaprow and his collaborators beginning in 1958. But he classes happenings as no more than a neo-avant-garde repetition of Dadaist manifestations, evidence that repeating historical provocations no longer has protest value. He concludes that art today

> can either resign itself to its autonomy status or organize events (*Veranstaltungen*) to break through that status; however, it cannot simply deny its autonomy status or suppose it has the possibility of direct effectiveness without at the same time betraying art's claim to truth (*Wahrheitsanspruch*). (Bürger, 1984: 57, translation modified)

Art's 'claim to truth', however, turns out to be a normative description of autonomy status itself. Following Adorno, Bürger accepts that it is only art's limited exemption from the instrumental reason dominating everyday life that enables it to recognize and articulate the truth – 'truth' here being understood not as a correspondence between reality and its representation but as an implicit critico-utopian evaluation *of reality*. Truth is not conformity to the given, but is rather the negative force of resistance generated by the mere existence of artworks that, obeying no logic but their own, refuse integration. Bürger's argument here merely endorses Adorno's. What it really says is: art can't give up its autonomy status without ceasing to be art. And the implication is that if art does manage to directly produce political and social effects, it thereby ceases to be art and is no longer his – Bürger's – concern.

But Bürger cannot escape the problem in this way. He has already argued that the aim to produce direct effects (i.e., the transformation of art into a practice of life, a *Lebenspraxis*) is precisely what constitutes the avant-garde. So he cannot now give his theorization of the avant-garde permission to ignore the avant-gardes when they do attain their aim. He also attempts to elude the same problem with a variation on the argument. Pulp fiction – in other words, the non-autonomous products of the culture industry – are what you get when you aim at a supersession of art into life (Bürger, 1984: 54). By 1974, there were serious counterexamples for Bürger's argument; the SI even went so far as to spell everything out for him in its own books and theorizations. In this case the blindness is devastating, for the gap between contemporary avant-garde practice and the theory that purports to explain why it is no longer possible invalidates Bürger's work.

This would be the case only if the SI accomplished successful supersessions of art without collapsing into culture industry. The collapse hypothesis is easily dispensed with, since the SI did not indulge in commodity production. But putting Bürger's theory to the test at least helps us to see that any evaluation of Situationist supersessions must take into account the fact that the SI cut its ties to the art institutions and repudiated the work-form of modernist art. For the same cannot be said of Bürger's 'neo-avant-garde'. Bürger's examples – he briefly discusses Andy Warhol and reproduces images of works by Warhol and Daniel Spoerri (Bürger, 1984: 62, 58) – are artists who submit *artworks to the institutions for reception*. Even the case of Kaprow, who is not named but can be inferred from Bürger's use of the term 'happening', doesn't disturb this commitment to the institutions. Kaprow wanted to investigate or blur the borders between art and life, but he did so under the gaze, as it were, of the institutions, to which he remained dependent. It is in this sense that every happening does indeed, as Bürger claims, take on the character of a work. At most, the happening-form achieved an expansion of the dominant concept of art, but not its negation. Ditto, in this respect, for the case of Fluxus. The subsequent appearance of the new medium or genre of 'performance art' confirms the institutional acceptance (and neutralizing assimilation) of this direction. (In my terms, the result of a successful capture or assimilation of a rebellious form of practice is another *expansion of the category* of institutionalized modernist art.)

The differences between the happening and the situation are decisive here. As an experimental event that never seriously put its autonomy status in question, the happening staged interactions or exchanges of roles between artist and audience – but in safe, more or less controlled conditions, and ultimately for institutional reception. Only when, as in the Living Theater in exile and also perhaps in Jean-Jacques Lebel's notorious 'Festivals of Free Expression' in the mid-1960s, happening-like events sacrificed the element of institutional reception (and its implicit appeal for institutional approval) did they become something more threatening to the institution of art. On the other hand, the staging of personal risk or even physical danger through the elimination of the conventions that put limits on audience participation, as in Yoko Ono's *Cut Pieces* of 1964-5 or Marina Abramovic's *Rhythm 0* (1974), are extremes of performance art that are indeed subject to the dialectic of repetition and the recuperation of protest pointed to by Bürger.

In contrast, a situation – a constructed moment of de-alienated life that activates the social question – does not depend on the dominant conception of art or its institutions to generate its meaning and effects. The Situationists themselves, who continued to criticize contemporary art in the pages of their journal, in 1963 published an incisive discussion of the happening-form and differentiated it from the practice of the SI:

> The happening is an isolated attempt to construct a situation *on the basis of poverty* (material poverty, poverty of human contact, poverty inherited from the artistic spectacle, poverty of the specific philosophy driven to 'ideologize' the reality of these moments). The situations that the SI has defined, on the other hand, can only be constructed on the basis of material and spiritual richness. Which is another way of saying that an outline for the construction of situations must be the game, the serious game, of the revolutionary avant-garde, and cannot exist for those who resign themselves on certain points to political passivity, metaphysical despair, or even the pure and experienced absence of artistic creativity. (Situationist International, 2002: 147)

Situations activate a revolutionary process, then, but do so by developing social and political efficacy within the found context of material everyday life, rather than through a displacement of everyday elements and encounters into the context of institutionalized art. In this sense, situations are indeed 'direct' by Bürger's criteria. The so-called 'Strasbourg Scandal' of 1966 is an example of a successful situation that contributed directly to a process of radicalization culminating, in May and June of 1968, in a wildcat general strike of nine million workers throughout France. There moreover is little danger of mistaking or perversely misrecognizing this kind of event with an artwork or happening. The conclusion seems inescapable that the SI renewed – and not merely repeated to no effect – the avant-garde project of overcoming art by turning it into a revolutionary practice of life.

It follows that what Bürger has named the 'neo-avant-garde' in order to dismiss it is not avant-garde at all. Those who, like the SI, renewed the avant-garde project were categorically excluded from the analysis. When the repudiation of institutionalized art and the work-form are given their due weight as criteria, then it becomes clear that the avant-garde project of radicalizing artistic autonomy by generalizing it into a social principle is a logic inherent or latent in the capitalist art system. It will be valid to activate this logic – and to actualize it by developing it in the form of practices – just as long as the capitalist art system continues to be organized around an operative principle of relative autonomy. It will be valid, that is, for artistic agents to reconstitute the avant-garde project through a politicized break with the dominant institutionalized art. True, actualizations of the avant-garde logic cannot be mere repetitions. Each time, they must invent practical forms grounded in and appropriate to the contemporary social reality that is their context. But because this logic amounts to a radical and irreparable break with institutionalized art, there is little risk that such a protest will be reabsorbed through yet another expansion of the dominant concept of art. The SI showed that art could be surpassed in this way in the very period in which, according to Bürger, only impotent repetitions are possible.

II

INSTITUTIONS OF EXODUS

10

Anthropology and Theory of Institutions

Paolo Virno

(Translated by Alberto Toscano)

The Animal Open to the World

There is no dispassionate inquiry on human nature that does not carry along with it, as a sort of clandestine passenger, at least the sketch of a theory of political institutions. The evaluation of species-specific instinct and drives, the analysis of a mind characterized through and through by the faculty of language, the recognition of the thorny relation between the single human animal and his fellows: all of this always harbors a judgment on the legitimacy of the Ministry of the Interior. And vice versa: there is no theory of political institutions worthy of the name which does not adopt, as its badly hidden presupposition, some representation or other of the traits that mark out *Homo sapiens* from the other animal species. To mention a high-school example, little is understood of Hobbes's *Leviathan* if one disregards his *On Man*.

Let us avoid any misunderstandings: it would be unrealistic, even farcical, to believe that a model of the just society could be deducible from certain bio-anthropological invariants. Every political program is rooted in an unprecedented socio-historical context (religious civil wars in Hobbes's case, a productive process directly based on the power of verbal thought in our own), confronting a unique constellation of passions and interests. Nevertheless, collective action is really contingent precisely because, while it seizes hold of the most volatile reality, it takes charge, in unpredictable and changing ways, of what is not contingent, which is to say of bio-anthropological invariants themselves. The reference to human nature does not dull, but rather accentuates to the highest degree, the particular and unrepeatable character of a political decision, the obligation to act in due time (*tempo debito*), the perception that yesterday was perhaps too early and tomorrow will be too late.

The link between anthropological reflection and the theory of institutions was formulated pithily by Carl Schmitt in the seventh chapter of his *Concept of the Political*:

> One could test all theories of state and political ideas according to their anthropology and thereby classify these as to whether they consciously or unconsciously presuppose man to be by nature evil or by nature good. The distinction is to be taken here in a rather summary fashion and not in any specifically moral or ethical sense. The problematic or unproblematic conception of man is decisive for the presupposition of every further political consideration, the answer to the question whether man is a dangerous being or not, a risky or a harmless creature [....] Ingenuous anarchism reveals that the belief in the natural goodness of man is closely tied to the radical denial of state and government. One follows from the other, and both foment each other [....] The radicalism vis-à-vis state and government grows in proportion to the radical belief in the goodness of man's nature [....] What remains is the remarkable and, for many, disquieting diagnosis that all genuine political theories presuppose man to be evil, i.e., by no means unproblematic but a dangerous and dynamic being. (Schmitt, 1996: 58–61)

Were man a meek animal destined to agreement and mutual recognition, there would be no need at all for disciplinary and coercive institutions. The critique of the State – developed with varying intensity by liberals, anarchists and communists – is fuelled, according to Schmitt, by the prejudicial idea of the 'natural goodness' of our species. An authoritative (*autorevole*) example of this tendency is represented today by the libertarian political stance of Noam Chomsky: he advocates with admirable tenacity the dissolution of centralized apparatuses of power, ascribing to them the mortification of the congenital creativity of verbal language, the species-specific prerequisite that could guarantee for humanity a self-government devoid of established [consolidate] hierarchies. However, if – as everything leads one to believe – *Homo sapiens* is a dangerous, unstable and (self-)destructive animal, the formation of a 'unified political body' that would exercise, in Schmitt's terms, an unconditional 'monopoly over political decision' seems inevitable in order to hold him back.

It is not wise to turn up one's philosophically sophisticated nose when faced with the crass alternative between 'man good by nature' and 'man bad by nature'. First of all, because Schmitt himself is well aware of such crassness: he expressly uses this shorthand to evoke the bio-anthropological background which, indifferent as it is to naïve moral qualifications, provokes instead no shortage of theoretical conundrums. But it is not wise to turn up one's nose especially for another reason. It is precisely that seeming crassness that allows us to state, without beating about the bush (*senza giochi di parole*), the historical-naturalist hypothesis that, by unsettling the conceptual schema outlined by Schmitt, becomes truly interesting. It is the following: the risky instability of the human animal – so-called evil, in brief – does not in any sense imply the formation and perpetuation of that 'supreme empire' which is state sovereignty. On the contrary. 'Radicalism hostile to the state' and to the capitalist mode of production, far from presupposing the innate meekness of our species, can find its genuine basis in the full recognition of the 'problematic' character of the human animal – which is to say its indefinite and potential (in other words, also dangerous) character. The critique of the 'monopoly over political decision', and generally of institutions whose rules function as compulsions to repeat, must rest precisely on the acknowledgment that man is 'bad by nature'.

The Excess of Drives and the Modality of the Possible

What does the 'evil' with which, according to Schmitt, every theory of institutions that demonstrates a smidgen of realism regarding human nature consist in? He refers, albeit in passing, to the theses of the most democratic among the founding members of philosophical anthropology, Helmut Plessner. I will limit myself to recalling a few key ideas of philosophical anthropology considered as a whole, leaving aside any distinctions (which are in other respects significant) between the different authors.

Man is 'problematic', according to Plessner and then Gehlen, because he is deprived of a definite environment, corresponding point by point to his psychosomatic configuration and the organization (*corredo*) of his drives. If the animal embedded in an environment reacts with innate assuredness to external stimuli, man, environmentally disoriented as he is, has to wrestle with a flood of suggestions devoid of a precise biological finality. Our species is characterized by its 'openness to the world' – if we understand by 'world' a vital context which is always unpredictable and partially undetermined. The overabundance of stimuli unconnected to any definite operative task elicits an enduring uncertainty and a disorientation which can never be entirely dispelled: in Plessner's terms, the animal 'open to the world' always maintains a non-adherence, or a 'detachment', with regard to the states of affairs and events he encounters. Openness to the world, with the rather high degree of undifferentiated potentiality it implies, is correlated, in terms of phylogeny, with low instinctual specialization, as well as with neoteny, which is to say the permanence of infantile characteristic even in adult subjects.

These rather generic indications are sufficient, however, to qualify the 'dangerousness' of *Homo sapiens*, which, according to Schmitt, is called upon by the modern theory of state sovereignty (and which, according to Freud, can only be attenuated by a normative order entirely comparable to the compulsion to repeat). The overabundance of stimuli which are not biologically finalized and the consequent variability in behaviors are accompanied by a congenital fragility in the inhibitory mechanisms: the animal 'open to the world' displays a virtually limitless intra-species aggressiveness, whose triggering causes are never reducible to a definite list (habitational density of a territory, sexual selection, etc.), since they are themselves infinitely variable (Lorenz, 2005: 297-336). Struggles for prestige alone, and even the notion of 'honor', have a very close relationship with the structure of drives of an environmentally dislocated living being, one which is, for this very reason, essentially potential in character. The lack of a univocal habitat makes culture into 'man's first nature' (Gehlen, 1985: 109). However, it is precisely culture which, as an innate biological *dispositif,* displays a fundamental ambivalence: it blunts danger, but, in other respects, it multiplies and diversifies the occasions of risk; it "defends man from his very nature", sparing him the experience of his "own terrifying plasticity and indeterminateness" (Gehlen, 1985: 97), but, being itself the principal manifestation of this very plasticity and indeterminacy, it simultaneously favors the full unfolding of the nature from which it was supposed to protect us.

So-called 'evil' can also be described by calling attention to some salient prerogatives of verbal language. Problematic – that is to say unstable and dangerous – is the animal whose life is characterized by Negation, by the modality of the possible, by infinite regress. These three structures encapsulate the emotive situation of an environmentally disoriented animal. Negation is inseparable from a certain degree of 'detachment' from one's vital context, sometimes even from the provisional suspension of sensory stimulus. The modality of the possible coincides with a biologically non-finalized excess of drives, as well as with the non-specialized character of the human animal. Infinite regress expresses the 'opening to the world' as chronic incompleteness, or even, but it amounts to the same thing, as the futile quest for that proportionality between drives and behaviors which is instead the prerogative of a circumscribed environment. The logical basis of metaphysics simultaneously (*a un tempo*) outlines a theory of the passions. Pain, empathy, desire, fear, aggressiveness: these affects, which we share with many other animal species, are reconfigured from top to bottom by negation, by the modality of the possible, by infinite regress. Then there are those affects which, far from being reconfigured, are even provoked by these linguistic structures: boredom, for example, is nothing but the emotional correlate of infinite regress, of the petrified movement that seems to remove a limit only to reconfirm it over and over again; or like anxiety (i.e., an indefinite apprehension, which is not bound to a specific state of affairs) is the emotive aspect of the modality of the possible. As for negation, it is precisely to it that we owe the eventuality of a failure of mutual recognition among co-specifics. The perceptual evidence 'this is a man' loses its irrefutability once it is subjected to the work of the 'no': anthropophagy and Auschwitz are there to prove it. Placed at the borders of social interaction, the possibility of non-recognition also has repercussions at its centre and permeates its entire fabric. Language, far from attenuating intra-specific aggressiveness (as Habermas and a number of contented philosophers assure us), radicalizes them beyond measure.

Ambivalence

The dangerousness of our species is coextensive with its capacity to accomplish innovative actions, that is actions that are capable of modifying established habits and norms. Whether we're talking about the excess of drives or linguistic negation, of a 'detachment' from one's vital context or of the modality of the possible, it is entirely obvious that what we are pointing to are not just the premises of subjugation and torture, but the prerequisites that permit the invention of factory councils or other democratic institutions based on that topically political passion which is friendship without familiarity. Both 'virtue' and 'evil' presuppose a deficit of instinctive orientation and feed on the uncertainty experience in the faced of 'that which can be differently than it is'. The bio-linguistic preconditions of so-called 'evil' are the same as the ones that subtend 'virtue'. Just think of negation again: it is capable of rupturing, or bracketing, the empathy among co-specifics guaranteed by the cerebral mechanism of mirror neurons (Gallese, 2003), making it possible to state something like 'this is not a man' in the presence of a Jew or an Arab. We must add, however, that the possibility of a reciprocal mis-recognition is kept at bay (precisely in a virtuous way) by the same faculty of negating any semantic content that made it possible in the first place. The public sphere – woven of persuasive discourses, political conflicts, pacts, collective projects – is nothing but a second negation with which the first one, that is, the syntagm 'non-man' is always stifled again. In other words, the public sphere consists in a negation of the negation: 'not non-man'. The patent identity between the species-specific resources enjoyed by virtuous innovation and the ones which nourish homicidal hostility does not authorizes us, even for a moment, to mitigate 'evil', to consider it as a peripheral nuisance, or worse, as the indispensable impetus behind 'good'. On the contrary: the only truly radical, which is to say inexorable and lacerating, evil is precisely and solely the evil that shares the same root as the good life.

The complete co-extensiveness between threat and shelter allows us to place the problem of political institutions on a firmer basis. This, for at least two reasons. Above all, because it introduces the suspicion that the apparent shelter (state sovereignty, for instance) constitutes, in some cases, the most intense manifestation of the threat (intra-specific aggressiveness). Furthermore, because it suggest a methodological criterion of some relevance: institutions truly protect us if, and only if, they enjoy the same background conditions which, in other respects, do not cease to fuel the threat; if, and only if, they draw apotropaic resources from the 'openness to the world' and from the faculty of negating, from neoteny and from the modality of the possible; if, and only if, the exhibit at each and every moment their belonging to the category of 'that which can be different than it is'.

Wishing to defuse the little dialectic scheme, according to which the (self-)destructive drives of the linguistic animal would be destined to empower and perfect always and evermore the synthesis represented by the state, contemporary critical thought – from Chomsky to French post-structuralism – has deemed it convenient to expel from its horizon, together with dialectics, the very memory of those (self-)destructive drives. In so doing, contemporary critical thought risks corroborating Schmitt's diagnosis that radicalism hostile to the State grows in proportion to the faith in the radical goodness of human nature. Everything suggests that we are dealing with a dead end. Rather than abrogating the negative if only to avoid the dialectical grindstone, it is necessary to develop a non-dialectical understanding of the negative. With this end in mind, three keywords show their usefulness: ambivalence, oscillation, the disturbing. Ambivalence: friendship without familiarity, the authentic nub of a political community, can always turn into the familiarity loaded with enmity that fuels massacres between factions, gangs, tribes. There is no pacifying third term, which is to day a dialectical synthesis or superior point of equilibrium: each polarity refers back to the other; or rather, it already contains it within itself, it already lets us glimpse the other in its own fabric. Oscillation: the mutual recognition among co-specifics is marked by a ceaseless back-and-forth that goes from partial achievement to incipient failure. Disturbing: what is frightening is never the unfamiliar, but only that with which we have the greatest acquaintance (the excess of drives, the infrastructure of verbal language) and which, in varying circumstances, has even exercised or could exercise a protective function.

Murmurs in the Desert

The relation between the redoubtable aspects of human nature and political institutions is without doubt a meta-historical question. In order to confront it, it is not much use evoking the kaleidoscope of cultural differences. However, as always happens, a meta-historical question gains in visibility and weight only within a concrete socio-historic conjuncture. The invariant, that is the congenital (self-)destructiveness of the animal who thinks with words is thematized as the 'argument' of a 'function' which is entirely made up of contingent crises and conflicts. In other words: the problem of intra-specific aggressiveness jumps to the foreground once the modern centralized state experiences a noteworthy decline, albeit one which is marked by convulsive restorative impulses and disquieting metamorphoses. It is in the midst of this decline, and because of it, that the problem of institutions, of their regulative and stabilizing role, makes itself felt in all its bio-anthropological scope.

It is Schmitt himself who acknowledges, with patent bitterness, the collapse of state sovereignty. The erosion of the 'monopoly over political decision' derives as much from the nature of the current productive process (based on abstract knowledge and linguistic communication), as from the social struggles of the sixties and seventies, and from the subsequent proliferation of forms of life refractory to a 'preliminary pact of obedience'. It is not important here to dwell on these causes or to rehearse other possible ones. What matter instead are the question marks that hover over the new situation. What political institutions can there be outside of the state apparatus? How is the instability and dangerousness of the human animal to be held in check, where we can no longer count on a 'compulsion to repeat' in the application of the rules which are in effect at any given time? In what way can the excess of drives and the openness to the world act as a political antidote to the poisons they themselves secrete?

These questions refer back to the thorniest episode in the Jewish exodus: the 'murmurs' in the desert, that is a sequence of singularly bitter internecine struggles. Rather than submitting to the pharaoh or rising up against his rule, the Jews took advantage of the principle of the *tertium datur*, seizing a further and unprecedented possibility: to abandon the 'house of slavery and iniquitous labor'. So they venture into a no man's land, where they experience unheard-of forms of self-government. But the bond of solidarity grows weak: the longing for the old oppression grows, the respect for one's comrades in the flight suddenly turns into hatred, violence and idolatry run rampant. Schisms, hostility, slander, polymorphous aggression: this is how, on the slopes of the Sinai, there appears. The narrative of the exodus is perhaps the most authoritative theological-political model for the overcoming of the State. This is because it projects the possibility of undermining the pharaoh's monopoly of decision by means of a resourceful subtraction; but also because, by drawing attention to the 'murmurs' it rules out the idea that this subtraction is based on the natural meekness of the human animal. The exodus refutes Schmitt: a Republic that is no longer a state enjoys a very close and open relationship with the innate destructiveness of our species.

Natural-historical Institutions

Not only does 'radicalism hostile to the State' not hesitate in recognizing the (self-)destructive drives of the living being endowed with speech, but it takes them so seriously that it deems unrealistic, or even intensely harmful, the antidote envisaged by the theories of sovereignty. I would like to elaborate some further conjectures on the form and functioning of political bodies that, though they closely tackle the fearsome aspects of human nature, nevertheless appear incompatible with the 'monopoly over political decision'.

I will try to develop these conjectures without alluding to what could be, but focusing my gaze on what is always already there. In other words, I will neglect for the time being the need to invent political categories worthy of current social transformations, in order to fix my attention on two macroscopic anthropological – or rather anthropogenetic – realities which constitute, to all intents and purposes, institutions: language and ritual. They are precisely the institutions that display with the greatest clarity all the prerequisites that my sequence of questions has just enumerated: acknowledgment of the impossibility of exiting the state of nature, back-and-forth between regularity and rules, reciprocal commutability between matters of principle and matters of fact, an intimate acquaintance with ambivalence and oscillation. These two natural-historical institutions, of which I will say the bare minimum, are not, however, political institutions. Nevertheless, we cannot exclude the possibility of finding in our tradition one or more conceptual devices that represent the properly political equivalent of language or ritual. In our tradition: even here, as you can see, I am not invoking what will come, but what has been. Concerning ritual, let me propose the following hypothesis: the manner in which it confronts and mitigates always anew the dangerous instability of the human animal has a correlate in the theological-political category of *katechon*. This Greek word, employed by the apostle Paul in the second letter to the Thessalonians and then repeatedly recovered by conservative doctrines means 'that which restrains', a force that always yet again defers the ultimate destruction. Now, it seems to me that concept of *katechon*, as the political aspect of ritual practices, is more than useful in order to define the nature and tasks of institutions that no longer belong to the state. Far from being an intrinsic cog in the theory of sovereignty, as Schmitt and company claim, the idea of a force that restrains so-called 'evil', without however ever being capable of expunging it (since its expunction would correspond to the end of the world, or better, to the atrophy of the 'openness to the world'), is instead well suited to the anti-monopolistic politics of exodus.

Language

Language has a pre-individual and supra-personal life. It concerns the individual human animal only to the extent that the latter belongs to a 'mass of speaking beings'. Precisely as freedom or power, it exists solely in the relation between the members of a community. Bifocal sight, the autonomous possession of every isolated man, can further be considered, rightly, a shared endowment of the species. Not so for language: in its case it is the sharing that creates the endowment; it is the between of inter-psychic relations which then determines, as if by resonance, an intra-psychic asset. Natural-historical language testifies to the priority of the 'we' over the 'I', of the collective mind over the individual mind. That is why, as Saussure does not tire of repeating, language is an institution. It is for this reason, in fact, that it is a 'pure institution', the matrix and yardstick for all the others.

Such a judgment would not be fully justified, however, if language, beside being supra-personal, did not also exercise an integrative and protective function. For every authentic institution stabilizes and repairs. But what lack does natural-historical language need to fill? And what risk must it protect us from? Both the lack and the risk have a precise name: the faculty of language. This faculty – that is the biological disposition to speak of each single individual – is a simple potentiality that remains devoid of actual reality, all too similar to an aphasic state. Language – as a social fact or pure institution – compensates for individual infancy, that is, for that condition in which one does not speak though one possess the capacity to do so. It protects us from the first and gravest danger to which the neotenous animal is exposed: a power that remains such, devoid of corresponding acts. The difference between the faculty of language and historically determinate laws – a difference which, far from being elided, persists into adulthood, making itself felt every time a statement is produced – confers an institutional tonality to the natural life of our species. It is precisely this difference that implies an extremely close link between biology and politics, between *zoon logon ekon* and *zoon politikon*.

Language is the institution that makes possible all the other institutions: fashion, marriage, law, the State – the list goes on. But the matrix is radically distinct from its by-products. According to Saussure, the functioning of language cannot be compared to that of the law or the State. The undeniable analogies reveal themselves to be deceptive. The transformation over time of the civil code has nothing in common with the mutation of consonants or the alteration in certain lexical values. The gap that separates the 'pure institution' from the socio-political apparatuses with which we are familiar is perhaps quite instructive for an investigation such as ours. If we wish to employ the terminology used hitherto, we could say that only language is an effectively worldly institutions, which is to say such as to reflect in its very way of being the overabundance of biologically non-finalized stimuli, not to mention the chronic 'detachment' of the human animal vis-à-vis its own vital context.

Language is both the most natural and the most historical of human institutions. More natural: unlike fashion or the State, it is founded on a 'special organ prepared by nature', that is on that innate biological disposition represented by the language faculty. More historical: while marriage and the law are suited to certain natural facts (sexual desire and the raising of offspring, for the former; symmetry of exchanges and the ratio between harm and penalty, for the latter), language is never constrained by an objective domain, but concerns instead the entire experience of the animal open to the world, and therefore the possible as much as the real, the unknown to the same extent as the customary. Fashion is not localizable in an area of the brain, yet it must always respect the proportions of the human body. On the contrary, language depends on certain generic conditions, but enjoys an unlimited field of application (since it is itself capable of always expanding it anew). Language mirrors the typically human lack of a circumscribed and predictable environment; but it is precisely its unlimited variability, in other words its independence from factual circumstances and natural data, which offers a perspicuous protection vis-à-vis the risks that are connected to that lack.

The pure institution, which is simultaneously the most natural and the most historical of institutions, is also however an insubstantial institution. Saussure's *idée fixe* is well known: language contains no positive reality, endowed with autonomous consistency, but only differences and differences among differences. Each term is defined only by its 'non-coincidence with the rest', which is to say by its opposition or heterogeneity with respect to all the other terms. The value of a linguistic element consists in its not being: x is something only and precisely because it is not y, not z, not w, and so on. The speaking being's capacity to negate some worldly state of affairs, sometimes even to the point of deactivating perceptual proof, is limited to the reprise and exteriorization of the 'complex of eternally negative relationships' which has always characterized the interior life of language. Negation, which is to say what language does, must be understood above all as something that language is. The pure institution does not represent any given force or reality, but may signify them all thanks to the negative-differential relationship entertained by its components. It is not the spokesperson or trace of anything, and it is precisely in this way that it shows its inseparability from 'a being founded primarily on detachment'.

Is it conceivable that a political institution – in the most rigorous acceptation of this adjective – borrows its own form and functioning from language? Is it plausible for there to be a Republic that protects and stabilizes the human animal in the same way that language performs its protective and stabilizing role vis-à-vis the language faculty, which is to say neoteny? Can there be an insubstantial Republic, based on differences and differences among differences, a non-representative Republic? I cannot answer these questions. Like anyone else, I too am suspicious of beguiling allusions and speculative short-circuits. Having said that, I think that the current crisis of State sovereignty makes such questions legitimate, stripping them of any vain or complacent air. The idea that the self-government of the multitude may conform itself directly to the linguistic character of man, to the disturbing ambivalence that marks him, should at the very least remain an open problem.

Ritual

Ritual registers and confronts all sorts of crises: the uncertainty that paralyses action, the terror of the unknown, the intensification of aggressive drives at the heart of the community. In the most significant cases, the crisis that ritual is preoccupied with does not concern however this or that determinate behavior, but rather involves the very conditions of possibility of experience: the unity of self-consciousness and the openness to the world. Ernesto De Martino refers to the crucial occasions in which the I crumbles and the world seems about to end as 'crises of presence'. In these circumstances, the partial reversibility of the anthropogenetic process is starkly manifest. In other words, the possession of those fundamental prerequisites that make a human animal into a human animal becomes insecure. Ritual fulfils a therapeutic function not because it erects a barrier against the 'crisis of presence' but, on the contrary, because it retraces all its steps and attempts to invert the polarity of each and every one of them. Ritual praxis bears out the extreme danger, dilates uncertainty and chaos, returns to the primal scene of hominization. Only thus, after all, can it perform a symbolic repetition of anthropogenesis, ultimately reaffirming the unity of the I and the openness to the world. According to De Martino, psycho-pathological collapse and the catastrophe of associated life are held back by 'cultural apocalypses', that is by collective rituals that mimic destruction in order to ward it off (*rintuzzarla*). Cultural apocalypses are institutions based on ambivalence and oscillation. This is the ambivalence of critical situations, in which only loss offers a chance of deliverance, and there is no shelter save for that which danger itself delineates. And it is the oscillation between something familiar that becomes disturbing and something disturbing which once again emits familiarity.

The crisis of presence follows two opposite and symmetrical paths. It can consist of a painful 'semantic defect', but also, inversely, of the uncontrollable inflationary vortex provoked by a "semantic excess which cannot be resolved into determinate meanings" (De Martino, 1977: 89). The semantic defect is inseparable from a reduction of human discourse to a finite series of monochord signals. The I is reabsorbed into a chaotic world whose parts, far from still constituting discrete units, merge into an unstable and enveloping continuum. In the first case we are dealing with acts without power; in the second, with power without acts: these are the specular ways in which the regression of the anthropogenetic process manifests itself, in other words, to adopt De Martino's terminology, as the risk of the 'end of the world'.

The cultural apocalypse is the ritual counterpart of the state of exception. It too implies the suspension of ordinary laws, letting certain traits of human nature emerge (the crisis and repetition of the same anthropogenetic process) in a particular historical conjuncture. Like the state of exception, the cultural apocalypse too delineates a domain in which it is impossible to discern with confidence the grammatical level from the empirical one, the general rule from the individual application, matters of principle from matters of fact. The cultural apocalypse, just like the state of exception, makes it so that every normative proposition shows that it is both an instrument of testing and a reality to be tested, a unit of measure and a measurable phenomenon. The state of exception has today become the enduring condition of associated life. It is no longer a circumscribed interval – inaugurated and closed by the sovereign – but a permanent tonality of action and discourse. This also goes for the ritual. The cultural apocalypse is not confined to a special space and time, but now concerns all the aspects of contemporary experience. The reason for this is simple. The institutional task of ritual lies in containing the extreme dangers that menace the openness to the world of the linguistic animal. Well, in an era in which the openness to the world is no longer veiled or dulled by social pseudo-environments, but can even be said to represent a fundamental technical resource, this task must be carried out without any pause (*senza soluzione di continuità*). The oscillation between the loss of presence and its restoration characterizes every moment of social praxis. The ambivalence between the symptoms of crisis and the symbols of deliverance pervades the average everyday.

It remains to ask whether cultural apocalypse, that is the natural-historical institution that holds back radical evil through oscillation and ambivalence, possesses a strictly political correlate. Whether ritual, besides spreading through all the interstices of profane time, may also give us some hints regarding the possible functioning of a Republic no longer linked to the state. My reply to these questions is affirmative. As I already suggested, I think that the ancient concept of *katechon*, of a 'force that restrains', constitutes the plausible political equivalent of cultural apocalypses; and that this concept, like that of cultural apocalypse, is by no means inexorably tied to the vicissitudes of State sovereignty.

Katechon

In his second letter to the Thessalonians, the apostle Paul speaks of a force that restrains the dominance of iniquity in the world, always deferring the triumph of the Antichrist anew. To restrain, to defer: these terms have nothing in common with 'expunging' or 'defeating', or even with 'circumscribing'. What restrains cannot keep its distance from what it restrains, but remains in proximity to it, and even cannot fail to mix with it. The *katechon* does not vanquish evil, but limits it and parries its strikes each and every time. It does not save from destruction, but rather holds it back, and in order to hold it back, it conforms to the innumerable occasions in which it may manifest itself. It resists the pressure of chaos by adhering to it, just like the concave adheres to the convex. The border line between the *katechon* and the Antichrist does not belong exclusively to either of the two adversaries: analogously to the ritual device described by Ernesto de Martino, this line is both the symptom of the crisis and the symbol of deliverance, the expression of iniquity and a physiognomic trait of virtue. Or better, it is the one only because it is the other.

In mediaeval and modern political thought, the *katechon* was initially identified with the temporal power of the Church, then with the centripetal institutions of the sovereign State, which, by imposing a preliminary pact of obedience, aimed to offset the disintegration of the social body. This is what Carl Schmitt writes in his *Nomos of the Earth*. This is certainly not the place for a detailed discussion of the conservative and state-worshipping use of the notion of *katechon*. Let a single observation suffice for the moment: Schmitt and his family album (Hobbes, De Maistre, Donoso Cortès) evoke a 'force that restrains' to indicate generically the stabilizing and protective role that befalls political institutions faced with the dangerousness of the disoriented and neotenous animal. Such a role is fundamental but does not represent a discriminating element: it may be claimed, in principle, by the most diverse types of political institution (to be clear: from an anarchist commune to a military dictatorship), as well as by innumerable non-political institutions (beginning with language and ritual). Grasped in its generic sense, the *katechon* is a ubiquitous and pervasive property, perhaps even a bio-anthropological invariant. The salient point in Schmitt and authors close to him is not at all in he reference to a 'force that restrains', but its unequivocal attribution to state sovereignty. The question of the *katechon* is freed from these associations once the necessity of an institutional protection is stipulated, while at the same time rejecting the idea that the State and its associated 'monopoly over the political decision' can guarantee it (given that it is precisely they which constitute the utmost danger). Since dissimilar, or even diametrically opposed ways of containing the risky instability of the linguistic animal are in competition, it seems legitimate not only to disentangle the idea of *katechon* from the 'supreme empire' of the State, but also to juxtapose the two. All of this does not hold, of course, for those who critique the State while trusting in the innate meekness of our species. For them, a 'force that restrains' is always deserving of contempt; for them, the appropriation of the *katechon* by authoritarian political thought is therefore entirely legitimate, or rather unimpeachable. But I'd rather disregard such stances.

If we equate the concept of *katechon* with the apotropaic function involved in any political (and non-political) institution, we are led to conclude that it surpasses and exceeds that of State sovereignty: between the two concepts there lies an insurmountable gap, the same gap that separates the genus from the species, the phrase 'linguistic animal' from the phrase 'university professor'. If we turn our attention instead to the truly peculiar aspects of the *katechon*, which is to say to what makes it a proper name, it is not difficult to recognize its radical heterogeneity with respect to the form of protection envisaged by State sovereignty (whose crux, as we know, is the exit from the state of nature and the preliminary pact of obedience). Let us follow this second path. In order to grasp the characteristic features of the *katechon* as a political institution, those aspects that relate it to cultural apocalypses and oppose it to the modern central State, we need to pause for a moment on its theological make-up.

The *katechon* is marked by an internal antinomy. It hold back the Antichrist, radical evil, polymorphous aggressiveness. But in the second book of the Apocalypse the triumph of the Antichrist constitutes the necessary premise for the second coming of the Messiah, the *parousia* which will accord eternal salvation to creatures by putting an end to the world. This is the double bind to which the *katechon* is subject: if it restrains evil, the final defeat of evil is hindered; if aggressiveness is limited, the ultimate annihilation of aggressiveness is forestalled. Of course, blunting ever anew the dangerousness of the species Homo sapiens means avoiding its lethal expression, but it also, and perhaps above all, means prohibiting its definitive expunction: that expunction, to be clear, that the theories of sovereignty seek by means of the stark caesura between state of nature and civil state. From a logical point of view, the antinomy that lurks in the institution-*katechon* is perhaps comparable to the paradoxical injunction "I command you to be spontaneous": if I am spontaneous, I am not, since I am obeying an order; if I obey the order, I am not really obeying, because I am being spontaneous. From a political point of view, the same antinomy becomes remarkably productive, inasmuch as it delineates a model of institutional protection according to which the (self-)destructive drives linked to the openness to the world can only be confronted thanks to the same bio-linguistic conditions (neoteny, negation, the modality of the possible, and so on) which constitute the foundations and guarantee of that very openness.

Let us reiterate once more the crucial point. By hindering the triumph of the Antichrist, the *katechon* simultaneously hinders the redemption at the hand of the Messiah. To restrain iniquity entails renouncing the restitution of innocence. The *katechon* – a radically anti-eschatological theologico-political concept – is opposed to the 'end of the world', or better, to the atrophy of the openness to the world, to the various ways in which the crisis of presence can manifest itself. Both evil triumphant and the total victory over evil imply that end, which is to say this atrophy. The *katechon* is a protection against the lethal instability that emanates from the Antichrist, but equally from the messianic state of equilibrium; it protects from terrifying chaos as well as from redemptive entropy. Not only does the *katechon* oscillate between the negative and the positive, without ever expunging the negative, it preserves oscillation as such, its persistence.

In strictly political terms, the *katechon* is a republican institution designed to forestall two catastrophic possibilities which can undermine the very root of social interaction: the case in which the regularity of species-specific behaviors becomes prominent, albeit devoid of any determinate rule whatsoever (semantic excess); and the diametrically opposed case in which a set of rules is in force which, having been sundered from regularity, require an automatic and uniform application (semantic deficit). Thus, the *katechon* is the republican institution that holds back the risks implicit in the instability of 'a being primarily founded on detachment', though it simultaneously counters the rather menacing ways in which the modern State has sought out a protection from those very risks. Not unlike the 'irregular institutions' (leagues, councils, assemblies) that characterize the political existence of the multitude according the Hobbes, the *katechon* is doubly tied to circumstances and occasions. It does not exercise a centralizing synthesis with regard to concrete forms of life, powers and local conflicts, but instead carries out a contingent and very precise task. The *katechon* is the institution best suited to the permanent state of exception, to the partial lack of distinction (or reciprocal commutability) between matters of principle and matters of fact that characterize it. In other words, it is the institution best suited to the state of exception once the latter, far from still being a prerogative of the sovereign, signals instead the action and discourse of the multitude.

11

What is Critique?
Suspension and Re-Composition in Textual and Social Machines[*]

Gerald Raunig

(Translated by Aileen Derieg)

> Critique does not have the premises of a thinking that conclusively explains: and this is what is to be done now. It must be an instrument for those who fight, resist, and who no longer want what is. It must be used in processes of conflict, confrontation and resistance attempts. It must not be the law of the law. It is not a stage in a program. It is a challenge to the status quo. (Michel Foucault, 'Roundtable, 20 May 1978')

In the manifold assemblages of concepts of resistance, an impression of confusion is not unusual; neither is arbitrariness in terms of a meaningful differentiation of these concepts. When Michel Foucault presents an entire battery of concepts of resistance in his governmentality lecture and weighs them – refusal, revolt, disobedience, resistiveness, desertion, dissidence, dissent, and, finally, counter-conduct – then the following question arises in relation to critique: Is there a specific place of critique in this assemblage of concepts, and if there is, then where? This is the question, the problem that I want to address in the course of this essay, beginning with Foucault and tying my own idea of this specific place of critique into his.

First of all, I would like to avoid a misunderstanding that might possibly arise about the title of the conference[1] that is the occasion for this text. 'The Art of Critique' is not in any way a reference to art in the narrower sense, nor to art criticism, even though the efforts undertaken by our institute do move in the neighboring zones of art production and art theory. The conference title was, first of all, a set piece of a quotation from 'What is Critique?' – the lecture that Michel Foucault held in late May 1971, which is also the leitmotiv of my text. The term 'art' here is closely related to the Greek word *techne*, which is why Foucault calls critique in his lecture not only an 'art' and a 'virtue', but also a 'technique'. This is not simply an idiosyncrasy of Foucault's, but rather a tradition that reaches back to the first uses of the term critique. The term first appears with Plato, in *Politicos* (The Statesman), in the combination *kritiké techne* (*Polit.* 260b), in other words the art, the craft of distinguishing, which is then translated in Latin as *ars iudicandi*. Calling critique both 'technique' and 'art' is found throughout the centuries and in various European languages.

Yet which practice makes up this technique of critique? Contrary to the commonplace use of the term, in Judith Butler's essay – inspired by Foucault's lecture and also entitled 'What is Critique?' – she refers to critique as "a practice that suspends judgment" (Butler, 2002). So instead of judging or condemning, critique specifically suspends judgment. Contrary to the notion of a purely critical position, a privileged place, upon which – and from which – the overview and authority of judgment arise, it is initially a matter of suspending judgment. In fact, this was already noted by the eternal head of the court of critique, Immanuel Kant, who wrote: "critical method suspends judgment." Nevertheless, he also continued with the explanation that this suspension of judgment has only one aim: "critical method suspends judgment, in order to reach [judgment]" (Kant, n.d.: 459). Butler, on the other hand, concurs with Foucault that critique goes beyond suspending judgment, that critique specifically does not return to judgment in this suspension of judgment, but instead opens up a new practice. This double figure of suspension and re-invention corresponds to the development of the two components of my own text.

1. Critique suspends judgment.
2. At the same time, critique also means re-composition, invention.

Foucault's 'What is Critique?' The Necessity of New Reversals of the Movement from the Critical Attitude to the Project of Critique

In my lecture at the opening of the Transform project in Linz in the Fall of 2005 (reprinted as chapter 1 in this volume), I focused primarily on the famous starting point of Foucault's lecture, which names critique as the attitude, the art, the will not to be governed like that, not in this way, not at this price, not by them (Foucault, 1997a). Judith Butler calls Foucault's starting point here the 'signature of a critical attitude' (Butler, 2002), and it is in fact inscribed in most practices of critique as a figure that derives its force of resistance primarily from the will to shift the relationship of power and resistance.

Foucault develops the figure of critique as an art of not being governed like that, consistently parallel to the expansion of the pastoral 'economy of the souls', into an art of governing people: the critical attitude is simultaneously 'partner and adversary of the arts of governing', which expanded explosively in the late Middle Ages. And while Foucault posits this unexpectedly early start of the genealogy of critique, in his lecture he picks up virtually all of the important threads of critique in European Modernism: he starts with the emergence of the *critica sacra*, the new bible criticism during the transition from the late Middle Ages to Modernity as the most important component of the modern foundation of critique. He ascribes to Kant's endeavor of critique the main moment of questioning knowledge about its own limits and dead ends, and he calls this the 'Kantian channel' (Foucault, 1997a: 63). With the term 'critical attitude' Foucault ties into the revolutionary, leftist Hegelian texts of the nineteenth century, and finally even takes a position of "fellowship with the Frankfurt School" (Foucault, 1997a: 44) – especially in relation to their "critique of positivism, objectivism, rationalization, of techne and technicalization" (1997a: 38) – whose critical theory embodied the last major boom of the concept of critique.

As my starting point for Transform was the thesis at the beginning of Foucault's lecture, that of critique as the art of not being governed like that, now at the close of our project I would like to start from the end of Foucault's lecture. There he poses a question that is difficult to understand. Following the familiar opening passage and longer epistemological passages in the middle section, he states his sympathy for certain aspects of the Enlightenment contrary to a form of critique that he increasingly begins to doubt in the course of his text. His question is, specifically, is it not necessary to reverse the path from the critical attitude to the question of critique, from the endeavor of the Enlightenment to the project of critique? The movement of the reversal is first of all to be examined in its heterogenesis, as a historical dissemination of Enlightenment, on the one hand, and the Kantian 'project of critique' on the other. It must be noted, however, that the reversal of the process cannot simply lead back to the pathos of Enlightenment, it also includes the leftist critique of the Enlightenment from the nineteenth and twentieth centuries, but understands the critical attitude as Enlightenment-critical 'enlightenment' in a different genealogy as the 'project of critique'.

Whereas critique and Enlightenment (*Aufklärung* in German) seem to be inextricably interwoven in a more general understanding, Foucault gradually unfolds both terms in the course of his lecture, finally polarizing them with a reserved polemic reference to Kant and his concept of critique: he writes that "this question of the *Aufklärung*, since Kant, because of Kant and presumably because of this separation he introduced between *Aufklärung* and critique, was essentially raised in terms of knowledge (*connaissance*)" (Foucault, 1997a: 48). In other words, a separation of Enlightenment and critique first took place with Kant, then the "movement responsible for reassessing the *Aufklärung* endeavor within the critical project" (Foucault, 1997a: 61). In this 'critical project'[2] now comprising both Enlightenment and critique, Foucault sees a procedure develop that focuses exclusively on testing the legitimacy of historical modes of knowledge.[3] Foucault, on the other hand, takes up and assails the question of how power and knowledge are interwoven.[4]

The problem of the Kantian position is that "Kant set forth critique's primordial responsibility, to know knowledge" (Foucault, 1997a: 36). Here a radical critique of knowledge is separated from every critical political activity. Instead of this form of critique understood as being necessarily limited, Foucault is interested in a practical critique that continuously transgresses the limit of knowledge that is not to be grasped as a 'law of laws'.[5] Whereas Kant is concerned with critique as knowing knowledge, therefore also and above all knowing the limits of knowledge, Foucault wants the critical attitude to be understood as a transgression of precisely these limits.

I read the direction of Foucault's demand for a reversal primarily as an attack on fixations and restrictions of the concept of critique to the critique of knowledge, as an attack on the extreme academicizing and narrowing of the Kantian concept of critique, which made it impossible in the early nineteenth century, at least in the German-speaking region, to use the concept of critique in political contexts. And what is perhaps even more important: I also read Foucault's suggestion that it is a matter of reversing the path from the critical attitude to the project of critique into a new productive repetition of leftist Hegelian discourses, which attempted a reversal of this kind around the mid-nineteenth century. The highpoint of this development in opposition to Kant's concept of critique – which is also posited, not least of all, dichotomously against revolutionary violence – is Marx' famous dictum from his *Critique of Hegel's Philosophy of Right*: "Clearly the weapon of criticism cannot replace the criticism of weapons, and material force must be overthrown by material force. But theory also becomes a material force once it has gripped the masses" (Marx, 1975: 251). Or less oratorically: what Marx and Engels called 'practical critical action' is already quite close to the Foucauldian concept of the 'critical attitude' in this emphasis on turning away from Kant's purely epistemological critical project. And since Marx, it is possible (again) to understand critique as 'practical' alongside revolutionary violence, and to grasp these two activities not as mutually exclusive, but rather as complementary components of social struggles.

And this was also possible before Kant. The intention of my essay is to insist on this complementarity. Critique and Revolution, critical discursivity and social struggles, the machines of textual criticism and the machines of social resistance do not have to be understood as mutually exclusive. When the relationship to text suspends the law of the law, then new social machines emerge. If a new social composition emerges in resistance, then a re-composition of the texts also results; the social organization form of an assemblage joins together with a new concatenation of conceptual and textual components. In fact, in my examples this social re-composition overlaps to a certain degree with re-constructive textual critique. To support this thesis, in the following I would like to investigate both components of machinic complementarity, the text machine and the social machine.[6] Instead of constructing and fixing the distance between two identical poles with terms such as 'scholarly text production' and 'people's revolt', I want to focus on the zones of proximity between these two machines, especially on the modes in which they impel the suspension of judgment and the practice of re-composition.

Critique as Discursive and Textual Machine

In the beginning of the modern history of the concept of critique, there is textual criticism, and it consists primarily of the suspension of judgment that was practiced by the clergy as a Medieval monopoly on interpreting the bible. The growing objections to the Christian principle of tradition and its privileging of the Fathers of the Church and the clergy as monopolists of exegesis took the scriptures away from the clergy as sole mediators.[7] In the high and late Middle Ages, when the art of governing was largely a spiritual practice closely linked to the doctrine of the scriptures, this was exactly the point where governing, guiding people was attacked, resistance ran, not least of all, through the search for a different relationship to scripture: "Not wanting to be governed was a certain way of refusing, challenging, limiting (say it as you like) ecclesiastical rule" (Foucault, 1997a: 29).

Foucault speaks here of a dimorphism, in which the clergy is on the one side and the laity on the other, an extreme development that represents "one of the starting points of pastoral counter-conduct" (Foucault, 2004a: 294). The monopoly on performing the sacraments, the practice of obligatory confession as a permanent tribunal, the inversion of asceticism into obedience, and not least of all the jurisdiction over the interpretation of the sacred scriptures, these are the central components of the pastorate. Counter to all of these components, however, there was also a pastoral counter-conduct in the form of short-circuiting, subverting and over-affirming the respective clerical coercion or monopoly. In the case of the scriptural monopoly this meant the repulsion of the pastor in the field of scriptures (Foucault, 2004a: 309). Critique as suspension of judgment meant here the suspension of the 'pastoral relay', suspension of the mediation of the scriptures through the clergy, suspension of teaching, and thus the self-empowerment of the readers.[8]

Following the late Medieval practice of resistance against the clerical scriptures monopoly, the concept of critique from antiquity was reanimated in the late fifteenth century.[9] Roughly a hundred years later, the term entered into English and French from Latin. A hundred years after that, the word *Kritik* appeared for the first time in German, specifically in Gottlieb Stolle's *Concise Introduction to the History of Practical Learning*. Here the early scientific systems theorist and historian Stolle (1673-1744) wrote a condensed definition of critique, summarizing its conceptual development in the last centuries and definitively closing, in a sense, the conceptual development from late Medieval resistance against the clerical scriptures monopoly. In this genealogy, Stolle's definition emphasizes the specific significance of text critique and provides a concise representation of the object of this critique:

> Critique commonly means an art of understanding the old authors, or making them understandable, of distinguishing what they wrote from what has been imputed to them or falsified, and improving or replacing what is spoiled. (Stolle, 1736: 117)

I would like to use this probably first appearance of critique in German to take a closer look at the dense definition proposed here. The source is a 'Historia Literaria', which essentially collects bibliographical references to certain specialized questions; the definition of critique is the sentence that introduces the 18-page chapter 'Von der Critica'. Gottlieb Stolle initially calls 'Critica' or 'Critic' an 'art'. He does so in the tradition of the philological line of the *ars critica*, as it dominated the concept of critique since the end of the sixteenth century, in other words, critique essentially as text critique. In keeping with the sense of *techne*, of *ars* from antiquity, we may presume that a technique, a technical procedure of the philological discipline is to be designated here, which is subsequently made concrete. The 'old authors' are defined as the object of critique, thus also seeking and establishing the familiar reference to antiquity and its theory protagonists, which takes up the line intended to suspend, skip and explode the Medieval *authority* of the clergy. Yet 'authors' — or as Stolle writes, 'auctores' — also indicates the central concept of authorship, subjectifying and specifying the origin, which — as we will see — is not to be interpreted as an essentialist figure, so much as a simple root: the Latin noun *auctor* stems from the verb *augeo*, for multiplying. *Auctor* is hence a person who multiplies something or brings together several components that do not necessarily belong together.[10]

What *Critic* first involves is *to understand* the old auctores. The next step, which was relatively surprising for the context of that time, expands this 'understanding' with *'making understandable'*. The crucial difference between 'understand' and 'make understandable' is the relation between a passive continuation of the tradition of interpretation in the old tracks of knowledge and 'making understandable' as a definitive productivity of critique. Critique is thus based not only on the appropriation of linguistic competence to be able to understand the texts, it also actively intervenes in the text production. It goes beyond obediently following the rules just as it goes beyond slavish re-construction of the original text.

Critique should nevertheless 'distinguish', it remains an *ars iudicandi*, a technique of distinguishing. But what does distinguish mean, what is to be distinguished here? That which the 'old authors' 'have written' from that which 'has been imputed to them or falsified'. It is not only the sense of an unambiguous writing that has been clearly passed on that is to be interpreted here; before that, critique seeks to distinguish what was written from what was falsified. For this, we must imagine the often fragmentary quality of the handwritten manuscripts as well as the manifold revisions, the complex interlocking of generations of manuscripts and the various degrees to which the texts have been 'spoiled' through various circumstances ranging from fire to less talented scribes. Evident here is the knowledge that text production and text critique are processes. Aspects of imputing and falsifying reveal a process, which multiplies authorship, shifting the focus to the interests of the respective historical contexts and their subjects in understanding, interpreting, shifting or even obfuscating the origin in their own interest. All of these revisions of the existing original material are to be understood as a productive process of re-composition. Instead of introducing the distinction as an essentialist excavation of an origin, it is instead a matter of reinstituting a heterogenetic process: not a pure tree schema, at the head of which there is an original text and an *auctor*, but rather a much more winding practice of continual re-combination.

And what results over the course of time is a gigantic and complex interlocking apparatus of philological method and auxiliary sciences, the visual representation of which in the positive or negative apparatus, which sometimes takes up a large portion of the page of a book, illustrates its apparatus-like character. Yet the history, linguistics, conjectures, translations, and the biographical and political contexts of the authors form not only a gigantic apparatus, but also a productive, abstract machine. The copyists not only copied and improved/deteriorated the texts, they also filled gaps with much imagination, sometimes refined the texts, corrected them ideologically, sometimes even continued them. Text critique involves more than distinguishing between the source and its multiple shifts, it also involves 'improving or replacing what is spoiled'. With the words 'improve' and 'replace', Stolle positions critique in the terrain of re-construction and re-composition. And the re- in both these terms does not necessarily indicate a return to an origin that must be re-produced, but rather a new, more suitable place. The result is a scope for re-composition, re-invention.[11]

Critique is thus to be understood as an interplay between the suspended *iudicium* and *inventio*, between the capacity for judgment, which in 'making understandable' clearly goes beyond the practice of empirically distinguishing in the sense of separation and exclusion, and invention that newly concatenates the (signifying) components.

Critique as Social Machine

Even before the re-invention of critique as text critique, Foucault discovered a resistive practice against the pastorate: in the religious struggles of the second half of the Middle Ages, in the revolts of mysticism, in the nests of resistance against the authority of clerical exegesis, not only was the Reformation prepared, but for Foucault they were also "the kind of historical limit upon which this critical attitude developed" (Foucault, 1997a: 64).[12] Both before and as scholarly resistance arose, the self-empowerment of philology against the clerical exegesis monopoly and the application of philological critique to the biblical scriptures, social machines against mediation by the pastor also arise. What especially interested me was the historical basis of what Foucault took as the starting point for his explanations, what he also mentions as questions that were still open for him in the discussion of his lecture from 1978. Here he asks:

> If we were to explore this dimension of critique, would we not then find that it is supported by something akin to the historical practice of revolt, the non-acceptance of a real government, on one hand, or, on the other, the individual experience of the refusal of governmentality? (Foucault, 1997a: 73)

Foucault himself left this question open in his lecture. In his lectures on the history of governmentality held in the same year, there are ideas that continue on from this. Especially in the eighth lecture from 1 March 1978, Foucault brings up numerous indications of the various resistances against the pastorate in the late Middle Ages (Foucault, 2004: 278). Yet Foucault did not really close the gap here either. His method remained eclectic and purposely on the surface. He listed the most important movements on the constantly shifting border between internal and external criticism of the church, referred occasionally to single specific features of these movements that tested a different conduct, a counter-conduct.[13] Not only witchcraft and the familiar heresies, but also a multitude of smaller and larger anormalities at the margins of ecclesiastical immanence are mentioned here. Waldensians, Utraquists, Calixtines, Taborites, Amalricans, Flagellanti, the mysticism of the Rhine nuns, the Society of the Poor and Jeanne Dabenton, Beguines and Beghards, the Brethren of the Free Spirit and Marguerite Porete populate the space and time of this marginal cartography of counter-conduct especially in the twelfth to the fifteenth century (Foucault, 2004a: 285, 306).

However, Foucault does not go into detail about any of these examples of counter-conduct. The reason for his limitation to a movement along the surface certainly has something to do with the precarious source material, which is marked by the fact that sources from the perspective of the actors hardly exist, because the Inquisition so thoroughly destroyed them. This forced fragmentarity, however, also has an implicit quality. This made it possible for Foucault to collect single aspects from every possible area, which constitute individual and collective counter-conduct in (not only) the late Middle Ages: the election and the option of deposing the pastor among the Taborites, the new forms of 'counter-society' among the Society of the Poor, the emphasis on communal property and the rejection of personal ownership of goods. All of these are components of an abstract machine that assails the dimorphism of priests and laity, in which the suspension of the Christian pastorate goes hand in hand with the re-composition and re-invention of social organization.[14] These forms of counter-conduct have their specific features, but this remains a "non-autonomous specificity" (Foucault, 2004a: 286). This means they develop in the connection with political revolts against power as sovereignty, with economic revolts against power as exploitation. Most of all, though, "these revolts of conduct, these resistances of conduct are equally linked with a very different, but decisive problem, namely the status of women" (Foucault, 2004a: 285).[15]

When I look more closely in the following at one of the movements central to this question, then I am exploring somewhat below Foucault's eclectic probing maneuver on the surface of counter-conduct in the high and late Middle Ages. I mainly limit myself to the thirteenth and early fourteenth century and to a single movement, but one that left traces throughout broad sections of Europe: the Beguines.[16] At the turn of the twelfth to the thirteenth century, a new type of religious or semi-religious form of living crystallized primarily in Belgium and the Netherlands, in the Rhineland and in northern Italy (Dinzelbacher, 1993: 21-23). The *mulieres religiosae*, the pious, honorable women who were soon called by the collective name Beguines (Leicht, 2001: 99), lived unmarried and in poverty, or more strongly formulated: in the rejection of the marital dominance of men and in the rejection of wealth, which was also understood at the time in the sense of a rejection of power and higher position.[17] However, they lived without a fixed ecclesiastical rule, such as that which defines life in a religious order. Not least of all, due to this lack of a rule, they could also leave the community at any time, because they had not taken a vow of eternal obedience. This means that the Beguines were border-crossers, who were always and from the start in danger of being thrown into the outside of ecclesiastical immanence.[18] Depending on the interpretation of the authorities, geographical and historical context and the conclusions of various practices of divine judgment, they were persecuted or revered, landed on the lists of heretics or later in the calendar of saints.

The rise of the Beguine movement emerged not at all primarily as a revolt against worldly rule, but rather out of the desire for a suspension of the clerical-patriarchal order and the everyday misogyny that permeated all classes in the twelfth and thirteenth centuries. As Foucault described it (2004a: 302-7), alongside the failed conduct of the clergy, it was primarily the growing dissatisfaction with the sacramental power of the priests that gradually incited a threatening perforation of the dimorphism between clergy and the laity. In the case of women there was an additional reason not to accept the alternative or early marriage or entry a cloister. The suspension of this alternative led them directly into the risky experiment of trying out a non-institutionalized, non-secured, non-protected way of living.

The desire for alternative forms of living generated essentially three practices of the Beguines, the withdrawal into the hermitage as an anchoress, the collective practice of living together without the rule of an order, and finally the nomadic practice of the mendicant wandering preacher.

1. First the mystical practice of the anchoresses: this is essentially a technique of radical self-isolation, but does not only consist solely of a

hermit existence, of the complete withdrawal of a hermit into solitude. The anchoress' hermitage was sometimes also attached to a church and furnished so that the anchoress could also take part in the mass. Ecstasy, trances, visions, and finally the *unio mystica* (mystic union as the bride of Christ) marked the anchoress' specific way of living; direct experience of God, the rapture or the *enthousiasmos* of God were the highest aim, and guidance from the confessor was the transformed remainder of ecclesiastical order. Here one should think about Foucault's distinction between asceticism and obedience that would even shift the ascetic practice of the anchoresses into a light of disobedience towards church power, or as Foucault says: "a kind of raging and inverted obedience" (2004a: 301). However, here is not the place to go into this in more detail and especially more critically, and what I am interested in here is primarily the aspect of re-composition in the context of the Beguines.

2. When the suspension of judgment is found here in the suspension of divine judgment (=ordeal) and clerical order, this means not only a movement of defecting from the extreme ecclesiastical order, but also a dangerous attempt to live without rule, beyond the discipline of the institutional order. The Beguines founded unofficial religious communities living in one or more houses, later entire city districts. A collective alternative form of living emerged in self-organization as fleeing from the practice of confession as a permanent trial, from penance and reconciliation imposed from outside, from the double domination by men and priests. Whereas entering a cloister was a final decision, leaving the community at any time remained open to the Beguines and with that also leaving the voluntary abstinence from sex.

3. Finally, however, along with these radically individual and collective practices of being settled in one place, there was also a Beguine form of living in movement: vagabond, nomadic Beguines who regarded themselves as homeless mendicants (Cohn, 1970: 163). Initially the nomadic existence of the Beguines was an analogy to their notion of a spiritual path leading through detours and wandering without plan or destination through a difficult terrain. Like their male counterparts, the Beghards, however, these Beguines concretely led a deliberately impoverished life of wandering based on the pillars of begging and preaching.

More or less public preaching, sometimes in more out-of-the-way places, sometimes in central squares, was probably imagined as an act of provocation. Women like Hildegard von Bingen or Marguerite Porete who appeared in public, tested a rare form of female presence, but probably provoked the authorities all the more for it. The Beguines were easily attacked, since they belonged to no order, but the forms of living they practiced and propagated were also subject to persecution: *recompositio* and *inventio*, re-composition and re-invention, take on a dangerous tone here, because the new, 'new fashions' and 'unheard of innovations' were terms associated with the *novi doctores*, the heretics (Dinzelbacher, 1993: 21-23). In this respect, the bishops attacked both the anchoresses' way of living, as the ecstasy of the brides of Christ was especially condemned as immoderate, and that of the nomadic Beguines, whose wandering way of life was also read as excessive (Dinzelbacher, 1993: 37).[19] What was left – although increasingly regulated – was only the middle form of communal living under the control of worldly and ecclesiastical authorities. Towards the end of the thirteenth century, the attacks became increasingly massive, the border between inside and outside the church was clearly drawn again[20]: some were integrated into Catholic order, were accommodated in manageable city districts, were compelled to withdraw into communities with orderly ecclesiastical surveillance, regulation and institutionalization; others were increasingly exposed to persecution, condemnation and burning (Cohn, 1970: 165), or they made the transition into the clandestine. It may be supposed that under this pressure there was a development similar to the one asserted by Norman Cohn for the Beghards: the wandering Beguines also withdrew from the public practice of preaching and begging in "conspirational understanding which they were able to develop with certain of the Beguine communities" (Cohn, 1970: 162). This results in a new re-composition, or at least a re-ordering of the functions of settled and nomadic Beguines. Whereas the nomadic Beguines were able to continue their practice of preaching in the community houses, through this clandestine combination of moving and static elements, even communication with far distant Beguine centers was maintained (Cohn, 1970: 166).

When I talk about a suspension of (divine) judgment in the context of the Beguine movement, I am not at all imputing a turning away from Christian practices, but rather the attempt to intensify, reinterpret and rewrite them, the excessive application and outdoing of the rule, the over-affirmation and exaggeration of the regulations: to the extent that Beguines exercised ecstatic practices, they were able to draw on non-biblical messages, the direct access to Jesus Christ in their mystical experiences. The knowledge of God grounded in experience (*cognito Dei experimentalis*) entered into competition with the mediating role of the church. The revelation experiences were thus not only supernatural, but also unmediated (self-)authorization, which went beyond the original authority of scripture, as well as beyond the mediating authority of the clergy.

Along with this privileged access to God, which was primarily reserved to the anchoresses, there was also a direct attack on the scripture monopoly of the clergy. The Beguines used their knowledge of the bible to develop their own form of living and to become autonomous from the monopoly of the clergy (Gnädinger, 1987: 223). The type of relationship the Beguines had to exegesis is evident not only in this emancipation process, but also in the fact that they already attempted to translate the bible into French in the twelfth century, that they presumably interpreted its mysteries and discussed it in secular assemblies and even in the street (Cohn, 1970: 161; Gnädinger, 1987: 223, 229). Not only the bible was interpreted and translated autonomously, but the Beguines also wrote texts. Even in the interweaving of experiential mysticism and theoretical mysticism, however, they did not use Latin as the language of scholars, but rather Middle Low German, other German dialects or French.[21] And these self-assured texts are, not least of all, also invectives against the established theology (Leicht, 1999: 108), implicit and explicit criticism of the clergy.

In this context, critique must also be seen as a search for alternative forms of living, different from the marital dominance, clerical and patriarchal order, and as a struggle for education, as a struggle over language, as a struggle for broader knowledge production. The social machine of the Beguines is not to be decoupled from the text machine that gradually and increasingly arose against the monopoly of the pastor. The concatenation of the two machines is the crucial indication of the quality of critique.

And this brings me back to the opening question of the specific place of critique in the conceptual assemblage of expressions for the forms and forces of resistance. Of course, there should not be an overly hasty link made here between the historical and the current; space must be left for querying historical shifts both in terms of the text function and in terms of the social re-compositions. The late Medieval concatenation of text critique and social machine undoubtedly follows a different mode than the opposition of an economic power as difficult to grasp as capitalism, which was central to the Marxian concept of critique in the nineteenth century. And if today we negotiate the position of the 'general intellect', a collective and militant intellectuality in post-Fordist cognitive capitalism, this in turn means a new challenge for the various forms of critique as suspension and re-composition. Nevertheless, the place of critique is there, where the social machines of resistance are concatenated with text machines. What has made the concept of critique so relevant and so controversial in various phases of modernism, is the struggle against decoupling text machines and social machines, their concatenations, overlaps and superimpositions.

Notes

*   For suggestions and critical advice, I would like to thank Aileen Derieg, Isabell Lorey and Stefan Nowotny.

1. This essay is a revised version of the introductory lecture for the eipcp conference 'The Art of Critique', at the Kunsthalle Exnergasse in Vienna in April 2008 (cf. http://transform.eipcp.net/Actions/discursive/artofcritique).

2. "[W]hose intent was to allow knowledge to acquire an adequate idea of itself" (Foucault, 1997a: 61).

3. Foucault contrasts this test of legitimacy with the strange concept of 'eventualization' (Foucault, 1997a: 49).

4. His question describes the movement of deserting from this specific connection to the figure of not being governed like that: "In what way can the effects of coercion [...] not be dissipated by a return to the legitimate destination of knowledge and by a reflection on the transcendental or semi-transcendental that fixes knowledge, but how can they instead be reversed or released from within a concrete strategic field, this concrete strategic field that induced them, starting with this decision not to be governed" (Foucault: 1997a: 60)?

5. Foucault (2005: 702): "The point in brief is to transform the critique conducted in the form of necessary limitation into a practical critique that takes the form of a possible transgression." This also illuminates the somewhat confusing conceptual shift from the critical attitude to the critical

project. What Kant originally describes as *Aufklärung* clearly separates from critique, and finally dissipates into a notion of critique that is solely a critique of knowledge, which for Foucault is "very much what I was trying before to describe as critique, this critical attitude which appears as a specific attitude in the Western world starting with what was historically, I believe, the great process of society's governmentalization" (Foucault, 1997a: 34).

6. These are also two main strands that Foucault indicates with his reference to pre-Reformation 'religious struggles' on the one hand and the "spiritual attitudes prevalent during the second half of the Middle Ages" on the other, when discussing the genealogy of the critical attitude (Foucault, 1997a: 64).

7. On the emergence of *critica sacra*, cf. Kosseleck (1976: 87-89); and Gürses (2006).

8. "The pastor can comment, he can explain what is unclear, he can name what is important, but this occurs in every case so that the reader can read the Holy Scriptures himself" (Foucault, 2004: 309).

9. The Italian humanist Angelo Poliziano, in his lecture about Aristotle's 'Analytica priora' in 1492, ties into the terminology from antiquity, ascribing to the *critici* the sole right to judge and improve writings.

10. Giorgio Agamben points this out in *State of Exception* (2005). Agamben sees the specific function of the *auctoritas* in contrast to *potestas* precisely where it is a matter of suspending right: "It is a force that suspends and reactivates right, but gives it no formal validity."

11. There is something involved here that Cicero and Quintilian already addressed in conjunction with critique, but still clearly *distinguished* from critique in the narrower sense, from *ars iudicandi*. The *recompositio*, the re-composition of the text, is also accompanied by a component of *inventio* or of *ars inveniendi*. Quintilian emphasizes, for instance, in the *institutio oratoria*, describing the meticulous and scrupulous character of the dialectical discussion of scholars, "that they claim for themselves both the part of invention and that of judgment, the first of which they call topic, the second critique." Quintilian (*Inst. orat.* V, 14, 28): "*ut qui sibi et inveniendi et iudicandi vindicent partis, quarum alteram topikén, alteram kritikén vocant.*"

12. And he continues: "[T]hese experiences, these spiritual movements have very often been used as attire, vocabulary, but even more so as ways of being, and ways of supporting the hopes expressed by the struggle" (Foucault, 1997a: 74).

13. Foucault (2004a: 282): "By that I mean that these are movements that have a different conduct as their goal, which means wanting to be conducted differently, by other conductors [*conducteur*] and by other pastors, to different goals and to different forms of salvation, by means of other

procedures and other methods." Cf. also Foucault (2004a: 288): "an aspect of the search for a different conduct, for a being-conducted-differently, by other people, to goals other than that which is provided for by the official, visible and recognizable governmentality of society."

14. At this point Foucault repeats the familiar figure that resistance should not be understood as a subsequent reaction: rather than a linear sequence of action (by power) and resistance, there is "an immediate and fundamental correlation between conduct and counter-conduct" (Foucault, 2004a: 284).

15. In the early 13th century policies for women were more prohibitive in recognized orders such as the Premonstratensians, and at the same time there was a strong increase in the number of women joining the Waldensians, who initially instituted religious equality. Here women were permitted to preach, baptize, grant absolution, and celebrate the Eucharist.

16. See Cohn (1970: especially 148-186); Gnädinger (1987: 215-39); Vaneigem (1993: especially chapters 31 and 32); Dinzelbacher (1993; 1998: 13-30); Leicht (1999); Jantzen (2001: 29-44).

17. Initially this development was based on intercessions from bishops and permission from the Pope. At the intercession of Bishop Jakob von Virty, Pope Honorius III allowed pious women in France and Germany "to live together without assuming an approved order in common houses and to hold sermons for their mutual edification" (Dinzelbacher, 1993: 36).

18. The Beguines moved at the margins of the pastorate and brought a certain change to its limits at the same time. This relationship between limit and immanence corresponds with a figure that I call immanent transgression: transgressing a limit that does not presume the existence of a radical outside, into which the transgression of the limit is supposed to lead, but rather which changes the limit and the immanence. In his 'Preface to Transgression' from 1963, Foucault writes about Bataille and transgression as a 'gesture that applies to the limit'. And many years later, in 1978, this concept of transgression returns: "This philosophical ethos may be characterized as a limit-attitude. We are not talking about a gesture of rejection. We have to move beyond the outside-inside alternative; we have to be at the frontiers. Criticism indeed consists of analyzing and reflecting upon limits" (Foucault, 1997a).

19. It is doubtful, however, that the promiscuity, negation of sinfulness, complete absence of moral ideals, such as Cohn (1970: 179) presumes for the Brethren of the Free Spirit as 'mystical anarchism', also applied to the Beguines.

20. Official stages of this development are 1274, the Council of Lyon, the Provincial Synodes in Cologne, 1307, and in Mainz and Trier in 1310, and finally the general ban of Begine forms of living by the Council of Vienne,

1311/12 (Leicht, 1999: 98). In 1317 the Bishop of Straßburg "organized the first regular episcopal inquisition on German soil" (Cohn, 1970: 165; Dinzelbacher, 1993: 55-58).

21. Hadewijch, Beatrijs von Nazareth and Mechthild von Magdeburg wrote in German, Marguerite Porete in French (Gnädinger, 1987: 225; Dinzelbacher, 1993: 20).

12

Attempt to Think the Plebeian: Exodus and Constituting as Critique

Isabell Lorey

(Translated by Aileen Derieg)

Critique is not a position outside the realm of modes of governing, it is an attitude that keeps struggles virulent. Critique is the ongoing questioning of the way of being governed. Against the background of these succinct theses by Foucault (1997a, 2000: 347), it is possible to focus on the fundamental fragility and instability of governmental circumstances. Questioning naturalized, stable circumstances means not only showing that things have become as they are and can therefore be changed again, but also, as Foucault says in his text on critique, always principally thinking the possible disappearance of certain relations of government.

With and beyond Foucault, I would like to propose an immanent manner of resistive critique, in which rejection and refusal can be understood as a productive practice. When I speak of refusal as critique in the following, I want to introduce refusal in a seemingly paradoxical movement not as a simple negation, but rather as productivity. In addition, I want to show how it becomes imaginable to elude certain relations of government, specifically not as entering an outside of power relations, but rather as an immanent exodus.

In the winter of 1977, a year before his text on critique, Foucault gave an interview entitled 'Powers and Strategies', in which he clarified his understanding of critique and resistance with the help of a new contextualization. In this conversation Foucault brought up, in a relatively abrupt and brief way, the example of the plebeians, the social formation representing a foundation of the Roman Republic.[1]

131

This brief reference from Foucault is also interesting, because the interview was conducted by Jacques Rancière, who would later base his political theory, not least of all, on the relationship of domination between patricians and plebeians. However, Rancière subjected ancient Roman history from the fifth century BCE to a relatively abbreviated and shifted reading that would not be an example for the understanding of critique and resistance that I want to represent here (Rancière, 2002: 35).

I find Foucault's brief mention of the plebeians considerably more interesting, although he does not historically analyze them, but instead introduces them as an abstract figure of resistance and critique (the plebeian). He writes:

> The 'plebs' certainly have no sociological reality. However, there is always something in the body of society, in the classes, the groups and in the individuals themselves, which evades power relations in a certain sense; something that is not more or less malleable or recalcitrant raw material, but rather a centrifugal movement, a contrary, liberated energy. (Foucault, 2003: 542)

This is an important thought for what I would like to show; here Foucault considers the recalcitrant as belonging to that which is 'formed', better perhaps as that which emerges through power relations. What evades them, on the other hand, he calls 'contrary', centrifugal. The centrifugal refers to the energy of fleeing away from the center. What evades power relations is a force that flees, e-vades, departs. Critique can be understood accordingly as fleeing.[2] Foucault continues:

> 'The' plebs undoubtedly do not exist, but there is 'something' plebeian. There is something plebeian in the bodies and souls, it is in the individual, in the proletariat, in the bourgeoisie, but with various expansions, forms, energies and origins. The part of the plebs forms less of an outside in relation to the power relations, but rather perhaps their boundaries, their flip-side, their echo. (Foucault, 2003: 542)

And further, this plebeian "reacts to every advance of power with an evading movement; this motivates every new development of the constellation of power" (2003: 542). For this reason, it is indispensable for every analysis of *dispositifs* of power to assume the 'perspective of the plebs', specifically that of the reverse side and the boundary of power. In order to think 'the plebeian', I would like to briefly recount a part of the more or less 'actual' history of the plebeians, specifically the start of the struggles with the patricians at the beginning of the Roman Republic. Let us return to the period in the early fifth century BCE. I will subsequently transform the strategic struggles of the plebeians into an abstract figure again, in order to understand critique and resistance as productive refusal.

In telling of the struggles between the patricians and plebeians, I refer primarily to the line of the historiography of Titus Livius. The Roman historiographer wrote a chronology of the political history of Rome beginning with the time of the kings in the sixth century BCE up to the time of his own life, the period of the principality of Augustus in the first century BCE. In other words, Livius was writing almost 400 years after the events to be recounted now. There are no written sources for this period, for which reason, among others, Livius' account has had such a strong historical influence. It is relatively certain that Livius would have had no interest in the reading I offer of what the plebeians were doing in the early fifth century BCE in Rome. In his historiography he was primarily interested in highlighting the strengths and the glory of Rome and representing the history in such a way that it necessarily culminated in the rule of Augustus. This is one reason why Livius, in all his detailed representations of conflicts, ultimately always emphasizes the concordia, the Roman concord.

The conflicts that interest me here are those between the patricians, the Roman aristocracy, and the plebeians, a very heterogeneous mixture of mostly Roman peasants, who were differently positioned, especially economically, but who were all considered 'free' in terms of personal status; they were not slaves, but they had few political rights. We find ourselves at the beginning of the Roman Republic. The last tyrannical king had been driven out a few years before, and a republic was established under the rule of the patricians. Republican order could not yet be characterized as stable, and patricians and plebeians did not form a homogeneous group. My focus on the events of the early Roman Republic consists of the question of how that which is called 'secession' in the ancient sources can be understood as a political division or separation, specifically as the departure of the plebeians from Rome. I would like to theorize this event as 'exodus'.

Livius places the history of the first of three secessions explicitly in the context of military service and indebtedness: according to his account, around 495 BCE the situation in Rome became increasingly tense in terms of both domestic and foreign policies. The conflict between the patrician senators and the plebs broke out especially because of the plebeians who had ended up in debt bondage, were in other words economically dependent on a patrician patron. Then these indebted plebeians protested increasingly audibly that they were permitted to risk their lives for the freedom of Rome, but in times of peace were kept in servitude as a kind of serf (Liv. 2,23,1-2).[3]

Following several victorious wars against the Volsci, Sabines and Aurunci, a promised edict was not granted, a decree that had promised the plebeians security and protection of property and *familia* during a campaign. Debt bondage was not ended. The patrician senators feared rebellions and conspiracies among the plebeians, but as creditors they supported the further disregard of the decree (Liv. 2,31,7 ff.; 2,32,1). For this reason, they attempted again to obligate the plebeians fit for military service to the existing pledge of allegiance and gave the legions the command march out of the city because of a presumably expected attack. According to Livius, "that accelerated the outbreak of outrage" (Liv. 2,32,1).

The armed plebeian men, following Livius' dramatic account, then considered whether they should murder the consuls to prevent conscription. Instead of implementing these kinds of ideas, however, the plebeians fit for military service did something completely different: they refused and withdrew, according to Livius, "without command from the consuls to the Sacred Mountain" (Liv. 2,32,2), to a hill outside the boundaries of Rome and thus beyond the sphere of influence of the patrician rulers. This exodus from Rome marks the first secession of the plebeians.

The exodus of the plebeians, going out of the city, beyond the boundaries of the city, means revealing the boundary of the patrician dominated power relations at the same time. Becoming aware of the boundary also means leaving, withdrawing, and thus no longer taking this boundary as an absolute horizon. Foucault writes that the plebeian "forms less of an outside in relation to the power relationships, but perhaps its boundary instead" (Foucault, 2003: 542). The exodus does not lead into a beyond the realm of power. Instead it involves a withdrawal and leaving that results in a centrifugal force, which motivates a "new development of the assemblage of power". The plebs dynamized the demarcation of patrician dominated power relationships, the structure of power in Rome began to move, to change.

The plebeians' strategy of fighting for their political, economic and legal goals with a secession is still extremely unusual today. No indications can be found in the existing sources that this could have involved a civil war, nor even a singled armed battle between patrician and plebeian men. The struggle against patrician rule consisted at first exclusively in disobedience. It was a refusal of obedience in both military and political terms, a revocation of the acceptance of constraining patrician power.

Those who refused, without using their weapons to fight, were the armed plebeian men.[4] In other words, they were the ones who, under other circumstances, defended Rome and thus always also its patrician dominated power relationships against warring attackers from the outside. These plebeians then withdrew from armed battle to enforce their internal political and economic interests. They refused allegiance to the patricians, both as commanders and as creditors.

This revocation of the acceptance of patrician power through refusal and exodus from political and economic limitation is an example for the questioning, the rejection of the acceptableness, the self-evidence of modes of governing that Foucault addresses in his text on critique. And according to the post-Operaist philosopher Paolo Virno, this revocation, this refusal can be called 'radical disobedience' (Virno, 2004a: 69), because with their exodus, the plebeians eluded the jurisdiction of laws and commands. It was important to Livius to write that it was "without command from the consuls" (Liv. 2,32,2) that the plebeians went out to the sacred mountain. The plebs eluded by leaving. They not only acted here on their own authority, but with their action they fundamentally questioned the *imperium*, the consuls' authority of command, in other words the structure of public rule in Rome.

In this respect the secession of the plebeians can be understood as exodus. However, it is not the form of exodus of the Israelites, who did not return to Egypt (Walzer, 1986). The exodus of the Plebeians signified a strategy of self-constitution as a political alliance. And at the same time, the exodus, the withdrawal through departure, is a means of pressure and threat to express political demands for rights.

When they arrived on the sacred mountain, as Livius continues the story, the plebeian men set up a strong camp without being attacked or attacking. During their stay on the sacred mountain, the plebeians formed an alliance with an oath and agreed in sacred laws to install plebeian tribunes for their protection and to achieve their political interests. These *tribuni plebis* were to be invulnerable, sacrosanct and have a right to aid for the plebs. Negotiators and the patriciate accepted these demands of the now constituted plebs. From this point on, the plebs were granted their own sacrosanct officials, and anyone who 'violated' the *tribuni plebis* faced the death penalty. Following the election of two tribunes the plebeians returned to Rome (Liv. 2,32,4-33,3; 3,55,7; 3,55,10).

The plebeians departed three times, three times they returned, as their struggle was for a republican political legal order in Rome. From the beginning, the plebeian exodus was thus not something 'new' in the sense of founding a city of their own with its own constitution. Yet it was also not solely a reaction, but rather an action specifically because this withdrawal was the first act for a newly invented constituting. This constituting, along with the plebeian power/order emerging in it, heralded the instrument and the weapon for intervening in the existing patrician power and rulership order that had become endangered and unstable due to the exodus. There was no new order thus created in a new place, but rather an 'alternative' order as a means of intervention (Fiori, 1996). First of all, however, the plebeian exodus called the power relationships radically into question, because secession meant eluding binarity, the binarity between command/law on the one hand and revolt on the other, in order to return again with a shared capacity and fight. In Livius' account, the capacity space of the plebeian, so to speak, is the sacred mountain a few miles outside the city. It is the space of alliance and organizing.

Without sufficient political rights and without any representation of interests, the plebeians invented themselves in a sense independently from the existing patrician order and structures of rule as capable of political action. Their strategy for this consisted primarily in a self-empowerment that I would like to consider with the term constituent power.[5]

In keeping with the various meanings of the Latin verb *constituo*, the term 'constituent' power moves in a semantic field of 'situate', 'together', 'set', 'settle', but also 'to decide', 'to create' and 'to determine'. The prefix con- imbues *constituo* with a strong meaning of the shared, of joint situating. This line of meaning is the basis for "common agreement and decision-making, 'con-stituting' in other words, found a common 'con-stitution'", as Gerald Raunig puts it in his essay in the last section of this volume.

Against this background the plebs assembled on the sacred mountain as a community of interests, as an alliance: according to Livius, they settled themselves there 'securely', in a strong camp with wall and moat and, as he emphasizes, "without leaders" (Liv. 2,32,4). No one forced or led the plebeians, they (re-)moved (themselves) together, giving themselves tribunes as representatives only in a second step. The formation as an alliance initially developed without leadership, without being led and governed. It was only in the process of constituting that representation first emerged, only then were the tribunes elected.

The plebeians decided to bind themselves together with an oath and to secure themselves politically and legally by their own authority through the alliance outside patrician-defined legality. When I speak of a 'plebeian' constituent power, I mean this capacity to join together, to protect and defend oneself based on a refusal of obedience.

This form of critique, the refusal of obedience is, in this sense, a productive practice. Productivity relates to the constituting, the composition, productivity refers to the centrifugal force and the constituent capacity. Constituent plebeian power is the capacity of composition, of constituting an order of one's own, which means the capacity for (self-)organizing. The plebeians constituted themselves as a political community of interests, not as a rigid order that separated itself permanently in Rome to oppose the patricians in an equally rigid dichotomous relationship. Rather, the constituent power of the plebs affected a flexible order, which instigated a political, legal and economic transformation process, ultimately leading in 287 BCE into the Lex Hortensia. This law determined that the plebiscite also officially no longer represented only the decrees and resolutions of the plebeians, but was now 'legally' binding for everyone living in Rome.

The plebeian constituent power, this capacity is thus instituted in several acts: first the withdrawal through departure, the exodus, then through the act of the oath and legislation, and finally through the creation of an office, the holders of which, the tribuni plebis, are to protect the plebs with the threat of the most severe punishment for their violation. With these acts the plebeians turned their meager political capacity into such a potent power that they were armed for conflicts with the patricians.

The exodus and the self-constitution of the plebs modified the power relationships in which the struggles of order between plebs and patriciate took place, instead of accepting the power of the patricians as an immutable horizon. Yet the battle strategy of the plebeian men is one that is in turn limited and does not question, revoke or reject relationships of power and domination beyond one's own interests. Throughout all the confrontations between plebs and the patriciate, the domination of the *pater familias* in the *domus* was not fundamentally questioned, just as little as slavery was.

For an abstract figure of resistive critique, it must also be stated again in this framework: the capacity of a constituent power always remains limited itself as well, produces exclusions and always also manifests certain relationships of power and domination instead of rejecting, reversing or even making them disappear. Eluding constraining power relationships is only possible to the degree, only with the means available for becoming aware of the limitation. There is not one way of rejection, not one way of withdrawal, not one way of critique, but always only specifically limited ways that are differently actualized. Nevertheless, what is true for plebeian struggles is that they change the contexts in which a problem emerges as a problem, rather than choosing one or another solution already offered. They change the assemblage of power and multiply the power relationships.[6]

Without the constituting of the plebeian, power relationships appear as the power, as relationships of domination without alternatives, the boundaries of which purportedly signify the horizon. The plebeian must be constituted, otherwise it remains a potentiality that inevitably emerges in power relationships. It is only when it is constituted as the plebeian and thereby evades limitations that it newly composes itself. The plebeian always signifies an immanent refusal; that is why it is productive. The plebeian is the capacity to productively refuse power relations and elude them in this way, whereby the assemblage of power permanently changes and one or the other constraining mode of governing vanishes.

Notes

1. My own reflections on the plebeian, which are only briefly sketched in the following, are part of a larger study of the Roman struggles of order between the patricians and the plebeians and a resultant political theory of immunization.

2. The concept of fleeing is not a slip on Foucault's part; in 1982, only a few years before his death, he wrote: There is "no relationship of power without the means of escape or possible flight" (Foucault, 2003: 346).

3. See Titus Livius (=Livy), Ab urbe condita, http://www.thelatin library.com/ liv.html.

4. The plebeian men fought with the exodus from Rome for their 'full' political freedom, meaning to be regarded as 'free' to the same degree as patrician men. The free Roman women, patrician and plebeian women, were regarded as free only to a limited extent, as they were subject to the authority of their *pater familias* or their husband. Female and male slaves had no personal rights at all in the Roman Republic, they were considered 'unfree'.

5. This not only ties into central theorems of political history, such as Antonio Negri's 'Repubblica Constituente: Umrisse einer konstituierenden Macht', published in Negri, Lazzarato and Virno (1998: 67-82), Raunig (2007: 59-66), and Negri (1999). The term 'constituent power' also ultimately signifies a continuation of appraisals of secession in antiquity studies (cf. Wieacker, 1988: 379; Mommsen, 1971: 274; and Ungern-Sternberg, 2001: 314).

6. Here I subscribe to Virno's ideas (2004a: 70).

13

Inside and Outside the Art Institution: Self-Valorization and Montage in Contemporary Art

Marcelo Expósito

(Translated by Nuria Rodríguez, supervised by Aileen Derieg)

This text was written on 1 October 2006 as a broad and immediate response (hence, its 'informal' style) to a short questionnaire posed by a Spanish digital magazine on contemporary art and critical theory. It was not published; it is reproduced here almost unaltered. The original questions have been replaced by epigraphs describing the subject matter that the different sections dealt with.

The title of this text paraphrases an important essay by the German-American art historian Benjamin H.D. Buchloh: 'Allegorical Procedures: Appropriation and Montage in Contemporary Art'. Written in 1982, Buchloh's influential essay sought to provide an explicitly political and historically grounded approach (going back to particular instances of politicization in the classic avant-garde movements, such as John Heartfield's photomontage) to specific practices that, beginning in the late 1970s but more emphatically during the 1980s, opposed the hegemony of the market within the arts institution – with its emphasis on strong notions of 'work' and 'artist' – through methodologies like the appropriation of images and the reinvention of montage. The (not quite fully-developed) hypothesis underlying my text is that the procedures analyzed by Buchloh were neutralized by the new hegemonies at the heart of the arts institution, which were, however, integrated into (or are in a sense the starting point for) the new forms of 'unbounded' politicization of artistic practice that have been taking place in synchrony with the laborious production of a new cycle of

141

struggles, which originated in the late 1980s and has filled the past decade with a series of explosions.

Another aspect of my hypothesis that needs to be developed suggests that the certain exhaustion of those same critical practices of appropriation and montage that Buchloh's essay tried to endow with critical and political meaning was precisely due to their 'confinement' within the margins of the arts institution, and the central importance they continued to give the very institution that they criticized because of its role as virtually the only space of legitimization and valorization. Some new forms of politicization of artistic practices based themselves on the assumptions established by these earlier critical practices, putting into practice various kinds of 'going beyond', as well as going 'in and out' of the institution and using other processes that deny, displace or relativize the arts institution's centrality as a space for valorization and legitimization. As explained below, it seems appropriate to apply the Operaist notion of the 'self-valorization' of labor to these processes.

A Critique of the Traditional Division of Artistic Labor

I don't know whether I can say anything new on this subject, because to me, the situation seems quite clear: this division was breached a long time ago and we've moved beyond it, although it probably continues to hold a contradictory symbolic and political hegemony in the art field. Part of my training took place in Spain's independent video movement of the 1980s and 90s, in which traditional role hierarchies were almost totally broken down. It was perfectly normal for activities like writing, criticism, the organizing of activities, editing and publishing, the creation and distribution of works and so on to be carried out by those who made up the network. This shouldn't necessarily be attributed to an unusually high level of political awareness. It can probably be partly explained by the fact that, at the time, video was developing on the fringes of the art institution, and we know that there have been similar experiences of hierarchies being dismantled and roles shared or interchanged on the 'periphery' of the institution at various times and places in history, not just in the recent past. It could be said that the breakdown of this 'traditional' division of labor is deeply rooted in the tradition of the avant-garde movements, and it is therefore, from certain points of view, quite 'traditional' itself.

So, I'm not really sure that practices which avoid falling into this particular division of labor can automatically be considered, as is sometimes tritely claimed, a 'negation' of a traditional model or a search for 'new' or 'other' paradigms. Rather, I think that at their best, they show their own strength, they enjoy their own ontological consistency when they are rooted in history, so they can't always be interpreted in terms of their 'alternative nature' in relation to the 'traditional' model. It was a long time ago now that I stopped seeing my own work in terms of putting forth an 'alternative' to a 'central' model, and started seeing it instead as a form of positivity, an exploration of independently consistent ways of working.

I began by describing the symbolic and political hegemony of a particular division of labor in the art field as contradictory because the vague 'artist-entrepreneur' model has become so widespread that it has burst its banks. In the cultural and the art field, labor now perfectly matches the 'communicative' labor paradigm that is at the centre of the post-Fordist mode of production, but division of labor still has a symbolic hegemony and is upheld by economic and institutional interests. Today, the work of cultural producers is de facto essentially communicative, linguistic and semiotic. It fundamentally involves the production, through language, of processes that are usually exploited by institutions when they valorize them exclusively at the moment that they materialize as objects or events that are profitable in economic, political and/or symbolic terms. The way I see it, the key to the contradiction lies in the fact that upholding one particular division of labor is no longer 'natural' – it isn't an inherent aspect of today's most highly developed forms of cultural production or most of its major trends: all it does is support that particular way of valorizing artistic labor – the moment of crystallization into marketable objects or certain kinds of events.

When the decision is taken to valorize artistic labor under different forms, in different places and times, through other processes, and, above all, to self-valorize artistic labor, this doesn't really mean negating or criticizing a certain model of the division of labor: it means that the instituted model simply loses its relevance.

That said, it is important to add that although within the art institution there is a growing acceptance of a particular, vague 'artist-manager' model (a slippery term, right? We could also add the ideas of the artist-entrepreneur, curator-artist and artist-'businessman', just as Maurizio Lazzarato speaks somewhat provocatively of the post-Fordist worker as an entrepreneur or 'businessman'...), this doesn't necessarily entail a critical or alternative practice, nor one that moves towards self-valorization. It did, to a large extent, thirty years ago, during the cycle around 1968, with its mood of widespread criticism of social institutions, just as it did with the explosive meeting of politics and the avant-garde in the period between the wars. Today it is an ambiguous model (just look at how different 'relational' artists and curators work). The way in which a 'traditional' function of artistic labor is currently being blurred corresponds, almost blow by blow, to the forms of the 'flexibilization' of labor in the context of production in more general terms. Just as in renewed capitalism overall, the 'flexibility' of artistic or cultural labor is profoundly ambivalent from the start. But the process is irreversible: we have no choice but to work within this contemporary condition.

Artistic 'Work' and 'Non-artistic' Work: On the 'Artisticness' of Art Labor

The distinction that is sometimes made in the work of certain artists (I count myself among them) between labor that is 'not strictly' 'artistic', and that which 'explicitly' is, corresponds to a hierarchical taxonomy based on the primacy of a somewhat old-fashioned idea of what an 'art work' is. Near the end of his life, El Lissitzky claimed that he considered the pavilions he had designed for the Bolshevik government in the early stages of the Soviet Union to be his most important art work. The historiographic distinctions that are usually made between 'artistic work', 'design' and 'works for the State apparatus' in order to taxonomize Lissitzky's career, are clearly an aggression against the nature of his practice. I think it would be much more useful to take his own statement seriously and ask ourselves: but where the hell is the 'art work' in his pavilions?

In historical terms, for many years I have considered names like Lissitzky, Klucis, Heartfield, Renau or the Benjamin of the 'reproducible work of art' and the author as producer to be the foundational paradigm (precisely because they are neither 'unique' nor isolated) of a particular way of surpassing a pre-existing traditional model. They marked an opening up to a type of practices that didn't start from scratch in any sense, but marked the start of forms that no longer 'negate' other, predominant models, but organize their own coherence, their own positivity. A pavilion designed by Lissitzky is a collective project that includes multidisciplinary dynamics, and contains 'art works' and other things that don't strictly qualify as such, as well as an infinite number of 'in-between' elements. It's a work based on co-operative principles and the sharing of many different kinds of skills. And it radically assumes two characteristics that strongly challenged the then-traditional model in order to leave it behind: its useful nature and its communicative dimension. When almost a century ago avant-garde art had to openly question its political function and face its communicative dimension, no longer questioning them in terms of content but rather incorporating them structurally, I think it marked the start of what we are now, or what we may still become.

(Incidentally, one of the artists whom I've most admired, Ulises Carrión, worked without rest and didn't produce much legible 'art work'. His practice largely consisted of interventions in the dominant communicative processes, or in producing others, constantly shifting the form and the moment of (self-)valorization, always changing. Interrupting communication channels, producing alternative communication and weaving together organization and networks – this was his labor.)

I think that in historical terms, certain avant-garde movements can teach us two things: firstly, that there can be 'art' without 'art works' (Godard used to say that cinema is one thing and films are another, and films often don't have anything to do with cinema: thus the history of cinema should be rigorously differentiated from the more usual history of films and directors. For some time now I've wondered: How can you write a history of art 'without art works', or where the usual notion of an art work is radically de-centred?); secondly, that it is possible to make a kind of art 'that doesn't appear to be so' (as soon as one looks outside the European scene and the 'classic' avant-garde movements, the examples increase exponentially). I don't think that the first lesson leads us necessarily to hackneyed academic chattering on the dematerialization of the object. Rather, it leads to the radical change of mentality that occurs at specific moments in history in which the valorization of artistic labor comes into focus as a relevant political problem, together with the definition of what 'new' forms, as a result, this labor has to take on in order to achieve self-valorization. The second lesson refers us to the contingency statute that characterizes artistic labor, which doesn't always have to give primary importance to being recognized as such in accordance with the primacy of current legibility criteria sanctioned by the corresponding institutional fields (the legibility criteria that determine an 'art work's' artistic status, which we now know to be contingent and which are themselves historical, in no way absolute and essential; in no way disinterested. In this sense, it's advisable to always keep in mind, for example, the lessons of feminist readings of the history of art and feminist film theory), in particular when the formalization of the work or its processes shift outside a particular institutional field, or flow in and out of it. In this latter case, it's particularly important to be aware that the 'artisticness' of work is not an identity or an essential or pre-existing condition: it is a contingency that can correspond to tactical or political functions, and its sanctioning as an 'art work' has to be disputed and challenged in discursive and material terms against the institution's 'common sense' through conflict and negotiation. This is why I think it is essential to practice writing and criticism, which shouldn't be understood as the occupation of those who emit inspired opinions, but as the field in which legitimacy criteria and the valorization of practices are negotiated through conflict (Butler, 2002).

Montage

In my opinion, the most momentous innovation that the artistic avant-garde movements contributed to twentieth-century culture and politics simultaneously, is montage. I'm not referring to montage as a stylistic exercise that folds in on itself, but the kind that, whether in Tucumán Arde, Heiner Müller or Alexander Kluge, constitutes a tool for thinking – for critical thinking. In this sense, montage brings heterogeneous things together into a fragmented whole that highlights its structural discontinuity, shattering the illusion of self-consistency and unity of both form and discourse, without relinquishing the production of meaning as a result. This convergence of a diversity of things deserves to be conceived as a part of a whole that in itself points elsewhere. I marvel at how much this invention can continue to contribute to the construction of forms and discursive practice at the same time.

I've always considered my incursions into editorial activities, for example, to be either fully or partly artistic projects. At least to some extent, the publishing projects I've participated in usually consist of taking elements that are at different stages of materialization and diffusion within larger networks or flows – which we consider ourselves part of – catalyzing through reorganizing. In very simple terms, the editorial process becomes a montage technique that discontinuously articulates a discourse that then enters into circulation once more. Inversely, I'm increasingly less likely to describe the 'artistic' research, teaching or curatorial projects that I've generally worked on as hybrids or interdisciplinary projects. Instead, I see them as suspended between the categories of art, criticism and editing; technically, they almost always consist of small exercises in construction and montage.

In short, I think that the usual distinctions that separate what some of us do into actual 'art works' and 'secondary' work (criticism, editing, writing...) is inappropriate when it comes to considering what needs to be done, because I believe, above all, in the labor of construction and montage that occasionally produces 'things' that can't necessarily be read as 'art works'. I've always felt suspicious of the ongoing presence of the surrealist object in certain kinds of contemporary art, as well as the way in which dominant conceptualism and its effects managed to reintroduce the fetishism of 'form' through the back door. I only have a little faith left in Dada now, whereas I'm still a believer in constructivism and productivism, modern political documentary and montage cinema. Almost all of the art that I still continue to learn from consists in constructing, (re)structuring, combining and putting together, in order to produce artefacts whose legibility is ambivalent, always site- and time-specific.

The Artist as 'Multifaceted' Worker: Contradiction, Adaptation and Complicity with the Institutional Medium

It may be interesting to pause for a moment and consider this strange adjective, 'multifaceted'. The history of modern Western art needed to create a narrative that would include, and thus 'normalize', the ruptures caused by some of the avant-garde movements, so it captured Soviet art, for example, articulated its (re)presentation by organizing it into a narrative that separated biographical lines into pieces that made up a 'plural' movement, and created a narrative for each of those separate and more or less isolated lines in turn, based on an organization that classified their 'art works' into different styles and formats. This taxonomy and juxtaposition produced the effect of simultaneity in the way artists used techniques, languages and media. At moments like this, the history of twentieth century art constructs the myth of the modern, 'multifaceted' artist. Alexandr Rodchenko and Varvara Stepanova never set out to be multifaceted artists. Their 'multifacetedness' is an effect of the way in which the history of modern art recovers the ruptures that these artists represent by incorporating them into a normalized narrative in which conflict has been tamed. Their work isn't multifaceted: if anything, it is conflictive.

In terms of work in general, today's workers aren't 'multifaceted': they are multi-exploited, or rather, subject to a regime of flexible exploitation.[1] It would be amusing to switch the concepts and consider how the illusion of the 'multifacetedness' that is now being required of workers in order to make the new form of capitalist control of the workforce more bearable is similar to the kind of flexible exploitation that Vladimir Tatlin or Liubov Popova are subjected to by the history of modern art in order to extract some kind of cultural added value that fuels its existence and in return distorts the nature of the original, simultaneously artistic and political, experience.

The other term that I find curious is 'complicity'. I appreciate the clarity with which it is stated, but it is based on a way of framing the issue that I find inoperative: What should one declare oneself, sitting on the bench of the accused? Guilty, innocent of acting in collusion or complicity with an institutional system? (I can't speak for anyone else, but I'm not in this in order to submit myself to a political trial or to earn myself a place in heaven). If the idea is to question whether 'critical' positions 'genuinely' question the state of things or, on the contrary, help to reproduce it, I think a very simplified answer would be: both. But this does not go far enough.

In this order of things, labor in art is no different to the way in which post-Fordist labor in general oscillates between self-valorization and control (subjugation), and it's often paradoxical because it operates under the conditions of autonomy and subjection simultaneously. For much of last century, artistic and cultural labor was an 'extraordinary' social activity – outside of the ordinary, exceptional. Today, the characteristics that have traditionally defined it (deregulated activity not subject to the same discipline as 'industrial work', with an emphasis on the value of self expression, giving maximum importance to subjectivity...) are increasingly becoming the paradigm for the core forms of labor in renewed capitalism.

In my generation, those of us who started off doing artistic work before political work, only gradually became aware of how our activities functioned within the arts. At the beginning, we didn't have the slightest idea that the flexible exploitation system we were subject to was intensive but discontinuous. Its discontinuous nature is precisely the key that makes sustainable exploitation possible. If your work is 'at the disposal' of an institution in a continuous, regulated way, you immediately consider entering a standard 'labor for wages' relationship. If your work is at the institution's 'disposal' in a discontinuous, deregulated way, then the relationship will be based on casual 'labor for income (honorarium)' terms. Discontinuous income, rather than a continuous wage, is what you get paid circumstantially for 'rendering services' on a casual basis; in this case, the rest of the time is 'yours'. But the work of self-education, training or testing, preparation, production and so on that is carried out in the periods when your relationship to the institution is 'inactive' is time that you use for producing, for the rendering 'of services', without remuneration. Thus, the exploitation of artistic labor is intensive, because it is exercised in the overall time that you commit to your work, but the key to its economical sustainability for the institution resides in the fact that it is formalized discontinuously: you only get paid for the specific project, exhibition or investigation or the number of hours 'you work'. The extent to which this kind of exploitation is widely accepted in the arts is because, obviously, your activity is presumably 'gratifying' in terms of vocational self-expression and freedom. Also because your subjection to the institution is irregular in terms of labor-income, but constant in symbolic terms and in its forms of subjectivization: the artist is taught to always turn to the institution as a guarantee of legitimacy and, above all, the 'relevance' of his or her own activity.

There was an inescapable structural contradiction for those of us who started to think about the politicization of our art practice without breaking out of the vicious circle of its valorization predominantly within the institution. The currents of thought based on a critique of institutions and certain forms of public and critical art, and some critical theory of the visual representations that fuelled us from the 1980s until part of the 1990s were like manna from heaven in the middle of the desert of the postmodern cultural counterrevolution (as Virno calls it). Nonetheless, it was becoming increasingly clear that critical practice would only be able to put forth its own consistent and powerful forms of creation (and self-creation!) through the same solution that some avant-garde movements adopted when they reached the same crossroads: a critique trapped within its own field. What they did was to look to other times, places and forms of the valorization of artistic labor apart from or as well as those that involved a relationship with the institutional apparatus. In terms of my own experience, I think this didn't start to take place until the 1990s, when the possibility arose for the self-valorization of artistic labor linked to new forms of protest and new social autonomy dynamics. I believe that this is behind the enormous importance of the new collaborative experiences of what where originally (mostly) artists groups such as La Fiambrera in Spain, Ne pas plier in France, Grupo de Arte Callejero (GAC) and Etcétera in Argentina, and probably many others that have either faded, or were less consistent, or we have yet to discover: they reinvented a way of valorizing artistic labor, at a time when art practice was already clearly paradigmatic of post-Fordist production overall. They brought it out of its state of subjection (even if it was a critical subjection) to flexible exploitation, and allowed this self-valorization to help strengthen the new social opposition dynamics that had emerged precisely from the post-Fordist neo-liberal hegemony.

This way of breaking out of the circle in which critical practices were imprisoned certainly didn't 'solve' all the problems involved in the ways in which critical work in the arts is subject to the institution – a complex relationship that includes aspects ranging from the symbolic to the economic. But it did favor conditions that allowed it to come to light and be approached from other material and political positions.

This condensed account seems to culminate in the idea that it would, therefore, be necessary to take this dynamic to the limit and bring about a pure and simple escape from the art institution or to relate to it from the outside in a merely cynical or instrumental way. I've never considered this to be the only possible conclusion; in fact, it doesn't seem to me to be necessarily a productive political position. For many reasons. One of these reasons is patently obvious: the production of artistic or cultural artefacts is not equivalent to the production of cars or weapons. The results of our kind of production have a complex function in semiotic capitalism. Regardless of the attractiveness of the post-Situationist perspective, there is no rule stating that cultural artefacts are not, or cannot be, anything other than (or as well as) goods or tools for the ideological control of consciousness. In empirical terms, it's not sustainable for all 'forms' of labor in the industry of the spectacle to be objectified, and I can't stand the hypothesis of the system's omnipotent capacity to recuperate or co-opt. I'm not saying I believe in the intrinsic goodness of culture or its essential legitimacy as a means of emancipation! But in the face of so much (both cynical and erudite) skepticism within our institutional field, I have no choice but to declare myself a believer (that is, of liberation theology!) in the potential of critical labor within art, cultural and educational institutions – not only to enlighten some minds but, above all, to influence the established modes of the production of knowledge and subjectivation. Nevertheless, I think that the operations carried out within the institutional field should seek to go beyond it, and above all valorize that which is produced, at least partly outside of it. To me, this is not just a political necessity but more importantly one of life's lessons. Because in this way, many of us found a way to break out of the desperate circle of critical theories that seems unable to do anything other than wait to be recuperated for the umpteenth time.

Whether a particular critical theory is recuperated or not isn't as important as what it was able to generate in addition to being put into practice. What counts is the direction in which your work contributes to mobilizing individual and collective energies, which it can do in many diverse ways and on a bigger or smaller scale. I don't think declaring each of us an 'accomplice' to a situation leads anywhere, except to widespread cynicism. Likewise, it disturbs me to hear people whose work I admire state that 'we're all on the inside', 'we're all institution' or 'we're all prostitutes' in the arts and leave it at that. These declarations are not only inaccurate, they also stop short, and I think that they provoke the responsibility to immediately respond: Then, what's to be done?

For quite a few years now, there has been an ongoing stream of projects that approach the relationship to institutions in ways that are neither cynical nor instrumental. They aim to generate critical practices within the institutions with the idea that they should be valorized there and at the same time at some other time and place, in other ways. The idea would be to move from the 'inside' to the 'outside' of the institution in a continuum that doesn't avoid the institutional mode of formalization, and even examines it, without making it the central or unique objective.[2] The production of networks and flows that don't heed pre-existing boundaries and instead establish their own kinds of public sphere – a concept that we're probably starting to find a bit static – is surely one of the most important inventions to have emerged from political creativity in this new cycle of protest.

But to understand the extent to which we are obviously dealing with difficult and problematic dynamics, we don't have to look any further than Desacuerdos.[3] In terms of what I am proposing here, I see Desacuerdos as a clear example of how extremely difficult it is to negotiate the simultaneity of different times and forms of evaluating art labor, especially when most of the labor comes from the outside or fringes of the field. That may have been the principal failure of those of us who were involved in co-ordination in different ways and with varying responsibilities: to have made it impossible for there to be compatibility, at the core of the project and in a complex way, between the different dynamics and interests in relation to valorizing the work put into it. It was important to try, and we can only hope there will be many more attempts. And I don't think that this negates the project's other, equally important accomplishments (you only have to look at the publications edited). But the fact that this particular failure took place amongst individuals and institutions that had spent a long time fighting in favor of precisely those kinds of principles, makes us take a much more cautious approach and exercise a greater degree of reflection and modesty. I think that the outcome of Desacuerdos inevitably demands that we consider the problems of scale, rhythms, the division of labor and the way decision-making processes are managed in critical production projects linked to institutions. In addition (to continue with the question of the relationship between criticism, art practice and art institutions), I think it demonstrates the need to turn the cliché that 'behind the institutions, in the end, are the people' upside down. Because in the end, there in the background, behind the people, are the institutions (that through inertia have many different ways of applying the microphysics of power), and all the other power relationships that play a part in the arts, outside of the institutions. In theory, this isn't a problem. Foucault would insist that his critique of institutions should not have a paralyzing effect, and that it didn't refer to an idea of essential freedom, because attempts at constructing freedom and the enjoyment of freedom itself could only take place inside given power relations. I think that the kinds of contradictory and complex ways of proceeding that I am dealing with here (and which I certainly don't claim will exclude others!) are essential in today's world, with all its difficulties. But I also think that future attempts through trial and error, conflict and negotiation, will need more politics, not better intentions.[4]

Notes

1. See http://en.wikipedia.org/wiki/Precarity
2. See http://transform.eipcp.net/calendar/1153261452,
   http://transform.eipcp.net/transversal/0406/crs/en,
   http://www.fridericianum-kassel.de/ausst/ausst-kollektiv.html#
   interfunktionen_english, http://www.exargentina.org/lamuestra.html,
   http://transform.eipcp.net/correspondence/1177371677
3. http://www.desacuerdos.org
4. Additional links: http://www.arteleku.net/4.0/pdfs/1969intro.pdf,
   http://www.arteleku.net/4.0/pdfs/1969-1.pdf,
   http://www.arteleku.net/4.0/pdfs/1969-3.pdf,
   http://transform.eipcp.net/transversal/0106/brumaria/es,
   http://usuarios.lycos.es/pete_baumann/marceloexpo.htm

14

The Rise and Fall of New Institutionalism: Perspectives on a Possible Future

Nina Möntmann

Only a few years ago, 'new institutionalism' was recognized as a curatorial intention to create 'an active space' that is 'part community center, part laboratory and part academy'[1]. I quote these attributes from the profile of the Rooseum in Malmö, which – under the directorship of Charles Esche and later Lene Crone Jensen – was one of the model institutions of this new experimental and multi-functional approach to curating. At the zenith of these activities and their discourse Jonas Ekeberg edited a publication with the title 'New Institutionalism', in which he defined this subject as an "attempt to redefine the contemporary art institution [...] ready to let go, not only of the limited discourse of the work of art as a mere object, but also of the whole institutional framework that went with it." He states further that new institutionalism was "far from peripheral, but rather central, even crucial, to the contemporary art scene" (Ekeberg, 2003: 9, 14). What Rooseum and other progressive art institutions had in common was that they were institutions of critique, which means institutions that have internalized the institutional critique that was formulated by artists in the 1970s and 90s and have developed an auto-critique that is now actively embraced by curators. Indeed, curators no longer just invite critical artists, but are themselves aiming to change institutional structures, hierarchies and functions. Reacting to the current developments, 'institutions of critique', from the mid- or late-1990s on, deployed a criticism of globalized corporate institutionalism and its consumer audience.

Since then, and within a very short space of time, these approaches, although successful in terms of opening up to new local publics and gaining international recognition in the art world, have been cut down to size and things have changed dramatically. To provide a few more examples: In 2004, during my time as a curator for the Nordic Institute for Contemporary Art (NIFCA), I worked with the Swedish artists Mike Bode and Staffan Schmidt on the project 'Spaces of Conflict: An audio-visual, research-based essay on institutional spaces'.[2] The project was based on close cooperation and exchange among curators and directors of seven international institutions in Berlin, Oslo, Copenhagen, Vilnius, Malmö and Helsinki. It is remarkable that almost all the institutions portrayed by Bode and Schmidt – the Rooseum, Kunst-Werke Berlin, the Museum of Contemporary Art in Oslo, the Contemporary Art Center in Vilnius, Kunsthalle Helsinki, the x-room in Copenhagen and NIFCA itself – are now in a period of profound change that demands a radical change of political course. The Rooseum is becoming a branch of the expanding Moderna Museet in Stockholm; the Museum of Contemporary Art in Oslo has been merged with other national museums in Oslo under the umbrella of the National Museum for Contemporary Art, Architecture and Design; Vilnius is suffering from severe budget cuts; in several places curators and directors have been replaced, which has a severe impact on the programmatic approach of the institutions, and in the case of NIFCA itself the institution has even been closed down. Most of the institutions seem to have been put in their place like insubordinate teenagers.

What is not wanted, in short, is criticality. Criticality didn't survive the 'corporate turn' in the institutional landscape. This is not only due to the larger institutions that are run like branded global companies in an obvious way, like the Guggenheim, which provides the clearest example of how an institution is conceived and staged by politicians and sponsors. More and more this also applies to mid-sized and smaller institutions, such as the German Kunstvereine or art associations, which are supposed to be experimental, but find themselves increasingly forced into curating programs similar to an established Kunsthalle.

This situation raises some crucial questions: What is 'new institutionalism' today? Is there still anything like an institution of critique, and what does it mean in the present context? Can the discussion of the conditions of production be carried out within the institutions themselves, and what are the consequences for their internal structures, functionality, programming and projections? Or, as Hito Steyerl poses it in her essay in the first section of this volume: "is it not rather absurd to argue that something like an institution of critique exists, at a time when critical cultural institutions are clearly being dismantled, underfunded, and subjected to the demands of a neoliberal event economy?"

This current situation, which goes hand in hand with the dismantling of the welfare state, produces an urgent need for emancipatory forms of action in the institutionalized art field and thus for new institutions. This brings us back, first of all, to a fundamental question: What do we actually expect from an art institution? What do we want an institution to stand for? What desires does an institution in the art field produce? In his essay for the publication *Art and its Institutions*, the Swedish philosopher Sven-Olov Wallenstein analyzes 'institutional desires' that are connected with art institutions and exposes a profound paradox by asking: "Why is there such a desire for institutions, and why does the very attempt to meet it only give rise to more dissatisfaction?" Referring to Guattari, he concludes that "the need for facilities is an illusion, or rather a retroactive rationalization." Instead it is the very institution which, he continues, "produces a certain structure of desire, it enables a certain space where signifiers and desires can circulate, and in this sense it is just as futile to dream of a fully de-institutionalized space as it is to dream of an institution that would work" (Wallenstein, 2006: 121). While you can't beat this argument on the one hand, on the other the conclusion cannot be – as Wallenstein also claims – to leave institutions completely aside in order to enter alternative spheres. I fully agree with the artist Gardar Eide Einarsson, who says, "It is a classical democratic problem, whether one should engage in order to change, or simply ignore in order to establish something else on the outside (the classical and in my view false distinction between alternative and oppositional)" (Einarsson, cited in Ekeberg, 2003: 83).

In the face of this dilemma, what is therefore required is the establishment of transgressive institutions that question and break with the current developments of privatization and simultaneously orient themselves towards other disciplines and areas besides the corporative business of globalized capitalism. In searching for participatory institution-forming activities, my attention has recently turned to the institutional situation in several regions in the Southern hemisphere.

There, the few official contemporary art institutions mostly are inaccessible for young artists and dysfunctional as part of the public sphere, and artists and curators don't have easy access to public or private funding. These kinds of local situations where there is a lack of access to institutional infrastructure often give rise to community projects, that are characterized by their institution-forming character, such as Sarai or Khoj in Delhi, PUKAR and crit in Mumbai, or ruangrupa in Jakarta. You often find collective and occasionally interdisciplinary activities by artists, sometimes together with curators, researchers, activists or new media workers. They start with a small space and very local programming, exhibiting their own work and that of artists they know, or using the space for other community activities such as discussions or parties. In the beginning there is thus a kind of community center or hangout for friends from the art field. In the regions I am talking about these activities are assuming a quasi-institutional status that often goes hand in hand with an expansion of their activity. They then start to fundraise internationally, to set up residencies, offer research possibilities, invite foreign curators and artists, organize film programs, edit magazines and so on.

In my opinion, what institutions in Western countries need to do is precisely to reduce the number of structures and standards, and disengage spaces from too many codes and contexts. Here, where we have an institutionalized art field – and consequently the opportunities to participate in semi-public spaces, but also the difficulties caused by the control mechanisms of these spaces – the options are somewhat different. Here there are inherently many categories and conventions for all kinds of art spaces, and alternatives are always measured against the official system that already exists and is increasingly defined by the politics of city marketing and sponsorship. It may seem paradoxical, but from this perspective, in fact we have less scope here and more control. Therefore, a conceivable new institution of critique would be one that maintains and expands its participation in (semi-) public space, and at the same time creates free unbranded spaces and negates dependencies.

It could counter the corporate globalization that neo-capitalism created, instead enabling an active and immediate global exchange of diverse public groups and individual voices, and a critique of the nation-state. It would have to widen its scope, consider cross-genre collaborations with established as well as alternative organizations, and initiate multi-disciplinary activities. This conceivable critical institution could, for example, take on the form of an internationally operating 'organized network', which strengthens various smaller, independent institutions and activities – be they alternative, artist-run, or research-based – and could also set up temporary platforms within bigger institutions. Ned Rossiter describes the potential of 'organized networks' for superseding modern institutions that are just "rebooted into the digital age" by "reconciling their hierarchical structures of organization with the flexible, partially decentralized and transnational flows of culture, finance and labor." The advantage of "organized networks" instead is the way they function as "social-technical forms that co-emerge with the development of digital information and communication technologies" (Rossiter, 2006; 2007). In the art field this new institution of organized collaborations could serve then as an information pool, a hub for various transdisciplinary forms of collaboration, in legal matters as a union, and as an entry for audiences to participate locally and exchange internationally.

The transformative public potential of an institution so structured lies in creating 'diasporic public spheres', that are described by Arjun Appadurai – who like Ned Rossiter derives his transferable model from an analysis of the globalized use of electronic media – as "phenomena that confound theories that depend on the continued salience of the nation-state as the key arbiter of important social changes" (Appadurai, 2001: 4). Precisely in this lies both an internationalization as well as a democratization of the art institution and its research facilities, which not only breaks down or questions certain dominant forms of institutional politics, but also opens up a "new role for the imagination in social life" (Appadurai, 2001: 4). On the level of funding, groundbreaking new private as well as public foundations are required to create self-sustainable, independent and powerful alternatives – a 'globalization from below', if you will.

Notes

1. Quoted from http://www.rooseum.se

2. For a detailed description of the project, see http://eipcp.net/transversal/0106/moentmann/en.

15

The Political Form of Coordination

Maurizio Lazzarato

(Translated by Mary O'Neill)

Based on the model of 'coordination', the struggle of the 'intermittents et précaires d'Ile de France'[1] is a veritable laboratory that could well highlight the demise of the political schema born of the socialist and communist tradition. Where this tradition places the emphasis on a logic of contradiction, of the political representation of an injustice that brings remarkable identities into play, the political form termed 'coordination' is meant to be resolutely expressive, transformist, attentive to the unstable dynamics of 'post-identitarian' identities, of which the reality of our world is woven. Coordination is aimed less at the formation of a common collective that seeks its members' equality, at all costs, than it is at the becoming of the singularities comprising it within an unstable, networked, patchwork-loving multiplicity – defying all theoretical definition as well as trade-union or state identification. It is a politics of experimentation that lays aside prior knowledge and opens up to the unknown, without which no new life can be envisaged.

Contemporary political movements are breaking radically with socialist and communist tradition. They are deployed not according to the logic of contradiction but rather to that of difference, which does not mean that there is no conflict, opposition or struggle. Rather, these are radically altered and deployed on two asymmetric levels. Political movements and individualities are formed according to a logic of 'refusal', of being 'against', of division. They seem, at first sight, to reproduce the separation between 'them and us', between friend and enemy, which characterizes the workers' movement or indeed politics itself. But this 'no', this assertion of division, is expressed in two

161

different ways. On the one hand, it is directed against politics, and it expresses a radical break with the rules of representation or of the staging of a division within the same world. On the other, it is the precondition for opening up to a becoming, to a bifurcation of worlds and to the way these are created, in a confrontational manner, not a unifying one.

On the first level, the struggle is represented as a flight away from institutions and the rules of politics. People quite simply escape – they walk away as the 'peoples of the East' walked away from real socialism, crossing the borders or staying in situ to recite Bartleby's formula: 'I would prefer not to'. On the second level, the individual and collective singularities that make up the movement deploy a process of subjectivation, which involves both a composition of common platforms (collective rights) and the differential assertion of a multiplicity of practices for expression and for living. Flight, politically elusive practices on the one hand; creation, strategies of 'empowerment' on the other. This new process renders the behaviors of movements and singularities opaque and incomprehensible to political scientists, sociologists, political parties and trade unions.

In France, one of the most interesting devices that movements employ to hold both levels together is that of 'coordination'. The coordination of the 'intermittents et précaires d'Ile de France' is the latest and most accomplished of the coordinations that, since the beginning of the 1990s, have organized all forms of struggle of a certain scale (coordinations of nurses, students, railway workers, the unemployed, teachers, etc). The refusal, the 'no' ('we're not playing any more') is what has pushed the intermittent workers from an ambiguous yet always individual relationship to the organization of the culture and communications industry into a new relationship to themselves and to the power that comes through the 'power of us'. Instead of being subjected to appropriation and exploitation by industry, all the characteristics of the intermittent workers' cooperation operate as drivers of the struggle.

Coordination is what the event of the struggle has made possible. In this event, we see what is intolerable about an era and at the same time the new possibilities for living that it enfolds. The de-structuring of what is intolerable and the articulation of new possibilities for living have a very real existence, but they are first expressed as a transformation of subjectivity, as a mutation of the mode of sensibility, as a new distribution of desires in the 'souls' of the intermittent workers engaged in the struggle. This new distribution of what is possible opens up to a process of experimentation and creation: experimenting with what the transformation of subjectivity involves, and creating the devices, institutions and conditions capable of deploying these new possibilities for living.

Speaking about 1968, Gilles Deleuze and Félix Guattari (1984) said: "Society must be capable of forming collective agencies of enunciation that match the new subjectivity, in such a way that it desires its own mutation" When we consider political action in the light of the event, we are faced with a twofold creation, a twofold individuation, a twofold becoming (creating a possibility and bringing it about) that is confronted with the dominant values. This is the point where the 'conflict' with what exists manifests itself. These new possibilities for living come up against the organization of governments in power and the manner in which these actualize this same constituent opening.

Coordination has developed the struggle on the two asymmetric levels in an exemplary fashion: refusal and constitution, de-structuring what is intolerable and deploying new possibilities. De-structuring what is intolerable, by taking a step alongside the codified and conventional forms of the unions' struggle (the meeting, the demonstration), will find expression in the invention of new forms of action, whose intensity and reach will increasingly open up towards harassing and unmasking the command networks of society-as-business. Deregulation of the labor market and social rights is being countered by a deregulation of the conflict that is following the organization of power right into the communications networks, into the expression machines (interruptions in television programs, recovery of advertising spaces, interventions in press editorial offices, etc.), something which those involved in the conventional union struggles ought not to ignore.

Coordination has coupled (not opposed) a diversifying of actions (by the number of participants, by the variations in objectives), using the 'just-in-time' method (by the frequency and speed of their planning and execution), to the unions' monumental mobilization tactics (strikes), which are concentrated in time and space. This gives some indication of what effective actions can be in an organization of mobile, flexible capitalist production, where the expression machines (television, advertising, press, cinema, festivals) are constituent elements of 'production'.

If de-structuring what is intolerable has to invent its modes of action, the transformation of modes of sensibility implied by refusal is only the precondition for opening up to another process, a 'problematic' one, of creation and actualization in relation to multiplicity. 'Problems' are what characterize the life and the organization of coordination. The subjectivities engaged in the struggle are caught between the old distribution of the sensible, already defunct, and the new, which is not yet in existence other than as methods for transforming sensibility and changing modes of perceiving the world. Coordination is not a collective but a mapping of singularities, composed of a multiplicity of committees, initiatives, forums for discussion and planning, political and union activists, a multiplicity of trades and professions, friendship networks, 'cultural and artistic' affinities, which form and break up at different rates and with different aims. The process of constituting multiplicity that is initiated here is not organic; it is, rather, polemical and confrontational. There are, engaged in this process, individuals as well as groups clinging desperately to the identities, roles and functions modulated for them by the organization of industry, and also individuals and groups involved in a radical process of de-subjectivation from these same modulations. There are conservative forms of behavior and expression and other, innovative, forms distributed among various individuals and groups, or coming through a single individual or group.

The word 'precarious', added to the name 'intermittent workers' of the coordination d'Ile de France, is the word that has caused passions to run highest and provoked the most vocal reactions. There are those for whom the term 'precarious' denotes a fact, an assessment (there are as many non-indemnified intermittent workers as there are indemnified ones, if not more; at any rate, 35 percent of indemnified workers are transformed into precarious workers by the new draft agreement). Others happily embrace it, seeing it as a reversal of the terms under which power is assigned (like 'unemployed person', *'errèmiste'*[2], 'immigrant', etc.), and as a rejection of the categories into which they are forced. Still others, paralyzed by the vague, negative terms of this attribution, demand the reassuring identity of 'artist' or 'live-performance professional', which are also categories but, in their minds, 'positive' ones. One can identify with the artist or the professional whereas 'precarious worker' is a form of identification by default. There are those too for whom the word 'precarious' is sufficiently ambiguous and polysemous to open up to multiple situations that go beyond 'live performance' and [for whom] it allows enough possibilities for becomings that elude the categories assigned by power. And there are yet others who demand 'existential precarity' and denounce 'economic precarity'. There are those for whom the term 'precarious' denotes the point where categories, attributions and identities become blurred (artist and at the same time precarious worker, professional and at the same time unemployed, alternatively within and outside, on the edges, at the limits): the point where relations, since they are not sufficiently codified, are – at the same time and in a contradictory manner – sources of political subjection, of economic exploitation and of opportunities to be grasped.

'Precarious' is the very model of 'problematic' naming, which poses new questions and seeks new replies. Lacking the universal impact of names like 'worker' or 'proletarian', it plays the role – as these once did – of that which defies, and it can only be named negatively by power as a result. All are in favor of neutralizing precarity as a weapon of political subjection and economic exploitation. Where division occurs is on the means by which to bring it about and on the significance of this achievement. Do we take the unknown aspects of problematic situations conjured up by precarity back to what is known in established institutions and their forms of representation: wage earning, the right to work (employment), the right to state benefits indexed to employment, the joint democracy of employers' and trade union organizations? Or do we invent and impose new rights encouraging a new relationship to activity, time, wealth, democracy, which exist only virtually and often in a negative way, in conditions of precarity?

We see that the economic questions, those affecting insurance and representation schemes, immediately pose problems of political categorization, which relate back to different processes of subjectivation. Fitting into the pre-fabricated mould of the capital-labor relationship, by viewing art and culture as their 'exception', or analyzing the transformation of the concept of work and the concept of art, and opening up to the becomings these very questions imply, by defining the 'artist' and the 'professional' in different terms. Or else bringing the 'precarious', that which has not yet been codified, back into the institutionalized conflict, which has already been standardized (and also includes the revolution of a great many revolutionaries!), or seizing the opportunity to develop struggles for identities still in the making.

The post-feminist movements have already wrestled with the knotty issue of becoming, the problem of the relationship between difference and repetition, through the 'aporetic' concept of post-identitarian identity: shifting identities, fractured identities, eccentric identities, nomadic subjects, where identity is both asserted and stolen, where repetition (identity) is in favor of difference, where the assertion of rights is not an assignment or an integration but, rather, a precondition for becoming. Here this same question takes over the more traditional field of law and of the institutional forms regulating social issues.

Different modes of behavior and expression are represented in coordination, as they become widespread like skills or 'collective bodies of expertise' (as the intermittent workers put it when referring to their activities), each time revealing the political 'objects' and 'subjects'. These skills and expertise, as soon as they are in operation, trigger a proliferation of problems and responses.

The production of an alternative model to the one proposed by the government is one of these skills that questions the organization of our societies generally, using the specific practices of live-performance professions as a basis. By analyzing the legitimacy of the division between experts and non-experts, the modes whereby the new model is constructed also put the division between representatives and represented to the test. The action of coordination may be extended to experimentation with devices for being together and being against, which repeat codified political procedures and, at the same time, invent new ones but which, all of them, also take great care to encourage the meeting of singularities, the arrangement of different worlds and universes.

The general form of the organization is not the vertical and hierarchical structure of political parties or trade unions, but that of the network in which different organizational and decision-making methods operate, which co-exist and are coordinated more or less felicitously. The general assembly operates on the principle of the majority vote without, however, selecting elites and vertical, directive or permanent structures. But the life of the coordination and the committees is based on the model of patchwork that allows an individual or a group to launch initiatives and new forms of action in a more flexible and responsible way. Organization in the form of networks is more open to learning and the appropriation of political action by all. The network favors the development of minority politics and decision-making.

The coordination has adopted a strategy that operates transversally within the divisions instituted by politics and the majoritarian models (representatives/represented, private/public, individual/collective, expert/non-expert, social/political, audience/spectator, employee/precarious worker, etc.). The opening of this instituting space fuels a tension between the assertion of equality proclaimed by politics (we all have equal rights), and the power relations between singularities which are always asymmetric: (in a meeting, a discussion, a decision-making process, the circulation of speech, of places and roles is never based on equality).

'Collective' rights are what define the conditions for equality; rights are for everyone. But this equality is not for itself; it is not in itself a goal. It is for difference, for everyone's becoming; otherwise, it is nothing more than a leveling out of multiplicity, an averaging out of subjectivities and an average (majority) subjectivity. The differences imposed by power are rejected, but the differences between singularities are arranged (on this second level, equality can only be the possibility for everyone not to be separated from what he/she is capable of, [for everyone] to be able to fully realize his/her potential). The hierarchy of the cultural industries is rejected and there is an arrangement of the asymmetric relationships between singularities that cannot be measured one against the other, "as it is in the worlds of artists, where there are no ranks but a variety of sites."

Coordination makes it possible to cross borders, to blur the divisions, categories and assignments into which intermittent workers, all of us in fact, are forced. The space of coordination is located transversally vis-à-vis the logic of equality and that of difference (freedom) by constructing their relationship as a problem, by trying to analyze the limits within which socialism and liberalism had separately considered and practiced them. Coordination is the contentious site for transforming multiplicity: from the subjected and enslaved multiplicity to a new multiplicity the outlines of which cannot be measured in advance.

More generally, we can say this: the form of political organization of coordination relates back to invention, experimentation and to their modes of action, not to a new form of warfare. We are currently living in conditions of 'planetary civil war' and a permanent 'state of emergency', but I think that the response to this organization of power is only possible if the logic of war is turned back (invaginated) into a logic of co-creation and co-implementation. The logic of war is the logic of conquest or of the distribution of one sole possible world. The logic of invention is one of creating and bringing different worlds into being in the same world; it hollows out power and at same time makes it possible for us to stop being obedient. This deployment and proliferation means extending singularities within the vicinity of other singularities, drawing a line of force between them, rendering them temporarily the same and making them cooperate for a time towards a common goal, without necessarily denying their autonomy and independence, without reducing them in a process of totalization. And this action is, in turn, an invention, a new individuation.

Coordination is set up according to modes that relate back to the unpredictability of propagation and distribution of the invention (by reciprocal capture, based on trust and affinity), rather than to the realization of an ideal plan or of a political line aimed at raising awareness. It succeeds only if it expresses a power in which singularities exist 'one by one, each one for itself'. It takes shape only if it expresses a 'sum that is not reduced to a total of its own elements'. The transition from micro to macro levels, from the local to the global, must not take place in a process of abstracting, universalizing or totalizing, but through the ability to hold together, to coordinate networks and patchworks gradually.

Compared to these dynamics of coordination, the instruments and forms of organization of the workers' movement are largely inadequate since, on the one hand, they refer to the cooperation of the Karl Marx and Adam Smith factory and, on the other, political action is not conceived of as an invention but merely as a revelation of something already there, the main operator of which is awareness and representation. Turning what is potential into something present, current, is an entirely different matter from representing a conflict. The political action of what remains of the workers' movement (in its institutional or left-wing form) is dominated as ever by the logic of representation and reductive totalization, which means exercising hegemony in one sole possible world (whether it is a question of taking power or sharing it), whereas coordination is a politics of expression.

The deployment of the political form of coordination calls first of all for the neutralization of these methods of operating and expressing politics. Where there is a hegemony of the organizational forms of the workers' movement, there can be no coordination. Where there is coordination, these organizations can be a part of it, but only by abandoning their claims to hegemony and by adapting to the constitutive rules of multiplicity – (we can also see this co-existence at work in the forms of organization mobilizing against neo-liberal globalization!). Coordination alone represents a public space that includes differences.

The activist in a coordination is someone who is committed and at the same time elusive. Contemporary political movements do not develop according to the 'mystical' modes of the transition from the individual to the collective. All creative activity stems originally, from singular initiatives (by a group or individuals) that are more or less small in scale, more or less anonymous. These initiatives cause an interruption, introducing a discontinuity not only in the exercise of power on subjectivity, but also and especially in the reproduction of the mental habits and the corporeal habits of multiplicity. The act of resistance introduces discontinuities that represent new beginnings, and these beginnings are multiple, disparate, heterogeneous (there are always multiple foci of resistance).

Rather than relating back to the position of warrior or to religious commitment, the activist in contemporary movements takes on the attributes of the inventor, the experimenter. The activist is committed and elusive as these are, since he/she too must escape for his/her action to be effective in the chain of 'prevailing habits and imitations' codifying the space of political action. The fascination that the figure of Subcomandante Marcos exercises is the result of all the elements present in his way of conducting and expressing himself. In a situation that is restrictive in a different way from our own, he asserts himself as a warrior, as a political and military commander; at the same time, using the same gestures and the same words, he immediately eludes the warrior identity, rids himself of the assigned role of commander, of military and political leadership. The situation that is appropriate for the action of beginning something new is expressed in the aporetic definition of 'subcommandante': subjectivation and at the same time de-subjectivation, each presupposing and re-launching the other reciprocally.

In contemporary militancy, the warrior dimension must be turned into an inventive force, into the power to create and realize arrangements and ways of living. The activist is not the one in possession of the movement's intelligence, who sums up its strength, who anticipates its choices, who derives his/her legitimacy from an ability to read and interpret the movements of power; rather, he/she is the one who, by introducing a discontinuity into what exists, facilitates an increase in the power of arrangement and connection of cooperation, the flows, the networks and the singularities that comprise it, according to modes of disjunction and coordination that are non-totalizing, non-homogenizing, non-hierarchical.

The intermittent workers say: we do not know what it is 'to be together' and 'to be against' in conditions where different worlds proliferate within a single world; we do not know what the institutions of becoming are, but we raise these questions by means of devices, techniques, arrangements, statements, and in this way we analyze them and we experiment. The traditional modes of political action are not on the way out, but are dependent on the deployment of this power of coordination. The constitution of the self as multiplicity is not sacrificed to the struggle against the imperatives of power. The activist continues to put forward initiatives, to be the originator of new beginnings, but not according to the logic of realizing an ideal plan, of a political line that sees what is possible as a readily available image of the real. [He/she does so] according to an actual understanding of the situation, which obliges him/her to put his/her very identity, his/her worldview and methods of action at stake. In fact, he/she has no other option since all attempts at totalization, at homogenizing generalization, at creating a relationship of force exclusively oriented towards representation, at instituting modes of hierarchical organization, lead to flight and the breakdown of coordination (of multiplicity).

Notes

1. Translator's Note: intermittent and precarious workers of the Ile de France.
2. Translator's Note: people living on RMI = *Revenu minimum d'insertion,* a form of income support.

III

INSTITUENT PRACTICES AND MONSTER INSTITUTIONS

16

Instituent Practices, No. 2:
Institutional Critique, Constituent Power, and
the Persistence of Instituting[*]

Gerald Raunig

(Translated by Aileen Derieg)

> Insurrection leads us no longer to let ourselves be arranged, but to arrange ourselves, and sets no glittering hopes on 'institutions'. It is not a fight against the established, since, if it prospers, the established collapses of itself; it is only a working forth of me out of the established. If I leave the established, it is dead and passes into decay. (Max Stirner, *The Ego and Its Own*)

Institution and Critique

An attempt to deconstruct, problematize and reformulate institutional critique, such as the one undertaken from several different perspectives in the *transversal* issue 'Do you remember institutional critique?'[1], published in early 2006, cannot avoid questioning the understanding of both institution and critique in the first two phases of artistic institutional critique, as well as the analogous figures in the history of leftist movements. Here one problematic pole of the critique of the institution could be regarded as the fundamentally critical approach of constructing an absolute outside of the institution, whether as a distorted image of the pathos of the artistic avant-garde (still evident in the 1970s) or as a phantasm of radical anarchisms: this approach ignores the techniques of self-government and the modes of subjectivation and contributes, beyond pure forms of rigid institutional subjection, to producing forms of 'machinic enslavement' (Deleuze and Guattari, 1987: 456-7; Lazzarato, 2006) – and with them the imagination of spaces free of power and institution.

173

The other pole – frequently found in institutional critique art practices since the 1990s – would be the self-obsessed self-critique that substantializes one's own involvement in the institution and crowds out the horizon of change from perception. This also includes the misconstrual of theoretical approaches from Foucault (the interpretation of his theory of power as a dead-end of a comprehensive *dispositif* of power allowing neither escape nor resistance) and Bourdieu (the hermetic interpretation of his field theory), in ways that reinforce what exists – what is established, arranged, striated and gridded – as the seemingly sole and immutable possible.

Avoiding both polarizations suggests a movement of exodus, of defection, of flight, but looking for a weapon while fleeing. There is a consistent thread running from Max Stirner's remark about 'leaving what is established', to Gilles Deleuze's concept of 'lines of flight', to Paolo Virno and Antonio Negri's more recent conceptualization of 'exodus': the differentiated construction of a non-dialectical way out of purely negating and affirming the institution. Seeking out these kinds of exits from the dead-ends of the critique of the institution also means, not least of all – and this is the basis of this essay – a conceptual movement of flight, a defection from the treacherous concept of institutional critique, a dissolving of its conceptual components and their re-composition in a different conceptual genealogy.

Against Closure of/in the Institution

Against the background of a renewed concept of critique, as that begins to emerge from the essays collected here, it is possible to take a closer look at the question of the institution. What is at stake is specifically not the institution as an unchanging structure and state apparatus, as a mere element of a dominant repressive system. If, instead, institutions are grasped as processes, then the problem goes beyond the terrain of the critique of the state and capitalism, for social movements and revolutionary machines cannot dispense with institutions, nor are they immune to the occurrence of structuralization, rigidification and institutionalization.

In 1844, Max Stirner, individualist anarchist opponent of the young Karl Marx,[2] wrote the remarkably post-Hegelian and proto-structuralist *Der Einzige und sein Eigentum* [*The Ego and Its Own*]. In it, we encounter a molar concept of revolution that specifically takes into account the structuralization and terror of the French Revolution. Against these,

Stirner poses the concept of 'insurrection': "The revolution commands one to make arrangements, the insurrection [*Empörung*] demands that he rise or exalt himself [*empor-, aufrichten*]" (Stirner, 1927: 287; 2001). This kind of rising up, this insurrection, which Stirner had to argue linguistically in this manner in order to avoid criminal prosecution,[3] does not want to arrange itself, does not want to accept the institutions, even those of the revolution as such, if they close themselves off again. Insurrection sets 'no glittering hopes' on institutions; a new state, a new people, a new party, a new society are not options for Stirner. The mode of subjectivation of the closure of/in the institution simultaneously means arranging oneself in the institution and adapting the self like all those arranged.

In his works on institutional analysis Félix Guattari demonstrated the tendency to 'structuralization', as he called the process of the closure of/in the institution. He developed his specific approach from what he experienced in diverse contexts: from the experience of the fight against the Stalinist and Euro-Communist variants of the state left and against the phenomena of the rigidifying of the New Social Movements after 1968, but also and especially from his experience in the micro-political field of the (psychiatric) clinic. In all of these contexts, Guattari was interested in institutional translations of revolution in its non-molar form:

> The revolutionary project as a machine activity of an institutional subversion would have to uncover these kinds of possibilities and ensure them in every phase of the struggle against structuralization ahead of time. (Guattari, 2003: 247)

As Guattari stresses, it is not enough to think of theoretical models of this institutional subversion, but rather it is specifically a matter of the practical testing and stuttering invention of machines that tend to elude structuralization:

> The problem of the revolutionary organization is basically that of setting up an institutional machine that is distinguished by a special axiomatic and a special praxis; what this means is the guarantee that it does not close itself off in various social structures, especially not in the state structure. (Guattari, 2003: 137)

Precisely this kind of elementary treatment of forms of organization, the permanent opening of social structures and assurance against their closure were and are the aim of offensive practices of insurrection and molecular revolution that generate something other than copies and variations of what already exists. Wherever state apparatuses tend towards the orgic and revolutionary machines simultaneously test new forms of organizing (Raunig, 2007), insurrection takes place as a fight against structuralization: in the Paris Commune, with the soviets and all the subsequent soviet-like modes of organization, in the Spanish Revolution and in May 1968, in the Zapatist revolts and the anti-globalization movement. Fleeing from what exists, however, by no means dispenses with the question of the institution. Focusing on institutions' tendencies to closure and structuralization is one side; fleeing from structuralization, on the other hand, corresponds to the complementary aspect of inventing other forms of institution and instituting.

Constituent Power and Instituting

Even without a prefix, the Latin verb *statuo* means roughly to establish, set (up), decide. On the one hand this means a process of setting up objects, the erection of buildings and the placing of objects or people in a certain arrangement, but on the other also such performative speech and positioning acts to establish an arrangement of rule – or even to found empires. As static as the noun *status* is literally as standing, position, state, the concomitant verb *statuo* is just as dynamic.

The prefix *con-* changes primarily the relationship between the subject and object of the im-position/in-stitution, now the com-position/con-stitution: an aspect of the collective, the common is added. In setting up bodies of troops, this may mean simply a multiplication of the placed objects, a co-location of multiple components. With the performative aspect of deciding, determining, founding, the compositum *constituo* takes on the meaning of collective subjectivation and common positioning. Common agreement and decision-making, 'con-stituting' in other words, found a common 'con-stitution'. As with especially the word *constituo*, it seems that a dynamic aspect of establishing, setting up, founding correlates with a closing aspect of defining, determining, deciding.

These two strands of constitution are differentiated in the concepts of constituent and constituted power. The pair of concepts emerges in the history of the constitutional process in the French Revolution. In his text 'What is the Third Estate', Emmanuel Joseph Sieyes, protagonist of the constitution of 1791, already distinguishes in 1789 between the *pouvoir constitué* and the *pouvoir constituant.* For Sieyes, constituted power corresponds to the written constitution as fundamental law, constituent power corresponds to the constitutional assembly, the *Constituante.*

The generally problematic aspect of constituent power as constituting assembly lies in the crucial question of how this assembly comes together, in the circumstances of legitimizing this assembly. In *On Revolution*, Hannah Arendt stresses this "problem of the legitimacy of the new power, the *pouvoir constitué*, whose authority could not be guaranteed by the Constitutional Assembly, the *pouvoir constituant*, because the power of the Assembly itself was not constitutional and could never be constitutional since it was prior to the constitution itself" (Arendt, 1990: 163). In other words, this was a constitution before the constitution, which it might be better to call an institution, and which implies in different contexts different ways of in-stituting, but also different formats of participation.

In this context Arendt particularly stresses the difference between the French and the (US) American Revolution. In France it was the National Assembly that developed the first constitution for the nation through its self-given *pouvoir constituant* according to a certain principle of representation in a 'division of labor'. Unlike in France, in the USA the constitution was thoroughly discussed in 1787, paragraph for paragraph down to the last detail, in town hall meetings and state parliaments and supplemented with amendments. In other words, it emerged from countless constituted bodies in a multi-stage process.

What is especially important to Arendt is the aspect of participation in the federative system of the USA, which she sees as leading to completely different relationships between the Constitution and the people in the USA and in Europe. At a closer look, however, the difference between the constitutional processes in France and in the US is not so fundamental as to explain Arendt's strong emphasis on the legalistic procedure of the (US) American Revolution. Aside from the multiple exclusions of all women, indigenous people and slaves, the constitutional process in the USA was one that was borne by constituted assemblies and dominated by the principle of representation.

Naturally, similar problems are also involved in contemporary examples of the relationship between constituent assemblies and constitution. Even in the case of the Bolivarian Constitution, it was President Chavez who invoked the constituent assembly following his election in 1999, and due to the relatively brief period of time between the election of the assembly (June 2000) and the referendum (December 2000), the issue of participation still remained limited despite all efforts to increase it. The top-down procedure of the European Constitution, in which self-organized debates did not spread throughout Europe at all, proved to be even less participative; and regardless of one's position on the issue of the rejection of the European Constitution in the referenda in France and the Netherlands in 2005, the hollow form of 'direct democracy' does not even begin to substitute for a deliberative process involving the whole population (Raunig, 2005). Thus the 'no' should be interpreted as a break turning against the form of the referendum in the question of the European Constitution, or more generally against the caricaturing limitation of constituent power to a dualistic yes/no mechanism of installing or not installing a new constituted power. Here is Stirner again:

> What constitution was to be chosen, this question busied the revolutionary heads, and the whole political period foams with constitutional fights and constitutional questions, as the social talents too were uncommonly inventive in societary arrangements (phalansteries and the like). The insurgent strives to become constitutionless. (Stirner, 1927: 287; 2001)

Stirner's anarchistic point goes far beyond the remainders of constituent power in liberal representative democracy, yet it does not assert the possibility of a state without any form of constitution. It rather describes the desire of the insurrectionist to resist the endless striation of desire production through imposing constitutions. In a similar way, in *Insurgencies*, his book about constituent power,[4] Antonio Negri (1999) attempts to shift the discourse from the abstract general of the constitution and the concomitant constitutional processes, to the concrete general of an 'absolute process'. For "once the constituent moment is passed, constitutional fixity becomes a reactionary fact in a society that is founded on the development of freedoms and the development of the economy" (Negri, 2003: 245). Negri thus no longer explains the differentiation of constituting into constituent power and constituted power in relation to the constitutional process, but rather on the distinction, which goes back to Spinoza, between *potentia* and *potestas*.

When Negri further develops the concept of constituent power as an absolute process of social organization, he also starts from the discourse on constitution, specifically from Jean Antoine Condorcet's statement, "to each generation its constitution." Even before the relevant principle was specified in the revolutionary French Constitution of 1793, Condorcet asserted that one generation may not subject future generations to its laws. Negri takes this demand literally and thus goes far beyond the former meaning of the *pouvoir constituant*. He presupposes that constituent power can not only not arise from constituted power, but that constituent power does not even institute constituted power (Negri, 1999: 20). Initially this means that even if there were a permanent process of constituting the constitution in Condorcet's sense, in other words a continuous adaptation of the constitution as abstract general to the concrete general, there would still be the fundamental problem of representation, of the division of labor between those representing and those represented, the separation between constituted and constituent power.

Negri logically pursues the question of how a constituent power is to be imagined, which does not engender constitutions separated from itself, but rather constitutes itself: con-stituent power as a com-position, which constitutes itself in a collective process. Stirner's individual anarchism summarizes the concatenation of singularities on a few pages with the peculiar terms of the 'union' [*Verein*] and (social) 'intercourse' [*Verkehr*] (Stirner, 1927: 192, 197; 2001). Negri seeks to place the common, the collectivity, finally a new concept of communism at the center of his immanent-transgressive ideas of constitution with a collectively envisioned self-constitution. Here constituent power constitutes itself, yet no longer as a unity in diversity like the French *constituante*, as a unity that represents diversity. Instead of the self-constitution of a nation as one body that drafts its constitution itself, it is the constituent power of a diversity without unity, without uniformization. This brings both Stirner and Negri to a way of thinking that consistently goes beyond the constitution: just as Stirner's insurgent strives for constitutionlessness, Negri's *repubblica costituente* is a "republic that originates before the state that emerges outside the state. It is the paradox of the constituent republic that the process of constitution is never closed and that the revolution never ends" (Negri, 2003: 80).

Stirner's statement about 'becoming constitutionless' is to be understood in exactly this sense: as an unfinished process and non-molar revolution/insurrection.[5] It indicates the possibility of an arrangement of singularities without constitution, yet not without constituent power and the instituting event. This instituting event should not establish a constituted power, but rather aims at instituting oneself, arranging oneself: Stirner says, "insurrection leads us no longer to let ourselves be arranged, but to arrange ourselves" (Stirner, 1927: 287; 2001). If constituent power is investigated in its relationship to the event and the process of instituting, then it is primarily the mode of instituting that comes into focus, in other words the question of how exactly the instituting event relates to the process of constituent power, which relationship of composition, which form the common, the con- of constituent power assumes in the process of instituting. The mode of instituting is not only symbolically effective, its tendency either toward authoritarian positioning or toward a com-position of the singular is decisive.

The Persistence of Instituent Practice

Particularly the genealogy of constituent power shows that the question of instituting is resolved in very different ways: the modes of instituting the constitutional process in France and the USA at the end of the eighteenth century were just as different as those of the present day, and the instituting event often decides the future of models of political organizing. I would like to discuss this question in more detail on the basis of artistic political practices of the 1930s, the 1950s and the 1990s, which developed various forms of instituting and thus also various qualities of participation. This leap from constitutional theory to specific micro-politics seems suitable to me for tracing the unfolding of both constituent power and 'instituent practice' – not at all as a counter-image to the macro level of major transformations, but rather as transversal processes thwarting the dualism of macro/micro in their concatenations.

A decade after the Soviet Proletkult had begun to open the theater to everyone, Bertolt Brecht responded to the question of participation and activation with a gesture of radical *closure* by developing the strict form of the *Lehrstück* ('learning play') from the various experiments with epic theater in the 1920s. Here the precisely specified audiences become 'active participants': "The learning play teaches by being played, not by being seen" (Brecht, 2001). By giving up the theater as a site of presentation, the audience as a receptive figure, the text as a finished form, Brecht conceived of a theater that is intended only for those conducting it, as communication exclusively among the active participants. The *Lehrstück* consists of playing (out) all the possible positions and roles in a constant change of perspective. For this reason Brecht repeatedly refused performances of *The Measures Taken* before an audience, calling it a "means of pedagogical work with students of Marxist schools and proletarian collectives", with workers choirs, amateur theater groups, school choirs and orchestras. There is no question, however, that the Brechtian act of establishing this activated public only lasted a brief period of time, and its preconditions were still found in solitary text production.

The Situationist International (SI), on the other hand, began as a collective that deployed the text more as a discursive and politicizing medium in manifestos and magazines, but not as a precondition for the practice of creating situations. From the beginnings in the 1950s, the point was neither an authoritarian and solitary act of instituting nor a passive drifting in quasi-natural situations. The question that arose for the SI was:

> What admixture, what interactions ought to occur between the flux (and resurgence) of the 'natural moment', in Henri Lefebvre's sense, and certain artificially constructed elements, introduced into this flux, perturbing it, quantitatively and, above all, qualitatively? (Situationist International, 1960)

That a conscious and direct intervention is required beyond 'natural moments' to construct a situation is already evident in the terms *créer* and *construire*, which are used in conjunction with the Situationist situation. The Situationist definition accordingly conveys the constructed situation as "a moment of life concretely and deliberately constructed by the collective organization of a unitary ambiance and a game of events" (Situationist International, 1958). Entirely in keeping with the Brechtian tradition, an important aspect of creating situations consisted, not least of all, in thwarting the fixation of the relationships between stage and audience space, between actors and observers. The role of the audience was to constantly decrease, whereas the proportion of those, who were now no longer *acteurs* but rather *viveurs* was to increase, at least ideally.

In terms of the concrete Situationist practice, however, the SI already limited the collectivity of the *viveurs* to a three-phase hierarchy in 1958. In this hierarchy a certain predominance is attributed to the director as leading coordinator, who is also permitted to intervene in events, whereas at the second level those consciously experiencing the situation directly participate, and finally at the third level a passive audience drawn into the situation by chance should be forced into action. Despite the collective form of instituting, the problem of participation was obviously not resolved at all, especially at the third level of the passive audience. It was not until just before and around May 1968 in Paris that the SI achieved an opening into the complex and unpredictable space of the revolutionary machine as a discursive arrangement, only to disband shortly thereafter.[6]

Numerous artistic-political practices arose in the 1990s, which developed in transversal concatenation with local and global social movements. In this way, the somewhat rigidified and hierarchized relationship between art and politics was loosened at certain hot spots. In the early 1990s in Hamburg an initiative of urban planning from below arose from the social contexts of the autonomous squatter movement in the Hafenstrasse, the alternative population of the red light district of St. Pauli and its social initiatives, and the collective art practices of the politicized visual art and the leftist pop scene affiliated with the Golden Poodle Club. In the beginning (around 1994), it was simply a matter of preventing the planned 'development'/blocking of the banks of the Elbe with the fake idea of a park. However, this soon turned into the fiction of a park of a different kind: Park Fiction. The self-organized arrangement of a hot spot of gentrification was not only intended to attack the state apparatus of traditional urban planning policies, but also the limited citizen's involvement that operates as controlled forms of activation in between participation and mediation as governmental pacification. The aim of Park Fiction was not so much an orderly process of alternative urban planning, but rather the opening of a wild process of desire production.

This idea of a proliferation of collective desire production was the foundation for a series of various events (Park Fiction 0-5) in 1995 and

1996. "Initially, we were less interested in analyzing desires. Or in other words, we saw it as part of our work to convey how to start desiring" (Dany, 1996: 56). Lectures on the theme of park and politics, exhibitions, raves, video evenings on unusual forms of parks impelled desire and knowledge production on the question of all that a park could be. These manifold impulses for desiring were intended to make the desires start to become grander.

In October 1997 the planning container was realized as a central element: for six months the planning office in a container installed on site was open at least two days a week. The strange tools for instituting desires included a kneading office, a desire archive, a garden library, utensils for crafts, painting and drawing, information material and conventional planning material. With over 200 visits to households and businesses, people who did not yet have access to the project were offered possibilities for involvement with a portable action kit (a miniature version of the planning container). An extensive presentation and discussion of the results took place at a city district conference in April 1998 (Schäfer, 2001).

The *Park Fiction Film* by Margit Czenki, which was completed in 1999, went far beyond classical documentary aspects as a constitutive part of the collective desire production for a park that still did not exist: 'Desires will leave the house and take to the streets' was the suggestive subtitle that conjoined the constituent power of desires with the promise of becoming public. And gradually the desires did actually escape the striated space that separates the private from the political. They ranged from bird voices on tape and a boxwood hedge trimmed in the shape of a poodle, a tree house in the shape of a ripe strawberry, mailboxes for young people whose mail is monitored by their parents at home, an open air cinema, an exercise hall with a green roof and wooden palms on rails, a women pirates fountain, platforms on rails for sunbathing and barbecuing, rolling sections of lawn, a boulevard of possibilities for which there is no room in the street, tea garden and fruit tree meadow, benches, flowers and a fire-breathing Inca goddess as a cooking sculpture, a dog racing track, a water slide into the (then clean) Elbe, all the way to a trash park made of the garbage of prosperity that is not further destructible, which would mirror the conditions in this part of the city.

As art in public space, not only this desire phase should be made possible through support from the city, but also the process of realizing the park. In the midst of this phase of the realization of construction, during which there were increasing conflicts with bureaucratic obstruction, Park Fiction was invited to take part in documenta 11. Instead of a spectacular, Thomas Hirschhorn-style site-specific intervention in Kassel, Park Fiction focused on documentation and archiving, once again with highly unconventional means. Finally in 2003, just in time for the congress 'Unlikely Encounters in Urban Space' organized by Park Fiction, in which activists from different corners of the world took part, the park of many islands was partially opened: the Flying Carpet and the Palm Island, a small amphitheater behind the Golden Poodle Club, the neighborhood gardens around the St. Pauli church and the boule grounds 'breakfast outdoors'. Three open air solariums were added in 2005, the tulip-patterned Tartan Field, the dog garden with poodle gates and a boxwood hedge in the shape of a poodle, the footbridge system Schauermanns Park, two herb gardens in front of the parish, and the bamboo garden of the modest politician. The women pirates fountain and the strawberry-shaped tree house are still waiting to be realized. Most of all, however, the untamed 'instituent practice' of Park Fiction is still waiting for an appropriate contextualization of its fixed 'objects': the process, through which the park emerged – and this is a more general problem of art in public space, which is otherwise hardly taken into consideration – is not recognizable in the 'objects'; the explosiveness of their creation, the linking of the singular and the collective in desire production remains hidden. Since more complex models of a walk-in archive have been made impossible by the authorities, Park Fiction finally developed plans for an 'exploding archive' with a sculpture boulevard of the non-realized desires and electronic access to the archive.

In a further development of Negri's conceptualization of constituent power, Park Fiction uses the term 'constituent practice' as a self-designation. From the description of the ongoing impulses for collective desire production, however, it is particularly the quality as an 'instituent practice' that should be clear here. In terms of the two interlinking main components of 'instituent practice', a stronger participation in instituting can be recognized in the pluralization of the instituting event: especially the concatenation of so many ongoing and diversely composed instituting events hinders an authoritarian mode of instituting and simultaneously counters the closure of/in the institution Park Fiction. The various arrangements of self-organization promote broad participation in instituting, because they newly compose themselves as a constituent power again and again, always tying into new local and global struggles. In the autonomous genealogy and presence of the Hafenstrasse in Hamburg, in the mixed context of the Golden Poodle Club and its small debate counterpart, the Butt Club, and the fraying social fabric of the neighborhood, Park Fiction is most of all a continuously insistent practice of instituting: countless smaller and larger impulses for collective insurrection and for the emergence of constituent power, a series of events, in which desiring is learned, a permanent new beginning, an 'instituent practice' that animates an astonishing amount and is incredibly persistent at the same time.

Notes

*   Thanks to Isabell Lorey, Stefan Nowotny and Alice Pechriggl for advice and critique.

1.   Online at http://eipcp.net/transversal/0106. The essays in the first section of the present volume, above, are drawn from this issue of *transversal.*

2.   There are intersections between Stirner's main work *The Ego and Its Own* (1845) and Marx and Engels's *The Holy Family, or Critique of Critical Criticism* (1845), and Stirner is directly criticized as 'St. Max' in Marx and Engels's *The German Ideology* (written 1845-6).

3.   "To ensure myself against a criminal charge, I superfluously remark explicitly that I choose the word 'insurrection' because of its etymological sense, not in the limited sense proscribed by the penal code" (Stirner, 1927: 288; 2001).

4.   In the original Italian version of 1992, the book is entitled *Il potere costituente: saggio sulle alternative del moderno*; it deals with the concept of constituent power based on analyses of Niccolò Macchiavelli, James Harrington, the (US) American Revolution, the French Revolution and the Russian Revolution.

5.   With the Deleuzian turn of 'becoming constitutionless', I would like to propose an interpretation of Stirner's 'insurrection' that emphasizes the molecularity and the aspect of process, thus also drawing a precarious boundary that separates this interpretation of Stirner from those of his right-wing readers.

6.   See my discussion in Raunig (2007) and Gene Ray's essay in this volume.

17

Governmentality and Self-Precarization: On the Normalization of Cultural Producers[*]

Isabell Lorey

(Translated by Lisa Rosenblatt and Dagmar Fink)

For some of us, as cultural producers,[1] the idea of a permanent job in an institution is something that we do not even consider, or is in any case something we decide to do at most for a few years. Afterward, we want something different. Hasn't the idea always been about not being forced to commit oneself to one thing, one classical job definition, which ignores so many aspects; about not selling out and consequently being compelled to give up the many activities that one feels strongly about? Wasn't it important to not adapt to the constraints of an institution, to save the time and energy to be able to do the creative and perhaps political projects that one really has an interest in? Wasn't a more or less well-paid job gladly taken for a certain period of time, when the opportunity arose, to then be able to leave again when it no longer fit? Then there would at least be a bit of money there to carry out the next meaningful project, which would probably be poorly paid, but supposedly more satisfying.

Crucial for the attitude suggested here is the belief that one has chosen his or her own living and working situations and that these can be arranged relatively freely and autonomously. Actually, also consciously chosen to a great extent are the uncertainties, the lack of continuities under the given social conditions. Yet in the following my concern is not with the question of 'when did I really decide freely?', or 'when do I act autonomously?', but instead, with the ways in which ideas of autonomy and freedom are constitutively connected with hegemonic modes of subjectivation in Western, capitalist societies. The focus of this text is accordingly on the extent to which 'self-chosen' precarization contributes to producing the conditions for being able to become an active part of neo-liberal political and economic relations.

No general statements about cultural producers or all of those currently in a situation that has been made precarious can be derived from this perspective. However, what becomes apparent when problematizing this 'self-chosen' precarization, are the historical lines of force (Foucault 1980; Deleuze, 1988) of modern bourgeois subjectivation, which are imperceptibly hegemonic, normalizing, and possibly block 'counter-behavior' (Foucault, 2004a: 292).

To demonstrate the genealogy of these lines of force, I will first turn to Michel Foucault's concepts of 'governmentality' and 'biopolitics'. We will not focus on the breaks and rifts in the lines of bourgeois subjectivation, but instead, on their structural and transformative continuities including the entanglement in governmental techniques of modern Western societies until today. What ideas of sovereignty arise in these modern, governmental *dispositifs*? What lines of force – i.e., what continuities, self-evidences, and normalizations can be drawn to what and how we think and feel as 'self-chosen' cultural producers that have been made precarious in neo-liberal conditions, how we are in the world, and specifically also in so-called dissident practices? Do cultural producers who are in a precarious state possibly embody a 'new' governmental normality through certain self-relations and ideas of sovereignty?

With the genealogy of the force lines of bourgeois subjectivation, in the course of the text I will differentiate between precarization as deviance, and therefore as a contradiction of liberal governmentality, on the one hand, and as a hegemonic function of neo-liberal governmentality on the other, to then finally clarify the relationship between the two based on the example of the 'free' decision for precarious living and working.

Biopolitical Governmentality

With the term 'governmentality', Michel Foucault defined the structural entanglement of the government of a State and the techniques of self-government in Western societies. This involvement between State and population as subjects is not a timeless constant. Only in the course of the eighteenth century could that which had been developing since the sixteenth century take root: a new government technique, more precisely, the force lines of modern government techniques until today. The traditional sovereign, for whom Foucault introduces the character from Niccolò Machiavelli's *The Prince* from the sixteenth century as a prototype, and Thomas Hobbes's contract-based voluntary community of subordinates from the seventeenth century, were not yet concerned with ruling 'the people' for the sake of their welfare, but instead, they were primarily interested in dominating them for the welfare of the sovereign. It was first in the course of the eighteenth century, when liberalism and the bourgeoisie became hegemonic, that the population entered the focus of power and along with it, a governing that was oriented on the life of 'the people' and making that life better. The power of the State no longer depended solely on the size of a territory or the mercantile, authoritative regulation of subordinates,[2] but instead, on the 'happiness' of the population, on their life and a steady improvement of that life.

In the course of the eighteenth century, governing methods continued to transform toward a political economy of liberalism: self-imposed limitations on government for the benefit of a free market on the one hand, and on the other, a population of subjects that were bound to economic paradigms in their thought and behavior. These subjects were not subjugated simply by means of obedience, but became governable in that, on the whole, "their life expectancy, their health, and their courses of behavior were involved in complex and entangled relationships with these economic processes" (Foucault, 2004b: 42). Liberal modes of government presented the basic structure for modern governmentality, which has always been biopolitical.[3] Or, in other words: liberalism was the economic and political framework of biopolitics and, equally, "an indispensable element in the development of capitalism" (Foucault, 1980: 141-142).

The strength and wealth of a state at the end of the eighteenth century depended ever more greatly on the health of its population. In a bourgeois liberal context, a government policy oriented on this means, until today, establishing and producing normality and then securing it. For that, a great deal of data is necessary; statistics are produced, probabilities of birth rates and death rates are calculated, frequencies of diseases, living conditions, means of nutrition, etc. Yet that does not suffice. In order to manufacture a population's health standard, and to maximize it, these bio-productive, life-supporting biopolitical government methods also require the active participation of every single individual, which means their self-governing. Foucault writes in The History of Sexuality:

> Western man was gradually *learning* what it meant to be a living species in a living world, to have a body, conditions of existence, probabilities of life, an individual and collective welfare, forces that could be modified, and a space in which they could be distributed in an optimal manner. (Foucault, 1980: 142, my emphasis)

Here, Foucault describes two things that I consider essential: the modern individual must learn how to have a body that is dependent on certain existential conditions, and, second, he or she must learn to develop a relationship with his or her 'self' that is creative and productive, a relationship in which it is possible to fashion his or her 'own' body, 'own' life, 'own' self. Philipp Sarasin shows the emergence in the context of the Western hygiene discourse of the waning eighteenth century and early nineteenth century, of "the belief that the individual was largely capable of determining its health, illness, or even the time of death" (Sarasin, 2001: 19). This idea of the ability to shape and fashion one's self never arose independent of governmental *dispositifs*.

In the context of liberal governmental technologies of the self, the attribute 'own' always signifies 'possessive individualism' (Macpherson, 1962). However, initially, self-relations oriented on the imagination of one's 'own', were only applicable to the bourgeois, then gradually towards the end of the nineteenth century, the entire population. At issue here is not the legal status of a subject, but structural conditions of normalizing societies: one must be capable of managing oneself, recognizing oneself as subject to a sexuality, and learn to have a body that remains healthy through attentiveness (nutrition, hygiene, living) and can become sick through inattentiveness. In this sense, the entire population must become biopolitical subjects (Lorey, 2006a).

With reference to wage workers, such imaginary self-relations[4] mean that one's own body, constituted as the property of the self, becomes an 'own' body that one must sell as labor power. Also, in this respect, the modern, 'free' individual is compelled to co-produce him or herself through such powerful self-relations, that the individual can sell his or her labor power well, in order to live a life that improves steadily.

Therefore, in modern societies, the 'art of governing' – which was another name given by Foucault (1991) to governmentality – does not primarily consist of being repressive, but instead, 'inwardly held' self-discipline and self-control.[5] It is the analysis of an order that is not only forced upon people, bodies, and things, but in which they are simultaneously an active part. At the center of the problem of government ruling techniques is not the question of regulating autonomous, free subjects, but instead, regulating the relations through which so-called autonomous and free subjects are first constituted as such.

Already in the second half of the seventeenth century, John Locke, who according to Karl Marx, "demonstrated ... that the bourgeois way of thinking is the normal human way of thinking" (Marx, 1999), wrote in *The Two Treatises of Government*, that man is "master of himself, and proprietor of his own person, and the actions or labour of it" (Locke, 1823). At the beginning of the modern era, property acquired a supposed 'anthropological meaning' (Castel, 2005: 24) for both the bourgeois man as a prerequisite for his formal freedom as a citizen, as well as for the worker, who owns his own labor power and must sell it, freely, as wage labor. It seemed to be the prerequisite with which the individual could become independent and free from the traditional system of subordination and security. With a biopolitical governmentality perspective, the meaning of property, however, surpasses the limited levels of citizenship, capital, and wage labor and is, in fact, to be understood as something entirely general. For in a biopolitical *dispositif*, relations of bodily ownership apply to the entire population as governmental self-governing, not only to citizens or workers.[6] The modern person is, accordingly, constituted through possessive individualistic self-relations, which are fundamental for historically specific ideas of autonomy and freedom. Structurally, modern self-relations are based – also beyond an economic interpellation – on a relation to one's own body as a means of production.

In this broad sense of economy and biopolitics, the lines of the labor entrepreneur, 'the entrepreneur of one's self' (Pühl, 2003) as a mode of subjectivation, reach back to the beginnings of modern liberal societies and are not an entirely neo-liberal phenomena.[7] This type of genealogy of course skips over the era of the social, the welfare state since the end of the nineteenth century, and ties together, the for the most part compulsively constituting self-entrepreneurs in the current reconstruction and deconstruction of the social/welfare state with fundamental liberal governmental methods of subjectivation since the end of the eighteenth century. With the interpellation to be responsible for one's self, something that had already failed in the nineteenth century seems to be repeating itself now, namely, the primacy of property and the construction of security associated with it. Property was introduced in the early stages of bourgeois rule as protection against the incalculability of social existence, as security against vulnerability in a secularized society and the domination of the princes and kings. Ultimately this applied to only a limited few, and at the end of the nineteenth century the nation state had to guarantee social security for many. However, it does not automatically follow that today the State must once again take on a more comprehensive social function of protection and security (Castel, 2005). For this would quickly reproduce the utterly flexible, Western nation state nexus of freedom and security with similar structural inclusions and exclusions, rather than break through it.

Normalized Free Subjects

In biopolitical governmental societies, the constitution of the 'normal' is always also woven in with the hegemonic.[8] With the demand to orient on the normal – which could be bourgeois, heterosexual, Christian, white male, white female, national – in the course of the modern era, it was necessary to develop the perspective of controlling one's own body, one's own life, by regulating and thus managing the self. The normal is not identical with the norm, but it can take on its function. Normality is, however, never anything external, for we are the ones who guarantee it, and reproduce it through alterations. Accordingly, we govern ourselves in the *dispositif* of governmentality, biopolitics, and capitalism in that we normalize ourselves. If this is successful – and it usually is – power and certain domination relations are barely perceptible, and extremely difficult to reflect on, because we act in their production, as it were, in the ways we relate to ourselves, and own our bodies. The normalizing society and the subjectivation taking place within it are a historical effect of a power technology directed at life. The normalized subject itself is, once again, a historical construct in an ensemble of knowledge forms, technologies, and institutions. This ensemble is aimed at the individual body as well as at the life of the population as a whole. Normalization is lived through everyday practices that are perceived as self-evident and natural.

Additionally, the normal is naturalized with the effect of actuality, of authenticity. We thus believe, for example, that the effect of power relations is the essence of our self, our truth, our own, actual core, the origin of our being. This normalizing self-governing is based on an imagined coherence, uniformity and wholeness, which can be traced back to the construction of a white, male subject (Lorey, 2006b). Coherence is, once again, one of the prerequisites for modern sovereignty. The subject must believe that it is "master in its own house" (Freud, 2000: 284). If this fundamental imagination fails, then usually not only others perceive the person in question as 'abnormal', but the person, too, has this opinion of him or herself.

Let's remain with the learned way of self-relation, which is so existential for the biopolitical governmental modern era, and which applies to the entire population in very different ways. This relationship with one's self is based on the idea of having an inner nature, an inner essence that ultimately makes up one's unique individuality. These kinds of imagined 'inner, natural truths', these constructions of actuality, are usually understood as unalterable, merely able to be suppressed or liberated. Until today, they nourish the ideas of being able to, or having to, fashion and design one's self and one's life freely, autonomously, and according to one's own decisions. These kinds of power relations are therefore not easy to perceive as they commonly come along as one's own free decision, as a personal view, and until today produce the desire to ask: 'Who am I?' or, 'How can I realize my potential?' 'How can I find myself and most greatly develop the essence of my being?' As mentioned, the concept of responsibility of one's own, so commonly used in the course of neo-liberal restructuring, lies within this liberal force line of possessive individualism and actuality and only functions additionally as a neo-liberal interpellation for self-governing.

Basically, governmental self-government takes place in an apparent paradox. Governing, controlling, disciplining, and regulating one's self means, at the same time, fashioning and forming one's self, empowering one's self, which, in this sense, means to be free. Only through this paradox can sovereign subjects be governed. Precisely because techniques of governing one's self arise from the simultaneity of subjugation and empowerment, the simultaneity of compulsion and freedom, in this paradoxical movement, the individual not only becomes a subject, but a certain, modern 'free' subject. Subjectivated in this way, this subject continually participates in (re)producing the conditions for governmentality, as it is first in this scenario that agency emerges. According to Foucault, power is practiced only on 'free subjects' and only to the extent that they are 'free' (Foucault, 1983).

In the context of governmentality, subjects are, thus, subjugated and simultaneously agents, and in a certain sense, free. This freedom is, at the same time, a condition and effect of liberal power relations – i.e., of biopolitical governmentality. Despite all of the changes that have occurred until today, since the end of the eighteenth century, this is one of the lines of force through which individuals in modern societies can be governed.

This normalized freedom of biopolitical governmental societies never exists without security mechanisms or constructions of the abnormal and deviant, which likewise have subjectivating functions. The modern era seems unthinkable without a 'culture of danger', without a permanent threat to the normal, without imaginary invasions of constant, common threats such as diseases, dirt, sexuality, or the 'fear of degeneration' (Foucault, 2004b: 101f).[9] The interplay of freedom and security, self empowerment and compulsion, also with the help of this culture of danger, drives on the problems of the political economy of liberal power.

Against this backdrop, all of those who did not comply with this norm and normalizing of a free, sovereign, bourgeois, white subject including its property relations were made precarious. Furthermore, in the context of the social state, which was meant to guarantee the security of modern insecurity, not only were women made structurally precarious as wives, through the normal labor conditions oriented on the man. Also those who were excluded as abnormal and foreign from the nation state compromise between capital and labor were likewise made precarious (Kleines Postfordistisches Drama, 2005a and 2005b; Mecheril, 2003). Precarization was, accordingly, until now always an inherent contradiction in liberal governmentality and, as abnormal, disturbed the stabilizing dynamic between freedom and security. In this sense, it was often the trigger for counter-behavior.

Presently, normal labor conditions oriented on a male breadwinner, a situation largely accessible only for the majority society, is losing its hegemony. Precarization is increasingly a part of governmental normalization techniques and as a result, in neo-liberalism it transforms from an inherent contradiction to a hegemonic function.

Economizing of Life and the Absence of Counter-behavior

The talk of the 'economizing of life', a discussion often struck up in the past several years, provides only very limited explanations of neo-liberal transformation processes: not only due to its totalizing rhetoric, but also because of the associated proclamation of what is supposedly a new phenomenon. 'Economizing of life' usually refers to certain simplified theses: no longer only work, but also life has fallen prey to economic exploitation interests; a separation between work and life is no longer possible and in the course of this, an implosion of the distinction between production and reproduction has also taken place. Such totalizing implosion theses speak of a collective victim status and distort the view of modes of subjectivation, agency, and ultimately of counter-behavior.

However, the thesis of the 'economizing of life' makes sense from a biopolitical governmentality perspective. It points to the power and domination relations of a bourgeois liberal society, which for more than two hundred years now has been constituted around the productivity of life. In this perspective, life was never the other side of work. In Western modernity, reproduction was always part of the political and the economic. Not only reproduction, but also life in general was never beyond power relations. Instead, life, precisely in its productivity, which means its design potential, was always the effect of such relations. And it is precisely this design potential that is constitutive for the supposed paradox of modern subjectivation between subordination and empowerment, between regulation and freedom. A liberal process of constituting precarization as an inherent contradiction, did not take place beyond this subjectivation, it is an entirely plausible resulting bundle of social, economic and political positions.

In this sense, the currently lamented 'economization of life' is not an entirely neo-liberal phenomenon, but instead, a force line of biopolitical societies, which today perhaps becomes intelligible in a new way. The associated subjectivations are not new in the way that they are usually claimed to be. In fact, their biopolitical governmental continuities have hardly been grasped.

Were living and working conditions, which arose in the context of social movements since the 1960s, really in no way governmental?[10] Indeed, the thoroughly dissident practices of alternative ways of living, the desire for different bodies and self-relations (in feminist, ecological, left-radical contexts), persistently aimed to distinguish themselves from normal working conditions and the associated constraints, disciplinary measures, and controls. Keywords here are: deciding for oneself what one does for work and with whom; consciously choosing precarious forms of work and life, because more freedom and autonomy seem possible precisely because of the ability to organize one's own time, and what is most important: self-determination. Often, being paid well hasn't been a concern as the remuneration was enjoying the work. The concern was being able to bring to bear one's many skills. Generally, the conscious, voluntary acceptance of precarious labor conditions was often certainly also an expression of the wish for living the modern, patriarchal dividing of reproduction and wage labor differently than is possible within the normal work situation.

However, it is precisely these alternative living and working conditions that have become increasingly more economically utilizable in recent years because they favor the flexibility that the labor market demands. Thus, practices and discourses of social movements in the past thirty, forty years were not only dissident and directed against normalization, but also at the same time, a part of the transformation toward a neo-liberal form of governmentality.

But to what extent are precarious modes of living and working, formerly perceived as dissident, now obvious in their hegemonic, governmental function? And why do they seem to lose their potential for counter-behavior? The following will offer a few thoughts without any claims of presenting a comprehensive analysis.

Many of the cultural producers who have entered into a precarious situation of their own accord, the people of whom we are speaking here as a whole, would refer consciously or unconsciously to a history of previous alternative conditions of existence, usually without having any direct political relationship to them. They are more or less disturbed by their shift to the center of society – i.e., to the place where the normal and hegemonic are reproduced. That does not mean, however, that former alternative living and working techniques will become socially hegemonic. Instead, it works the other way around: the mass precarization of labor conditions is forced upon all of those who fall out of normal labor conditions along with the promise of the ability to take responsibility for their own creativity and fashion their lives according to their own rules, as a desirable, supposedly normal condition of existence. Our concern here is not with these persons forced into precarization, but those who say that as cultural workers they have freely chosen precarious living and working conditions (Kuster, 2006; Panagiotidis, 2005).

It is amazing that there are no systematic empirical studies of this.[11] The common parameters of cultural producers, however, should be that they are well or even very well educated, between twenty-five and forty years-old, without children, and more or less intentionally in a precarious employment situation. They pursue temporary jobs, live from projects and pursue contract work from several clients at the same time, one right after the other, usually without sick pay, paid vacations, or unemployment compensation, and without any job security, thus with no or only minimal social protection. The forty-hour week is an illusion. Working time and free time have no clearly defined borders. Work and leisure can no longer be separated. In the non-paid time, they accumulate a great deal of knowledge, which is not paid for extra, but is naturally called for and used in the context of paid work, etc.

This is not an 'economizing of life', that comes from the outside, overpowering and totalizing. Instead, these are practices connected with desire as well as adaptation. For these conditions of existence are constantly foreseen and co-produced in anticipatory obedience. 'Voluntary', – i.e., unpaid or low paying jobs in the culture or academic industries, for example – are all too often accepted as an unchangeable fact, and nothing else is even demanded. The necessity of pursuing other, less creative, precarious jobs in order to finance one's own cultural production is accepted. This forced and, simultaneously chosen, financing of one's own creative output constantly supports and reproduces precisely those relations from which one suffers and of which one wants to be a part. Perhaps those who work creatively, these precarious cultural producers by design, are subjects that can be exploited so easily because they seem to bear their living and working conditions eternally due to the belief in their own freedom and autonomy, due to self-realization fantasies. In a neo-liberal context they are exploitable to such an extreme that the State even presents them as role models.

This situation of self-precarization is connected to experiences of fear and loss of control, feelings of insecurity through the loss of certainties and safeguards, as well as fear and the experience of failure, social decline and poverty. Also for these reasons, 'letting go' or forms of dropping out and dropping off of hegemonic paradigms are difficult. Everyone has to remain 'on speed' otherwise you might fall out. There are no clear times for relaxation or recuperation. This kind of reproduction has no clear place, which, in turn, results in an unfulfilled yearning and a continuous suffering from this lack. The desire for relaxation to 'find oneself' becomes insatiable. These kinds of reproductive practices usually have to be learned anew. They are lacking in any self-evidence and have to be fought for bitterly against oneself and others. In turn, this makes this yearning for reproduction, for regeneration, so extremely marketable.

As a result, not only the side of work, of production, has become precarious, but also the so-called other side, which is often defined as 'life', the side of reproduction. Do production and reproduction therefore coincide? In these cultural producers, in an old, new way, yes. What they reveal is that in a neo-liberal form of individualization, parts of production and reproduction are deposited 'in' the subjects. Panagiotidis and Tsianos (2004: 19) also argue along these lines when they state: "The progressive vanquishing of the division of production and reproduction does not occur at home or at the workplace, but instead, through an embodiment of the work itself: a reflexive way of precarization!" Though what is materialized in the bodies, beyond the work, is also always the governmental life, as biopolitical governmental power relations function doggedly through the production of hegemonic, normalized bodies and self-relations.

The function of reproduction consequently changes in the present context of precarious immaterial, usually individualized work and 'life'. It is no longer externalized with others, primarily women. Individual reproduction and sexual reproduction, the production of life, now becomes individualized and is shifted, in part, 'into' the subjects themselves. It is about regeneration beyond work, also through work, but still, quite often beyond adequately paid wage labor. It is about regeneration, renewal, creating from one's self, re-producing one's self from one's own power: of one's own accord. Self-realization becomes a reproductive task for the self. Work is meant to guarantee the reproduction of the self.

Presenting 'precarized' cultural producers (that is, cultural producers who have been made precarious) in their entire heterogeneity in such a uniform fashion, it is possible to say that their subjectivation in neo-liberalism has obviously been contradictory: in the simultaneity of, on the one hand, precarization, which also always means fragmentation and non-linearity, and on the other, the continuity of sovereignty. The continuity of modern sovereignty takes place through the stylizing of self-realization, autonomy, and freedom, through the fashioning of and responsibility for one's self, and the repetition of the idea of actuality. An example of this is the (still) widespread idea of the modern male artist subject, who draws his creativity from himself, because it supposedly exists within him, there, where Western modernity also positions sex and has made it the nature, the essence, of the individual. In general, for the cultural producers described here, sovereignty seems to rest mainly in the 'free' decision for precarization, therefore, self-precarization. Yet this, in turn, could be a central reason for why it is so difficult to recognize structural precarization as a neo-liberal governmental phenomenon that affects the entire society, and is hardly based on a free decision. Cultural producers therefore offer an example of the extent to which 'self-chosen' ways of living and conditions of working, including their ideas of autonomy and freedom, are compatible with political and economic restructuring. How else can we explain that in a study of the living and working conditions of critical cultural producers, when asked what a 'good life' is, they had no answer?[12] When work and life increasingly permeate one another, then that means, as one interviewee expressed: "work seeps into your life." But obviously, not enough ideas of a 'good life' seep into the work, whereby this could then, in turn, transform into something that could collectively signify a 'good life'. The counter-behavior with the view to a better life, which has less and less of a governmental function, is missing.

Apparently, the belief in precarization as a liberal governmental oppositional position can be maintained with the help of contradictory subjectivation, between sovereignty and fragmentation. However, in this way, continuing relations of power and domination are made invisible and normalization mechanisms become naturalized as the subject's self-evident and autonomous decisions. The totalizing talk of 'economizing of life' only contributes to this by causing hegemony effects to disappear from view and with them, struggles and antagonisms. One's own imaginations of autonomy and freedom are not reflected on within governmental force lines of modern subjectivation, other freedoms are no longer imagined, thus blocking the view of a possible behavior contesting the hegemonic function of precarization in the context of neo-liberal governmentality.

What is the price of this normalization? In neo-liberalism, what functions as the abnormal? As the deviant? What can't be economically exploited in this way? Rather than focusing on the messianic arrival of counter-behavior and new subjectivities, as Deleuze rhetorically formulates with the question: "Do not the changes in capitalism find an unexpected 'encounter' in the slow emergence of a new self as a centre of resistance?" (Deleuze, 1988: 115)[13], I believe that it is necessary to continue to work further and more precisely on the genealogies of precarization as a hegemonic function, on the problem of continuities of bourgeois governmental modes of subjectivation, also in the context of notions of autonomy and freedom that look upon themselves as dissident.

Notes

*   Thanks to Brigitta Kuster, Katharina Pühl, and Gerald Raunig for critical discussions.

1. 'Cultural producers' is used here as a paradox designation. It refers to an imagination of the designated subjects: that of their own autonomous production and of fashioning their selves. But at the same time it is about the fact that these ways of subjectivation are instruments of governing, thus functional effects of biopolitical govermental societies of occidental modernity. Therefore the term 'cultural producers' has a contradictory meaning and does not in first place concern artists. With this conceptualization I also refer to the definition by the group kpD/kleines postfordistisches Drama ('little post-Fordist drama') to which I belong, along with Brigitta Kuster, Katja Reichard and Marion von Osten. (Translators' note: The abbreviation KPD, all capital letters, stood for the Kommunistische Partei Deutschlands, the German Communist Party.) "We employ the term 'cultural producers' in a decidedly strategic way. With it, we are not speaking of a certain sector (cultural industry), nor of an ascertainable social category (for example, those insured by artists' social security in Germany, which is a health, pension and accident insurance for artists and writers) or of a professional self-conception. Instead, we are speaking of the practice of traveling across a variety of things: theory production, design, political and cultural self-organization, forms of

collaboration, paid and unpaid jobs, informal and formal economies, temporary alliances, project related working and living" (Kleines postfordistisches Drama, 2005b: 24).

2. Mercantilism was also oriented toward the growth of the population, but oriented more in terms of quantitative aspects than quality of life 'of the people'.

3. For one of the few places in which Foucault points out the inseparability of modern governmentality and biopolitics, see Foucault (2004b: 43). On biopolitical governmentality as a socio-theoretical concept, see Lorey (2006a).

4. Following Louis Althusser's thoughts, these imaginary self-relations cannot be separated from 'real living conditions', which are here the governmental techniques for ruling the population which, for example, materialize in the constitution of bodies.

5. I assume that it was not first under neo-liberalism that self-management shifted 'inward' and replaced a regulatory principle. Regulation and control are not techniques that were first established under neo-liberalism to oppose discipline (Deleuze, 1992; Hardt and Negri, 2000). Particularly when reproduction technologies along with hygiene and health are attributed a central biopolitical productivity of (gendered and raced) bodies, then for the bourgeoisie the introduction of these practices of subjectivation must be positioned at the beginning of the modern era, at the end of the eighteenth century, at the latest.

6. This biopolitical subjectivation is, conversely, differentiated through gender, race, class affiliation, religion, and hetero-normativity, which I cannot go into in detail here. Generally, the text focuses solely on these force lines of bourgeois subjectivation. It is not aiming at a comprehensive look at the problem of ways of subject constitution.

7. Foucault (2004b) on the contrary, speaks only in connection to the formation of neoliberal governmentality in the U.S. of the self employer; as does the research based on his work (Bröckling, 2000; Pieper and Gutiérrez Rodríguez, 2003). Lemke et al. (2000: 15) argue, for example, that first when the liberal regulation of 'natural freedom' transformed into that of 'artificial freedom', was it possible to detect "entrepreneurial behavior of economically-rational individuals". Yet what is this 'natural freedom' other than the effect of governmental techniques and social struggles? And what, in contrast, is 'artificial freedom'?

8. In his genealogy of governmentality, Foucault does not draw any explicit connections between the normal and the hegemonic. In order to understand the dynamic and meaning of governmentality, normalization mechanisms must be viewed explicitly in connection with the production of

hegemonic discourses and the related struggles. On the connection between Foucault and Gramsci, see Hall (1997) and Demirovic (1997).

9. Biopolitical governmentality structures modern societies in a specifically paradoxical way. "It enables", as Cornelia Ott so succinctly states, "people to come to understand themselves as unique 'subjects', and at the same time, brings them together as an amorphous, unified, 'population mass'. ...Hereby, the flipside is always the 'right to life' rather than the exclusion or annihilation of life" (Ott, 1997: 110). On the connection between biopolitical sociation and colonialism, see Lorey (2006b).

10. Boltanski and Chiapello (2001), in contrast, assume an appropriation. According to their study, the changes in capitalism since the 1960s can be traced back to a specific integration and strategic reformulation of an 'artistic critique', a critique that complains of the uniformity of a mass society, a lack of individual autonomy, and the loss of authentic social relations (see also Lemke, 2004: 176-78).

11. Initial approaches can be found in Böhmler and Scheiffele (2005); the study by Anne and Marine Rambach (2001) on precarious intellectuals in France; the theses by Angela McRobbie (2004) on the functionality of artists for the new economy; or the study by kpD (2005b).

12. As part of the film project *Kamera Läuft!* (*Action!* Zürich/Berlin 2004, 32"), at the end of 2003, the group kpD (kleines postfordistisches Drama, see note 1 above) interviewed fifteen Berlin cultural producers (including kpD) "with whom we work together for a specific form of political practice in the cultural field or whose work we use as a reference. ... Our questions were based on those from Fronte della Gioventù Lavoratrice's and Potere Operaio's questionnaire action carried out in early 1967 in Mirafiori, 'Fiat is our University', which among other things, also asked about the ideas of a 'good life', and organization. ... With regards to a potential politicization of cultural producers, we were, however, also interested in collective refusal strategies and in the associated wishes for improving one's own life, the life of others, and ultimately, social change. The only thing that was present at a general level in all of the interviews was the suffering from a lack of continuity. ... We, too, found almost no alternative life concepts in our horizon of ideas that could counter the existing ones with anything clear or unambiguous" (2005b: 24; 2005a).

13. An extreme example of a current messianic idea is naturally the end of the book *Empire* by Hardt and Negri (2000), but also, although different and in a greatly weakend form, Foucault (1983) with his demand for new subjectivities.

18

To Embody Critique:
Some Theses, Some Examples

Marina Garcés

(Translated by Maribel Casas-Cortés and Sebastian Cobarrubias/ Notas Rojas Collective Chapel Hill)

Not only does it matter which principles we chose but also which forces, which people will apply them. (Merleau-Ponty)

1. The problem of critique has traditionally been a problem of conscience. Today it is a problem of the body. How do we incarnate critique? How does critical thought acquire a body? If critique was used traditionally to combat darkness, today it must combat impotence. The global world is completely illuminated. Our minds are enlightened. There is nothing that we don't see: misery, lies, exploitation, torture, exclusion, etc. – all are completely exposed and brought to light. Nonetheless we are capable of doing so little. About ourselves. For our world. We can say it all and nonetheless we have nothing relevant to add. To embody critique is not to find the correct wording, nor to become complacent in the gardens of good conscience, nor to sell the cheapest solutions to existing institutions. To embody critique means to ask how to subvert one's life nowadays in such a way that the world can no longer remain the same.

2. The critique that historically fought ignorance had a hero: the artist-intellectual. His words and his actions were bearers of light: analysis, metanarratives, denunciation, provocation… These were the tools of an intervention made before and about the world. The artist-intellectual worked from his desk, from his studio. That was his balcony. From there, his word could remain pure or sell itself to the powers that be, sacrifice itself for the cause of the struggle or return the stability to the current order. This word could be right or wrong,

faithful or treacherous. The artist-intellectual could even abandon his balcony and join the multitude. A critique that battles impotence does not have a hero, or it has many. Its expression is anonymous, without a face. Its place of enunciation is wandering, intermittent, visible and invisible at the same time. Today, who is the subject of enunciation of critical thought? Where will we find it? If we cannot name it, that is because it is an anonymous and ambivalent subject. Composed of theory and practice, of word and action, this subject is brilliant and miserable, isolated and collective, strong and weak. Its truth does not illuminate the world, rather its truth contradicts it. If the world claims: "This is all there is", there exists a we that responds: "That cannot be all."

3. Impotence is not the consequence of a historical weakness of social movements or of any other kind of political subject that we can think of. Their weakness is the result of a big change in social relations, where a logic of pertinence has been replaced by a logic of connection. This means that the inclusion/exclusion of each one of us is decided not through our relationships of pertinence to some wider collective (a people, community, class) but rather in our capacity of connecting. Connections that must be fed and renovated permanently, maintained by each person throughout all activities in which s/he is completely invested. In the network-society, everyone is on their own in their connection to the world. Everyone fights their specific battle in order to avoid losing that connectivity to the world, to avoid remaining outside, to avoid making a story of exclusion out of their own biography. To spend one's life looking for work, to risk one's life crossing borders: those are the two paradigmatic movements, the biographies of the precarious one and the immigrant one that we all are. The logic of pertinence had it own forms of domination. The logic of connection is simple and binary: either you are connected or you are dead. With this reformulation of social links – which could be understood as a result of the historic defeat of the workers' movement – every life is put into motion toward the world. No one is sure of where they are: connections, personal and non-transferable, are inseparable from the threat of dis-connection. For this reason, this new social contract converts us into producers and reproducers of reality, in knots that strengthen the network: established unilaterally through each person. This network obligates through self-obligation, controls through self-control, represses through self repression.

4. Impotence is not the result of a historical weakness of social movements, nor is it the result of an incapacity of the 'I'. 'I don't do/cannot do anything': not for society, not for the preservation of the planet, not to stop war… Nothing. This is the declaration of self-contemplation by a subject that can only move between culpability and cynicism. It is the voice of that 'I' that is isolated in its connection to the network. Alone in a lonely world. Alone with all the rest. From its precarious and depoliticized connection, that 'I' is prey for moralism, opinion, and psychology. This 'I' moves between the spheres of some values that orbit around the world, with which s/he judges and is judged; the marketplace of opinions that offer this 'I' a position in society and the restrictive environment of discomfort/comfort.

5. Fighting impotence and embodying critique must pass firstly through attacking that 'I'. Attacking the values with which we fly around the world, attacking the opinions with which we protect ourselves from the world, attacking our own particular and precarious comfort. If critique can define itself as a theoretical-practical discourse that has emancipatory effects, the principal objective of critique today must be to free ourselves from the 'I'. The 'I' is not our singularity. The 'I' is the device that simultaneously isolates and connects us to the network-society. Each person with their values, opinions, and states of mind can remain calm before the world, can remain impotent before the world. Cynical and guilty, the 'I' always knows where it must remain.

6. Against the grain of the modern tradition, developing critical thought does not mean bringing the subject to its highest degree of maturity and independence but rather, uprooting the 'I' from that place that maintains it continuously in 'its place' before the world. The modern ideal of emancipation was linked to the idea that to free oneself really meant to 'takeoff' from the world of necessity, to undo the link until achieving a god-like self-sufficiency, individually or collectively. This would be the path from the kingdom of necessity toward the kingdom of liberty in its diverse forms. In our network-society, the question of a critical or emancipatory thought should perhaps be different: to ask what is our capacity to conquer liberty in the act of networking itself. Nowadays, liberation has to do with our capacity to explore the networked link and fortify it: the links with a planet-world, reduced to an object of consumption, a surface of displacements and a depository of wastes; as well as the links with those 'Others' who, while always condemned to being 'other', have been evicted from the

possibility to say 'we'. To combat impotence and embody critique then means to experience the 'we' and the 'world' that is amongst us. This is why the problem of critique is no longer a problem of conscience but of embodiment: it does not concern a conscience facing the world but rather a body that is in and with the world. This not only terminates the role of intellectuals and their balconies, of which we have already spoken, but also disposes of the mechanisms of legitimation of the intellectuals' word and their mode of expression.

7. The principal challenge for critique today is to challenge the privatization of our existence. In the globalized world, not only have goods and land been privatized but our very existence as well. The experience that we have of the world refers us to a private field of references: individual or collective, it is always self-referential. This privatization of existence has two consequences: first, the depoliticizing of the social question. This means that we have enemies but we don't know where our friends or allies are. We can perceive the foci of aggression against our lives, but not the line of demarcation between friend/enemy. We can speak of financial speculation, precarity, mobbing,[1] borders, etc. But how do we name the 'we' that suffers and struggles with these realities? By the same mechanism, the 'enemy' also becomes privatized. Every person has their own enemy, in their own particular problem. The multiple fronts of struggle are difficult to share. They infiltrate into every cell of our everyday misery, which is miserable precisely because in this everyday everyone is on their own, as an individual or in their small ghetto. But the privatization of existence also has a second consequence: the radicalization of the social question, which sinks its roots directly in our own experience of the world and not someone else's. To ask for this 'we' requires starting from the only thing we possess: our own experience. The fragmentation of meaning contains this paradoxical virtue: we are obliged to start with ourselves. Here we discover the importance of abandoning the third person, which dominated the traditional critical thinker, and exploring our own fields of possible experiences. The quest for the common today requires the courage to drown oneself in their actual experience of the world, even if it is naked and empty of promises. This is what it means to embody critique.

8. In Barcelona 2002, a project emerged from the necessity to begin a practical and collective form of critical thought. Collective, not because this thought does not have any proper names, but because in

each one of those names a 'we' echoes. Practical, not because it excludes the theoretical dimension but because the world is not the object of study or contemplation for this project of critical thought. Rather the world is the area of operations of this project's collective body. We call this project Espai en Blanc, Blank Space in Catalan (www.espaienblanc.net). Linked to the antagonistic practices occurring in the city over the past few years, this project opened a breach where critical thought could circulate outside of the spaces of specialists and in/through the hands of the protagonists of real movements, in their fragility, their intermittence, and their anonymity. Out of the works and projects in which Espai en Blanc has participated, three examples will be mentioned to indicate what to embody critique might mean today: the report *Barcelona 2004: el fascismo postmoderno* (Barcelona 2004: postmodern fascism, 2004); the movie *El taxista ful* (The Full Taxi Driver, 2005); and the series of encounters 'La tierra de nadie en la red de los nombres' (No man's land in the network of names, 2006).

9. The first example, the 'Barcelona 2004: postmodern fascism' report, demonstrates how a theoretical intervention can be embodied in the city. This intervention took place in the framework of the campaign against the Forum Universal de las Culturas (Universal Forum of Cultures), a large international event organized by city institutions in Barcelona 2004. Espai en Blanc contributed an analysis that uncovered the mechanism by which the project for a multicultural city being proposed by the municipality was in reality the implementation of a new device of de-politicization and neutralization of conflicts. What we call 'postmodern fascism' is based in mobilizing all the existing differences in the city towards a single project for that city, towards a single reality. However, what could be done so that this analysis didn't just float above and out of Barcelona but could actually intervene and interfere in the city's movements? The idea, together with the Bellaterra publishing house and other critical collectives in the city, was to edit and compile this analysis, together with other materials in a free book.[2] The book was released at a large public gathering, and two distribution points were selected. Those people interested in the book, would have to personally go and get it and could only obtain one copy each. In two weeks 3,000 copies were distributed. Even more interesting, though, is the fact that the appearance of the book provoked a mobilization. People had to decide for themselves how far to let their interest take them, travel to another part of the city, and personally relate with the

editor and with the collectives that were promoting the book. All kinds of people arrived: teachers, activists, politicians(!), and most of all, many anonymous folks whose intuition led them to identify with the words in the title or the description of the book. Many bodies were mobilized in order to share their rejection, rage and critiques against a model of the city that was getting more hypocritically aggressive everyday.

10. The second example, the movie *El taxista ful* (2005), is an example of how all critique is done with and on our very body, with and on our own life, especially when our life is understood as a common problem. This project was born out of a long collective initiative dealing with the critical consequences of precarity. For years, this assembly called Dinero Gratis (Free Money) was wondering, how could one refuse to work when the factory and stable jobs no longer exist? From that perspective a series of campaigns, actions and writings were carried out that called to attention the problems that our relations with money, both individual and collective, present nowadays. The film director Jordi Solé (Jo Sol) proposed a film project about these issues. The interesting thing was that it wasn't about producing a documentary about a political movement or a social problem, but rather using film to interrogate our own practices, and call to the film spectator at the same level. We worked without actors and without a written script. We were both subject and object of the process of creating this film. Together with Jo Sol and the non-actor Pepe Rovira, a very real fiction entered our lives: the story of a man that robbed taxis in order to work. This was a guy who wanted to have a normal life, that continued to aspire to this normal life, and that in the process of pursuing this dream, had become a thief and a lunatic in the eyes of the law and society. What would this guy think of us? How would he relate to us? Two lines of flight, two forms of resistance to the violence of work and money are found in a story of friendship, our true story of friendship. We don't have a solution to the problem of money, nor do we have an ideology that explains and resolves our relationship to precarity. We have the capacity to present ourselves, to learn and struggle from our own field of possible experiences. The movie speaks form there. The movie calls to the audience from there.

11. Finally, the third example is about the gatherings called 'La tierra de nadie en la red de los nombres' (No man's land in the network of names) taking place in 2006. This initiative is an example of how critical thought is produced amongst us. That is to say, the production of

critical thought happens when we break the hierarchy 'thinker-audience' in order to constitute a thinking 'we', in order to build a collective word capable of advancing through the problems that are truly problems. For five months, Espai en Blanc called for an encounter every last Thursday of each month in a local coffee-bar. Each gathering dealt with a specific problematic (social disquiet, border spaces, the experience of 'we', and speaking up) and began with a series of questions and materials for consultation that were distributed through a blog site. The attendance was made of those that wanted to be there: no announced conferences, no coordinating committee, no turns to speak or rebuttal. Throughout the 5 months, more than a hundred people, most of whom did not know each other, gathered together in order to think collectively. This anonymous self-called assembly opened a space for politicizing our language and our lives. Against the privatization of our existence, a world amongst 'us' appeared. In today's metropolises there are many collective happenings, we could even say that the majority of happenings are collective. Nonetheless, the city had completely lost the ability of calling itself to assemble. Its happenings are empty of a 'we'. 'We' only move if someone calls us, if there is a programmed activity, and if we're told what to do. At these gatherings, we didn't know what would happen, who would come, what direction the discussions would go in, or when silence would devour us. We came with knots in our stomachs. And every time, one after another, the encounter worked. With more or less tensions during the course of the discussion, each time a 'we' emerged that gave the happening meaning. Thanks to this we could think in another way. During these processes lives are shaken up. We no longer walk the same way when we return home. Maybe we don't even know exactly what we think. Perhaps, an empty space was opened, a blank space where other ways of living could be explored together with other people. Another consciousness? No, a body better prepared to battle fear, a body more exposed and less isolated. A body that knows that its life does not belong solely to itself, and everything depends in that which goes beyond itself.

Notes

1. Translators' note: 'Mobbing' refers to many types of harassment and psychological pressures used to coerce, stress or defeat someone with serious emotional and physical results. The term is used most often in reference to the workplace and when there is some involvement (or

tolerance) of management. It is not the same as sexual or racial harassment though the lines may be difficult to draw. Mobbing has also been referred to 'bullying', 'psychological terror' and 'emotional violence'.

2. This book can be downloaded at http://www.ed-bellaterra.com/uploads/pdfs/FOTUT%202004X.pdf

19

The Double Meaning of Destitution

Stefan Nowotny

(Translated by Aileen Derieg)

"What do we do with what we have done?" (Colectivo Situaciones, 2003: 34). The practical self-reflexivity of this question assumes a special meaning, when that which was 'done', which the sentence refers to, involves an insurrection, one that can certainly be regarded as 'successful', but not in the sense that the 'success' of this insurrection consisted in taking over power. Had the latter been the case, then the meaning of the question would inevitably have been unambiguous: a 'revolutionary' break would separate what is to be done now from all actions that first created the preconditions for what is currently to be done; and this break would make the conducting of the insurrection appear, more or less clearly, as the subject matter of a specific historiography on the one hand, whereas on the other it would open up the terrain, in which the current task field of governing could appear (although its formulated objectives would certainly be expected to maintain a certain congruence with those of the insurrection). But what if no break of this kind prefigured the double sense of (past and present) actions? What if it was not a matter of "appropriating a truth about what had happened" – a truth that simultaneously presupposes and actuates the described break – but rather of "probing the newly opening perspectives for action" and 'elaborating' the becoming that is articulated in what happened? (Colectivo Situaciones, 2003: 34).

Destitution as Opening: Insurrection and Deposition

Let us look at the social and political situation, in which the opening question – taken from a book by the Colectivo Situaciones, a group active in Buenos Aires – is specifically located; we will need to work out the implications that are only briefly and provisionally outlined there. This relates to the Argentinean insurrection movements that became manifest especially on 19 and 20 December 2001, which formed at the apex of the Argentinean state, economic and financial crisis induced by the neo-liberal policies of Carlos Menem and, in the end, the lack of international financial aid, after private savings accounts had been frozen, among other things, on 1 December of that year, to protect the parity of the Argentinean peso with the US dollar. Borne by a multiplicity of social actors, ranging from the Argentinean middle class, loudly expressing their resentment about the freezing of their savings in *cacerolazos* ('pot-banging demonstrations'), to the unemployed people of various *piqueteros* groups and their specific forms of action (street barricades, collective meals, parades, etc.), the movements found their point of unification especially in the demand *¡Que se vayan todos!* ('All of them should go!') (Colectivo Situaciones, 2003). This demand had some measure of success, at least in the form of a whole series of resignations of respectively appointed state presidents at the end of 2001 and beginning or 2002.

What primarily interests me here is less a detailed discussion of the events in Argentina in December 2001 (see also Moreno, 2005) than a close observation of the motifs that the militant research of Colectivo Situaciones sees in them (and in which they took part): the motif of destitution or the deposing, destituting insurrection. What is striking about this motif in the analysis of Colectivo Situaciones is certainly that it dissolves the link between the destituting movement and the specific institutive gesture, which ties the deposition or disempowerment of the ruling political forces a priori to the political purpose or end of a re-institution, a renewed institution and occupation of the – even if possibly reformed – organs of the exercise of power in the sense of governing:

> The sovereign and creative forces incited a rebellion, to which they tied no intentions of instituting power – as it is anticipated by the political doctrine of sovereignty –, but instead exercised their power to depose the established political forces. This is probably the paradox of the days of 19 and 20 December. An entirety of instituting forces far removed from founding a new sovereign order, which instead delegitimized the politics carried out in their names. (Colectivo Situaciones, 2003: 35)

At first glance, this suspension of the institutive end appears as a pause at exactly the point that is capable of evoking the political *horror vacui* par excellence: an abhorrence of the vacuum of political power and its functions of founding laws and social order. The political effects of this *horror vacui* are numerous: they range from the legitimization figures of an authoritarian, sometimes putschist power of order over the attempt to prevent the emergence of this kind of vacuum (invoking the specter of ungovernability, alleviating social tensions, pushing security doctrines, etc.), all the way to the themes, dominant in the history of leftist political theory, of possible (new) ways to fill this vacuum (revolutionary takeover of power, renewal of the legal systems, institutional apparatuses, governing techniques, etc.). The latter lead back to the initially mentioned configuration of the question "What do we do with what we have done?" which subsequently interprets the 'vacuum' simply as a 'break' – in other words, to the configuration that is specifically undermined by the motif of destituting power.

However, the vacuum is only a vacuum to the extent that it is measured against the aforementioned functions of political power and the representation of political 'subjects' linked to them. Relying on the described *horror vacui* in analyzing destitution decoupled from re-institution would hence mean identifying the question of the political or political power with just these functions, specifically by disregarding a social positivity, which I would like to call political appearance here. Yet it is precisely this question of political appearance – especially under the name of 'social protagonism' – that concerns the Colectivo Situaciones:

> Destitution is a process of the greatest significance: if the politics previously carried out by a sovereign power is realized in the state constitution of the social, the destituting action appears to be a different form of conducting politics or expressing social transformation. Destitution holds no a-political stance: the refusal to maintain representative politics (of sovereignty) is the condition – and the premise – of a 'situational' thinking and of all the practices, whose potentials for meaning can no longer be demanded from the state. (Colectivo Situaciones, 2003: 36)

The "practice of destitution that expands the field of the possible" can thus be linked "with conducting social protagonism that is not limited to the functions of founding sovereignty" (Colectivo Situaciones, 2003: 36) and gives expression to the aforementioned potentials of meaning outside the realm of the figures of state representation. From this perspective, as the research of the Colectivo Situaciones shows, not only can demonstrations, neighborhood assemblies, barter practices or new forms of political organization be analyzed, but also looting, for example. To the extent that one is willing to abandon the view linked with the *horror vacui* described above, which makes the mere fact of looting appear exclusively as (ultimately abstract) evidence for the 'war of all against all' in the absence of a state power of order, looting shows itself to be an ambivalent network of social agency permeated by differences and linked with gestures of self-constraint.[1]

Yet other political-social struggles can also be regarded from the same perspective of a social protagonism, such as the struggle of the Sans-Papiers, which is situated exactly on one of the central intersections of state political representation, namely that of coupling political citizenship with belonging to a (nation-) state. Not only would it be obviously absurd to understand migrants without papers as a 'revolutionary subject' of the type seeking to take over power in some form, but the struggles of the Sans Papiers can also not be reduced to fighting for inclusion in the existing apparatuses of political representation – unless one disregards the structural zone of intersection between the (juridical, economic, etc.) *dispositifs* of the nation-state and its supra-national extensions as well as the *dispositifs* of the globalized economies and politics engendering new dependencies and forms of exploitation, in which these struggles are located and which are made manifest by them. Destitution is expressed here in practices of 'becoming invisible' (in the face of state powers of control), which are linked with specific knowledge productions and networks of social agency, as well as in new forms of political organization and the affirmation of a newly conceived political situationality.

Let us note three moments of the concept and the practice of destitution as demonstrated here, which may shed a somewhat clearer light on the notion of political appearance at the same time:

1. First, the concept of destitution is to be detached from a certain dialectical grid, which may appear obvious at first glance: it is not the 'work of negativity' that is centrally effective in destitution, but rather a 'positive no' (Colectivo Situaciones, 2003), which in the rejection of a certain figure of representation simultaneously – and not first through taking over or influencing to change institutional political functions –

produces a 'self-changing' affirmation that engenders new practices and modes of subjectification, from which the 'no' first derives its force. Understood in this way, destitution is neither a deposition relating to the purpose or end of a re-institution of the fullness of power, nor simply a rejection in the sense of a disinvolvement, but rather indicates, first of all, a social practice.

The motif is not entirely new, even though it arrives at a new topicality in the contexts described. It is one of the central motifs in Walter Benjamin's 1921 essay 'On the Critique of Violence', specifically in the form of the question of the positivity of the strike. More precisely, Benjamin distinguishes the 'proletarian general strike' from the 'political general strike;' the latter merely seeks to achieve ends that are external to labor and to one's own action, and which thus achieves no transformation of labor and action. The proletarian general strike, on the other hand, eludes, according to Benjamin, the 'dialectical rising and falling' in the historical political 'formations of violence' continued through law-making and law-preserving, because it is like "an upheaval that this kind of strike not so much causes as consummates" (Benjamin, 1978: 292). The logic of action described here is that of a de-position, which is not oriented a priori to framework conditions of action modified for a performative new positing or re-institution, but rather to the opening of a field of changing possibilities for action (Hammacher, 1994: 360).

2. In all of this, however, a misunderstanding is to be avoided, which frequently occurs in social romantic form, grounded, however, in a certain – often Spinozist-influenced – variation of metaphysical natural law theory conceptions: the misunderstanding that the described affirmation is already necessarily emancipatory per se. The book by Colectivo Situaciones is not entirely free from this itself, yet it supplies clear evidence for the problems that are linked with a perspective of this kind:

> The most diverse slogans could be heard, first in the city districts of Buenos Aires, then in the Plaza de Mayo. 'Anyone who doesn't skip along is an Englishman'. – 'Anyone who doesn't skip along is a military'. Or 'Traitors to the fatherland against the wall'. 'Cavallo – you are a pig'. – 'Argentina, Argentina'. And the cry most frequently heard on 19 December: 'You can stick the state of emergency up yours'. And later the first *Que se vayan todos*. The potpourri of demo slogans made

the struggles of the past newly manifest in the present. (Colectivo Situaciones, 2003: 27)

And it is not difficult to recognize that with these struggles of the past, the nationalisms and chauvinisms of the past also reappear. Not only is the indeterminacy of the affirmation in the destituent movement, as a "collective affirmation of the possible" (Colectivo Situaciones, 2003: 28), open to very different codings, it is also borne by ambivalences and historical political structurings of affect, which are by no means emancipatory per se or a purely rebellious present (just as little as they engender pure violent chaos, as the other – in short, Hobbesian – variation of natural law theory imaginaries would claim). Instead, they are permeated by re-actualizations of political and probably also personal 'struggles of the past', which underlay that which is possible with a pre-formed reality and – literally – reactionary facilitations.

3. It thus seems all the more important to pay attention to the difference that the texts cited above introduce into a series of political concepts: they speak of 'sovereign and creative forces', which do not seek, however, to found a 'new sovereign order'; of 'instituent forces', although these are not linked with 'instituting intentions'. We can certainly come to an understanding about this difference that appears in the terminology, based on the difference between *potentia* and *potestas* that is currently frequently cited in political theory. In the following, however, the focus is on the question of the institution or instituting, the virulence of which has an obvious connection to the motif that was the starting point for these reflections: the motif of destitution and its relation to an expansion of the 'field of the possible'.

Destitution as Destruction: Subject Condition, Subjectification and the Question of Instituent Activity

Let us first consider a meaning of the concept of destitution that appears to be diametrically opposed to the one discussed so far. In the final section of his book *Remnants of Auschwitz*, Giorgio Agamben outlines an interpretation of the modalities of possibility (to be able to be), contingency (to be able not to be), impossibility (not to be able to be), and necessity (not to be able not to be), which detaches these modalities from their classical roots in logic and ontology, relating them to a theory of subjectivity. Agamben reads the first two – possibility and contingency – as 'operators of subjectification'. In contrast, "impossibility, as negation of possibility [...] and necessity, as negation of contingency [...], are the operators of de-subjectification, of the destruction and destitution of the subject" (Agamben, 1999: 147). Agamben takes over the concept of destitution from Primo Levi, who spoke of the experience of 'extreme destitution' (*destituzione estrema*) in the Nazi death and concentration camps. Here it means anything but a deposing power; instead it characterizes an impotence that is not simply the absence of any capacity, but rather the experience of the annihilating separation of the subject from his or her executive capacities, experience of de-subjectification reaching to the limit of the capacity for experience:

> [Possibility and contingency] constitute Being in its subjectivity, that is, in the final analysis as a world that is always my world, since it is in my world that possibility exists and touches (*contingit*) the real. Necessity and impossibility, instead, define Being in its wholeness and solidity, pure substantiality without subject – that is, at the limit, a world that is never my world since possibility does not exist in it. (Agamben, 1999: 147, trans. modified)

It is hardly necessary to say that a world, which is only my world to the extent that possibility exists in it, is also the only world that is open to change, a world in which 'another world' is possible. However, it is also a world that is principally in danger of being set up as 'pure substantiality', which annihilates every possibility.

Agamben's considerations do not at all seek to re-establish classical subject theory conceptions. Instead they explore a thinking – from the extreme of its annihilation – of living subjectivity, which is only a different name for a historically politically situated capacity of subjectification, a "a field of forces always already traversed by the [...] historically determined currents of potentiality and impotentiality, of being able not to be and not being able not to be" (Agamben, 1999: 147). This capacity of subjectification is exposed to the condition of a fundamental passivity, in which its specific possibilities and the capacity of expanding these possibilities are grounded, in which, however, also its seizure, its injury and its boundless destruction are located (cf. Blanchot, 1969: 200; and Kofman, 1987).[2] It is exactly at this point that the theory of testimony is located, which Agamben develops in conjunction with the passages quoted and based on a specific interpretation of the problem of linguistic reference as verbally actualized contingency and touching the real. A detailed discussion of this theory is not possible here; I limit myself to referring to the conjunction between the possibility of testimony and that of resistance, which is implicitly at stake in it.[3]

What is crucial for the considerations developed here is that the concept of destitution, which previously appeared as destituent power, as a name for a capacity of subjectification – releasing the possible – now indicates a subject condition, which exposes every capacity for subjectification not only to negation or 'alienated' representation, but also the extreme of its systematic annihilation. In fact, Agamben's analysis does not relate simply to the counterpart of 'representative politics' in a sense that might be situational but is also capable of generalization in many respects, but rather to the institutional apparatus of an industrialized politics of annihilation that directly takes hold of those it persecutes, a politics that eludes any generalization. It is a politics that nevertheless undoubtedly mobilized its own – predominantly anti-Semitic – figures of representation and never carried out its work of annihilation independently from strategies of symbolic annihilation. What destitution means in the experience of the Nazi camps is, in Adorno's words, "worse than death" (1975: 364), namely the disintegration of subjective existence with the mobilization of all institutional power.

Ultimately, however, the situational is not decided by what is capable of generalization, but rather by what is 'generally valid' in a different sense: namely by what, in every situation, can be actualized or robbed of its possibilities of actualization.[4] The problem that Agamben's analysis poses is thus, after all, that of the interlocking of the double meaning of 'institution' (as a function of political representation, setting up the scope of the possible, regulating, constraining, managing it – and still managing it in the will to annihilation – on the one hand and as 'instituent practice' on the other) with the double meaning of 'destitution' (as the release of a 'field of the possible' and as the destruction of the – always contingent – possibility of subjectification as such). Institution and destitution, also in this sense, are by no means in a relationship of a dialectical opposition, the opposition, for example, that has long made insurrection appear as an irresolvable problem of political juridical theory (Nowotny, 2003b). Rather, what should be presumed is a relationship of complex implications, which opens up the field of political struggles and, to return to our initial theme, makes an instituent moment that is not an end manifest in the midst of the destituent insurrection.

Despite the apparent conceptual opposition, destitution as 'destituent power' would thus yield the outlines of an instituent activity, which is emancipatorily different from the institutional apparatuses that limit the field of the possible and which, incidentally, perhaps cannot be grasped with – here largely omitted – conceptualizations of 'constitution'. In this sense, talk of 'instituent forces' (Colectivo Situaciones, 2003) is not to be over hastily regarded as an example of a 'new constitution of the multitude' (Negri, 2007), but rather to be taken literally. It is possible that the reason for the frequently lamented poverty of political (and not only immediately political) institutions is specifically that the function of institutions has almost always been regarded as dependent on a constitution in the sense of an antecedent composition. And this may also be the reason why the opposition of constituent and constituted power, which undoubtedly seeks to undermine the antecedence of the composition, results in a practical paradox – that of the permanently 'constituting republic' (Negri, 2003) – that leaves little scope for a new understanding of the institution or the instituent. At this point, however, it might be possible to attempt a re-conception of the instituent, which would not ignore the critique of the institutional and the power of destitution described above, but would instead focus on a positivity of the instituent action against this background.

In his lectures at the Collège de France in 1954/55, devoted to the question of instituting/institution, Maurice Merleau-Ponty placed the concept of the institution not in a hierarchical functional conjunction with the concept of the constitution, but rather in opposition to it. Merleau-Ponty's reflections start from a critique of the philosophy of consciousness, which remains inscribed in the language in which these reflections are formulated; nevertheless, they can certainly also be read in the sense of the thinking of the capacity for subjectification outlined above, and explicitly aim, not least of all, for a thinking of subjectivity in its political social historicity:

> Yet if the subject is instituent, not constituent, then one can understand that it is not limited to its momentary being and that the other is not the negative of my self. What I have started at certain crucial moments, is neither in a distant past as an objective memory, nor is it current as a

lived memory, but is found instead in this in-between realm [*l'entre-deux*] like the field of my becoming during this period of time. Hence my relationship to others could not be reduced to an alternative: an instituent subject can co-exist with an other, because that which is instituted is not the immediate reflection of its actions. This can be taken up again subsequently by itself or by others without being a complete re-creation. In this way it is like a hinge between the others and me, on the one hand, and between me and my self, on the other, as consequence and guarantee of our belonging to the world. (Merleau-Ponty, 2003: 123)

It seems that it is this kind of shared field of becoming that is meant – translated into the language of the political – in the question quoted in the beginning, "What do we do with what we have done?" which the power of destitution aims to open up, and whose potentials of meaning cannot be redeemed by the figures of existing institutional structures. It may become visible in events such as those of 19 and 20 December 2001, and yet it does not exist independently from an instituent activity that is not completed in these events and does not end with them.

Notes

1. As one mother, whose son was involved in looting a butcher shop, relates: "My son said that some of them first went to work on the cash register. So he threw the cash register on the floor so that the others could not get to the money, but should only take the food that they needed. Then a fight started and my son left. But first he took food for all of us and even brought some cheese" (Colectivo Situaciones, 2003: 107).

2. At the same time, at the theoretical level Agamben's thinking is permanently in discussion with a 'certain vitalism' in post-structural theory construction, evident for example in Foucault and Deleuze, which refutes every substantialization of 'life', only to see in this concept, nevertheless, the cipher of immanent processes of subjectification (self-affection: 'self'-actualization and 'self'-effectuation).

3. This is a conjunction that was already prefigured by Ferdinand Bruckner in 1933, in his drama *Die Rassen* (Bruckner, 1990: 418): "Helene It is our only paltry resistance, – / Karlanner (nods) You fight. / Helene – that nothing is covered up, that all testimonies remain preserved." The scope of this conjunction, which calls for a break in the understanding of testimony after Auschwitz, was hardly to be foreseen in 1933.

4. Cf. the distinction between the precondition of a 'capability of generalization' of (just) ends by law, which abstracts from situationality, and situation-specific 'general validity' as criterion of justice in Walter Benjamin's writing (1978); this distinction should also be noted by all those who, with critical intentions or not, attribute to Agamben the claim that the entire contemporary world is a Nazi camp.

20

Towards New Political Creations: Movements, Institutions, New Militancy

Raúl Sánchez Cedillo

(Translated by Maribel Casas-Cortés and Sebastian Cobarrubias)

A set of recurrent symptoms is forcing us to imagine, remember, project and build institutions. Particular dates and events can guide us as a compass in understanding the necessity of institutional construction: 1 January 1994, the day the EZLN rose up in arms against the Mexican government and against world-wide neo-liberal power. More than thirteen years have already passed since that event marked a way out from what Félix Guattari called the 'years of winter'. Slightly less distant are the days of Genoa, 20-22 July 2001, which, without a doubt, marked an inflection point in the capacity of political creation/creativity of the so called movement of movements. The declaration of war on the movement by the G8 (through the Berlusconi administration) and, during the same year, the instauration of the regime of global war after September 11, closed the democratic political space that the global movement was building since its 'foundational' moment, on 30 September 1999 in Seattle. As we know, the movement against the war in Iraq was qualified by the *New York Times* as the 'world's second superpower'. This time, though, it was about the potential of public opinion, a new pole of influence within the 'democracies of opinion', that is to say, a domesticated and neutralized potential. This was six years ago, and the *in nuce* political space that the movements were prefiguring – currently maintained by only a few experiments such as the Euromayday process – seems to be closing in leaps and bounds. This closure has been even more pronounced since the rejection by French and Dutch voters of the European Constitutional Treaty, paradoxically reinforcing the undemocratic, purely confederal and inter-

223

governmental character of the process of European construction, Sarkozy *docet*.

The consequences of this closure of political space are political impotence, organizational weakness and the dispelling of subjectivity – or, said in another way, the crisis of subjectivity production, a crisis of its consistency and self-organization. Those seem to be the central traits of the current crisis of the movement form in the European territory. This translates itself into an incapacity, in the first place, to build local and regional struggles that can express force relationships. For example, specific struggles in the terrain of the precarization both of salary and social rights; and more generally, struggles against the emergent form of governance intimately linked to the general mobilization of society as a production machine, to workfare and to warfare, which nowadays inform the current 'social policies' and labor relations in the continent whose center of gravity is the European Union.

Departing from these brief notes on the current 'conjuncture', what use or heuristic potential is offered by the creation and/or replacement/destruction of institutions? There is indeed some use for reflection on institutions, especially if we are able to simultaneously circumscribe concrete problems to concrete and current situations and situate ourselves within the large quantity of critique and theory focused on contemporary institutions in the current conjuncture. This conjuncture is marked by the neutralization of the constituent power of social movements. It is also situated in a context where life is equally political and productive, in such a way that it is only formally possible to establish distinctions between the process of politicization of individual and collective lives on the one hand, and the matrixes of a new productive power (outside and/or against measures of value). That is to say, from the point of view of the capacity of capture and control over cooperative singularities, the technologies and mechanisms of networked biopower are only capable of dictating sequences of economic value in accordance with a social relationship among subjects, among creative individuals who are able to influence each other, to exercise power over each other, (and thus to change their own attitude), in accordance with mobile relationships and within an open notion of space-time. These criteria are marked by the generalized market of all forms of life, which is also a decisive dimension of the project, within which all the competencies of the subject should be concatenated in order to obtain the goals of self-valorization.

In this sense, the individual (as a form) as well as its relationships, interactions, experiences, etc. becomes essential for this neo-liberal ontology of production and of government. It is possible to pose the following hypothesis: for this productive individual, the current regime of war – as a constitutive element of her/his own vital world- works in two ways. The war regime, within the concrete parameters of different levels of life stability, works both as a pile of risks and uncertainties, as a deficit of information, of fear and hope, as well as an incentive for its own performance within the productive network of total social mobilization, as a constant confirmation of the finitude and fragility of his/her own project.

Thus, an active selection of available tools and experiences becomes necessary. Let's make an effort to orient ourselves. Let's start by delimiting what we are referring to with the notion of 'institution' itself. I think the theme of institutions is of crucial and extraordinary relevance in its relationship with the problem of social and thus political counter-powers, with the project of a network of counter-powers able to bear a discontinuous and unpredictable dynamic proper of constituent exodus happening within the complex device of capitalism-governance-war. What does this active selection imply? As was mentioned before, it would chiefly imply a radical distancing from the contents and goals of previous periods, contexts and projects of institutional critique and require the imagining of a new world of libratory institutions. It becomes evident that, outside of the conditions of contextualization and situation discussed earlier, we run the risk of inventing a new environment from scratch, separated and isolated from the problems of conflict, organization, subjectivity production and counter-power in new social movements. We run the risk then of making a virtue out of a necessity. We run the risk of using a generic reference such as 'institutions' to cover the emptiness that critical practices hate or religiously adore, as well as to conceal the solid neutralization of the political space currently afoot within the European territory.

Institutions, *da capo*

Let's come back to the term. Let's depart from the extremely problematic notions of *institutio* and *instituere*. The term *institutio* refers to a foundation and a plan, a project, an elaborated intention, while *instituere* means to prepare, to arrange, to establish, but also to organize something that already exists, and to form and to instruct. These meanings are without a doubt quite generic; however they are interesting in order to productively focus on the question. The goal is to depart from the epistemic and political imaginary blockage that arises with the 'question of institutions', which includes references (images or icons sometimes) as serious as the state apparatus, as well as institutions such as school, prison, hospital, political parties, museums and other public infrastructures. In this way, we can get out, at least for a moment, to the open air offered by *instituere* and the instituent.

Gilles Deleuze offers a series of simple and stark considerations about the creative, positive and affirmative dimensions of generating institutions, in contrast with the law, with the violence of the norm. These considerations are written in a brief piece, linked to his work on David Hume, called 'Instincts and Institutions' (in Deleuze, 2004a: 19-21). According to Deleuze, on the one hand, institution and instinct share the search for satisfying tendencies and necessities; and on other hand, they distinguish themselves in the moment that the institution works as an organized system of means for satisfaction, an institutional means that is able to a priori determine social modalities that frame individual experiences. Institutions are, in contrast with laws, the main structures where the social is invented, where an affirmative and not limiting or exclusivist know-how is produced.

In this way, we are able to get beyond the exclusive fixation on the object of 'institutions' in its meanings used by other trains of thoughts and by critical practices, from the dialectics of the inauthentic and the alienated essence that even today inform some Situationist and neo-Situationsist positions, as well as the institutional critique defended by the circles of art and 'artivism', to the analysis of disciplinary institutions, including its diagram power-resistances (psychiatric ward, hospital, prison, school) linked to the 'apparently' more 'politicized' period of Michel Foucault's work and public life. But we know there are 'other' Foucaults. The later Foucault, mainly developed and lived in the North American territories (USA and Canada), offers us notes full of inspiration, even in reference to the question of institutional creation. The emergence of the themes around techniques of the self and its relationship with governmentality, and with the technologies of the government of populations, is intimately linked to Foucault's own experience and close relation to the minorities of desire and their political as well as academic expressions, from the late 1970's until his death (Lazzarato, 2006b).

In studying contemporary neo-liberalism, Foucault discovers a self-limitation practice on the part of government, a critique of the *raison d'etat* which is internal to the very problematic of 'governmentality'. The condition of this self-limitation practice is the definition of an absolute reference: 'society', in which populations are inserted. Within society it is possible to discover of dynamics self-organization, processes that are autonomous in relation to governmental interventions; to the point that excessive interventionism on the part of the sate, the proliferation of unnecessary legal interventions, may contribute to the failure of the very same goals defended by the problematic of governmentality.

Institutions and Movement: The 'Great Tactic'

Let's get back now to our own contemporary problems and ask ourselves about the following question: to what degree is an institutionalization process able to positively displace a neutralized political space? That is to say: could a concrete recognition and specific work on the issues of institutional formation be a relevant factor to support movements, and strengthen struggles against the regime of cognitive capitalism and against the regime of war/state of emergency, regimes that are informing the current system of governance both at the global and European levels? Before trying to provide a temporary answer to that question, we could look for inspiration in perspectives working on this issue, produced in the initial moments of the movements that followed the 'existential revolution' of 1968. This is the case in a text by Antonio Negri's work dedicated to the critical – fatal, in retrospect – period of the social proletarian movement in Italy in the late 1970s. This urgent, preemptory and practically unknown piece was submitted for publication from prison after the blitzkrieg attack of the Italian state on 7 April 1979. The piece was called *Class Politics: Five Campaigns* (Negri, 1980).

The situation at the time was one of total crisis of the different Italian autonomous political structures and perspectives. However, the text in question tried to interpret the crisis as a possibility for a total renewal of the movement, as a break with old and alien facades, tools, discourses and institutions, used by the political structures of the new movement. It attempted to grasp the crisis beyond the terms of 'autonomy from the political', beyond 'the worse the better' enunciated by terrorist groups, and beyond the catastrophic positions of capitalist elites. Negri's approach to the crisis as a creative crisis was based on a project of political mediation, both internal as well as external to the new movement, as a project of building its own similar and friendly political space.

According to Negri, the problem to be resolved consisted of breaking with the quagmire proper of the social counter-powers produced by the movement in a symmetric, purely military, relationship. This relationship was also 'dialectic', that is to say, dependent on the initiative of capital and the party system, especially in regards to spaces and times of conflict. Behind this approach, it is possible to see the difficulty of imagining a 'transition' outside the frameworks, deformed ones, of a Leninist-Bolshevik 'seizure of power'. Negri looked for this 'transition' in the exercise of collective effort (normative production by movements and the capacity to impose it), as well as in the deployment of inventive potential, and the potential of cooperating in common in the process of social transformation. The combination of both, the exercise of power and the transformation of ways of life, liberation of production and of singularities, was presented as an insolvable puzzle.

For Negri, the solution to this puzzle would come from the side of institutional dimensions – that is to say, from the new forms of productive cooperation used by the social proletariat, oriented towards expressing the power of freedom as well as of individual and collective enjoyment, both always expansive and open. This is what Negri calls 'communist production'. These new forms of cooperation are inseparable from the invention of a 'proletarian entrepreneurship', understood as the defining/determining of institutional creation.

In this way we arrive at what we could call an antagonistic use of Schumpeter's 'creative destruction' in the realms of the self-valorization by proletarian subjects and the creation of institutions as means of self-organization of those very same processes. The operator of this institutionality is, according to Negri, negative work.

The definitive defeat of the movements both of the social proletariat and of the minorities of desire during the 1980s, in Italy as well as Europe in general, paralleled the processes by which social life (material production and the production of subjectivity) was then being fully subsumed under the logic of capital, severely undermining traditional identities linked to labor. Despite that defeat, it would be difficult to refute the validity and urgency of Negri's proposal for "building, within the social, centers of alternative and independent *projectuality*, communities of negative labor, completely free and antagonistic towards the planning and programming of the reproduction of power of control." This is then the inspirational force of the approach towards institutional building as an element of a 'big tactic' of reformulation of contemporary anti-systemic movements and their political potential.

No one is unaware of the complicated (in the anthropological, ethical, political sense) status of the new labor force – cooperative, cognitive, relational and affective – born out of the conjunction of these diverse historical processes. Some of these incommensurable processes extend from the rejection of the Fordist labor by anti-systemic movements of the 1960s to the post-Fordist restructuring of society from the early 1980s on, and even from the impulse of massive schooling before and after 1968 in Europe to the new precarious subjects whose living labor is mainly cognitive, relational and affective. These are processes whose concomitant efficiency have, not without catastrophic results, produced a hybrid and monstrous species, definitely distant from the organic framework of capitalist modernity, as well as from the emancipatory counter-models of alternative modernity, including radical liberalism or socialism.

Nowadays, the identity crisis around labor mentioned above, confuses this identity with an individual's life/vital activity, poses a series of additional problems to the design of institutional restructuring. The notion of negative labor used by Negri, the self-valorization practices used by proletarian subjects needed of a temporal, rigidly dualist, and transitional dimension for the development of communist capacities on the part of all those exploited subjects, working towards the self-determination of such subjects. In contrast to this, though, living labor today is a priori presented as multiplicity, and the deployment of common cooperative capacities is inseparable from the process of singularization of each of its operators. However, it is precisely from this process that new models have emerged, new agents of enunciation consistent with other machinations and developments of knowledge, political cooperation and enunciation. Ex post facto, it is possible to draw a counter-genealogy, a diagram and program of those combinations, emphasizing their discontinuities of subjectification, of re-appropriation of cooperative nexuses and of the creation of new political machines. This is the case with various experiences in different parts of Europe. These experiences have desired to transform their communicative, relational, formative, creative lives, into a political life. That is to say, a life made of an interface between singularity and commonality. This is the case of institutions such as squatted/occupied social centers; the political forms of global activism; internet use and the inverted juridical engineering of copyleft licenses and hacker cooperatives; and action-research groups and networks that are starting to grow within the (precarious) interstices of a university system in crisis and undergoing almost definitive restructuring.

This is why the institutionalization of the movement is proposed as a means, of course. However it is a means towards self-determination, the free constitution of individual and collective subjectivity departing from a re-appropriation of the conditions of production and reproduction of the self.

It should be said that this institutional revolution is inseparable from the ability to express counter-powers. This is to say, the capacity to carry out a metropolitan strike against the total productive mobilization of the populations. Is it possible to think about defeating the regime of war/exception/emergency outside of this capacity to exercise a collective and ethically regulated potential against the violence proper of the total mobilization of the metropolis? This kind of strike is only feasible as a result of trial and error, of material processes of composition and cooperation, of multilateral networking among the multiplicities that nowadays constitute metropolitan living labor in an irreversible way.

Institution as a Political-productive Machine and Existential Territory: For the Immediate Present

However, the *ex ante* multiplicity of forms of life and figures of living labor do not directly imply an antagonistic value, nor an automatic resistance to the production of forms of life subsumed by the capitalist circuit of imitation and differentiation. Our problem is precisely one of the consistency and resistance to the lamination of the production of political subjectivities, as well as its coefficients of transversality, its disposition towards an experience of metamorphosis. In order to analyze this problem adequately, we need a much richer concept of subjectivity production than those that are circulating among most political groups and movements. The most common concepts currently in circulation avoid contrasting the forms of subjectivity compatible with total productive mobilization, with pre- and trans-personal terrains. Additionally, they render invisible many everyday life experiences in which impulses of freedom and transformation are lived within the microphysical registers of perception, affect and the *agencements* of 'non-significant' enunciation. These are experienced by each subject in his/her relations within the productive and communicative networks that constitute the material and machinic support of the so-called 'cooperation among brains' (Lazzarato, 2006a).

Félix Guattari (1995) offers a formal definition of subjectivity production related to what he calls the procedure of 'meta-modelization'. This refers to a theoretical discursivity capable of reaching the maximum number of ontological descriptions or cartographies, saving the inherent pluralism of the cartographic practice. This allows us to trespass established domains and to avoid the anti-productive restrictions of legality in each of the paradigms in dispute (Guattari, 1995). For Guattari, subjectivity is an effect of the consistence and existence of the agglomeration of entities that we can map according to four ontological functions: material and semiotic flows; concrete and abstract machines that work on those flows, the embodied universes of reference and adjacent value to each *agencements* of subjectification; and, last but not least, the existential territories marked by their precarity and finitude. These are the decisive elements in contemporary subjectivity production, and this is why they are in the center of the problematics of resistance and autonomy in new political creations. This subjectivity production, insofar as it is oriented towards rupture and battle against its capture, control and exploitation on the part of the mechanisms of new forms of capitalism, should be up to the task of being able to 'navigate' regimes of signs, and capitalist semiotics. This semiotics, in which one 'swims' and 'bathes', are concatenated in pragmatic montages, in straight-up capitalist agencies and institutions of enunciation. They saturate and distort efforts of both individual and collective singularization.

We may ask ourselves now: could the institution be a privileged site or topos for the production of non-controlled subjectivity, a topos which is also able to ethically treat that subjectivity and care for its consistency? And at the same time, would not this notion of institution imply its permanent openness, a condition of continuous process and self-critique, subordinated to the irruption of metamorphoses, by new *agencements* of enunciation and of life?

Experiences of institutions in this sense are not lacking. These experiences are intimately linked to the formation of cartographic tools of schizoanalysis and the coining of notions such as 'transversality' and 'group-subject'. Transversality is nowadays almost a requirement for technical use in group dynamics, in departments of human resources and so forth, although it goes without saying that these are a distortion of the original concept. We can blame this distortion in great measure on the 'systemic' and official diversion/drifting of the trend of institutional analysis, a problem of which Guattari was aware even during the same period when those notions were being elaborated. It is interesting, then, to remind ourselves that transversality "works in groups as a dimension which is both contrary to and complementary of structures that generate pyramidal hierarchies and transmission modes that sterilize messages" (Guattari, 1964).

The coining of terms such as transversality and group-subject happened in the midst of a political, institutional and existential adventure that is relatively well known. However, the particularity that the institutional invention supported by *bande à* Guattari created is not so well known. This invention intended to achieve the potential to politically act, think, write, intervene, and exit those apparatuses of capture of intellectual labor and political militancy. The most relevant and foundational experience of this domain of entrepreneurship for political minorities (minor politics) and subjectification was the CERFI (Centre de études, recherches et formation institutionnelles). According to François Fourquet, one of its founding members:

> It was founded in 1967 in order to finance, thanks to contracts for social research, the functioning of a federal organ, the FGERI (Fédération des groupes d'études et de recherches institutionnelles) [...] In contrast with the paralyzed apparati of the communist party and other leftist organizations, in contrast with those activists fascinated with and fooled by the hierarchies common to those organizations [...], it was about forming a new race of militants able to encourage, not a party, but a network of autonomous groups that would discuss among themselves and would act together. Also, these groups would be able to recognize and affirm their unconscious desires, the denial of which was, for us, the main cause of the political paralysis of many leftist factions. (Fourquet, 1981)

Another founding member, Anne Querrien, insists on the CERFI as an *agencement* of life for a small network of activist intellectuals and technicians. Today it is difficult to understand that a small group of radicals could achieve research contracts with French public ministries, with total freedom to do what they wanted. Those contracts allowed around twenty people to live, research and organize, and even to be in charge of 'analyzing' the very unconsciousness of the State at work with the 'advanced' civil servant with whom they dealt:

> In some way, the CERFI was about resisting our own tendency to become public employees, university members or part of a union's or political party's bureaucracy, [...] Our lives can be perceived as failures, but also as brief testimonies that resistance was possible. [...] Felix's and my own main hypothesis was that our institutional patrons were as schizophrenic as us, and that our schizoanalysis did not have to limit itself to the analysts' office, to the hospital walls or the interior of our group [...] In this sense we were neither inside nor outside power structures, we had a schizoanalytic relationship with several people on the inside of different structures of power that at the same time had relations among themselves. [...] The scale of our *tentatif* was too small to be able to last for a long period. The global context restructured power forces and our intellectual guerrilla may have merely contributed to reinforcing some countertendencies. (Querrien, 2002)

Today our challenge is to reinvent such gestures, impulses and modes of operating in the context of our current conditions. Our problem is very concrete: to transform those active minorities of intellectual and artistic labor into operators of a perspective capable of re-launching the movement.[1]

Above all it is about promoting those modalities of experimentation within those domains mentioned earlier. Those domains are related to capture of creative capacities by new forms of networked power, market institutions of cognitive capitalism and juridical structures of labor markets. Such creative potential is also captured by those modules or molds of subjective expression and identification inscribed within the new tendencies of the neo-liberal possessive individual, who is now creative, cooperative, owner of (fixed) capital which is itself inscribed mainly in her/himself, in his/her capacity for adaptation and discrimination among the possibilities offered by the market.

Another substantive problem to be resolved, according to my view, is that of forming real networks of political research, thinking and action. These networks would not be exclusive, identity-based, nor 'action-ist' nor 'campaign-ist'. Networks that would go beyond the banality of the 'new paradigm' and would passionately tackle the question of their own destructive and constitutive effectiveness. They would know how to generate and give birth to political and communicative war machines, suitable, finite and irreverent war machines.

It is time then for creating an (in many senses) unknown terrain of political invention, organization and growth. It is a terrain based on the self-organization and institutionalization of the collective production and processing of knowledges. We have also discussed that the very co-extensivity of such dynamic in regards to the networking of precarious collective intelligence allow us to do certain things. For example, to apply our forces, to form our recombination values in a variety of metropolitan territories, such as: from universities to social centers, and from museums and cultural agencies to peripheries in which there of plenty of groups and cooperatives of educators, social workers and intercultural mediators. The ethical and political subjectification of those spheres is a necessity and a task that is in our hands to carry out. Given that the path walked by different collectives (hackers, 'info-artists', independent musicians, interns/researchers, etc.) is long enough to be able to overcome astonishment we can move to putting a series of initiatives into practice to change the current tide: from the property-based offensive towards a recombination (in a public sphere yet to be created) of the communities of 'info-production', creation, research and education. It is about putting together an *'aguascalientes'*, a *'caracol'* formed out of the cooperation among brains.

In the final analysis it is about creating an instrument or way of doing things, that if not literally union-like, then at least one that is capable of promoting the care and guarantee of a new set of rights and the struggles against exploitation in cognitive capitalism. This would be done on the basis of an institutional collective enunciator that is both polyphonic as well as autonomous with respect to the institutions of cognitive capitalism and the capitalization of productive and aesthetic (producers of the sensitive) excess. This instrument would put into practice new prototypes of collective subjectification based on 'class' (so to speak) capable of including within that subjectivity all the multiplicity and heterogeneity of the new forces of contemporary living labor. This would be done from a perspective and promotion of the maximum existential singularity of each of its components. More precisely, the attempt is to impose the statute on the basis of the networks of cooperation, breaking in the first place, the individualization of cooperation with such institutions, which constitutes one of the primary means of vulnerability and division of collective intelligence. How? By imposing from the get go, negotiation and hiring/employment as a network of cooperation, finite, concrete, but open and political in its own definition.

The figures of the curator, of the intern and researcher in break speed competition in order to obtain their project or financing, the precarious worker who is employed intermittently on crappy little jobs in museums and cultural institutions: in a few months any of these figures may come back to the same museum or institution, but this time with the status of 'artist' or 'creative activist' with better or different work conditions. Faced with these practices, we are trying to impose collective hiring/contracting and autonomous management of resources on the part of the network of cooperation and artistic-intellectual-political work (that, let it be understood, should make the effort to build itself as a new type of institution, not a union, not a party, note a 'creative club', but a new political machine). In second place, we are trying to make all property common: all the products of the labor of networked collective intelligence, especially of those created by members of that particular network. Daily use, the legal battles around copyleft licenses and the disputes and negotiations with operators of art and knowledge institutions over the privatization of such products are other elements of this new 'charter of rights under permanent drafting'. We could imagine that from this type of panorama of the precarization of subjectification and political organization of 'immaterial' living labor in the European metropolitan regions we could see a significant swerve in favor of the 'monstrous' return of class struggle and constitution (always multitudinous) of the commons in the coming years.

Notes

1. See Vercauteren (2007), who constructs schizoanalytic theoretical tools from the practice of militant groups, based on ten years of common work and collective experience with new movements in Belgium.

21

Mental Prototypes and Monster Institutions:
Some Notes by Way of an Introduction

Universidad Nómada

(Translated by Nuria Rodríguez)

Mental Prototypes

For quite a while now, a certain portmanteau word has been circulating in the Universidad Nómada's[1] discussions, in an attempt to sum up what we believe should be one of the results of the critical work carried out by the social movements and other post-socialist political actors. We talk about creating new mental prototypes for political action. This is due to the importance, in our eyes, of the elusive and so often unsuccessful link between cognitive diagrams and processes of political subjectivation. That is, the link between the knowledge that allows powers and potentials to be tested, on one hand, and, on the other, the semiotic, perceptual and emotional mutations that lead to the politicization of our lives, become personified in our bodies, and shape the finite existential territories that are channeled into or become available for political antagonism. We believe there is a need to create new mental prototypes because contemporary political representations, as well as many of the institutions created by the emancipatory traditions of the twentieth century, should be subjected to a serious review – at the very least – given that, in many cases, they have become part of the problem rather than the solution.

In this respect, the anniversary of the 1968 world revolution – an unavoidable reference given the month in which we are writing this text – shouldn't be used as an excuse to wallow in amorphous nostalgia for the passing of the 'age of revolutions'. Just the opposite – it should be used to demonstrate the extent to which some of the unsuitable signs of

237

that world revolution are still present in a latent state, or, to be more precise, in a state of 'frustrated virtuality'. '68' interests us because, even though it didn't come out of the blue, it was an unforeseeable world event – a historical fork in the road that left a trail of new political creations in a great many different parts of the world. Ultimately, it motivates us because its unresolved connections and even its caricatures allow us to consider the problem of the politicization (and metamorphosis) of life as a monstrous intrusion of the unsuitable into history (the history of capitalist modernity and postmodernity).[2]

Over the last forty years this latency has been subject to a series of quite significant emergences. The latest and perhaps most important, the one that is generationally closest to us, is the one in which the 'movement of movements', or the global movement, played a central role. But in spite of its extraordinary power, it hasn't always been fruitful enough in terms of generating the 'mental prototypes' that we believe are so necessary. At least, it's not clear that it has been able to produce prototypes that are sophisticated, robust and complex enough to generate innovative and sustained patterns of political subjectivation and organization that make it possible to at least attempt a profound transformation of command structures, daily life and the new modes of production.[3] We've decided to avoid a merely speculative approach, and to remain as far as possible from declarations of how the political forms of the movements 'should-be'; rather, we try to present a series of experimentations – not to exemplify, but more in the manner of case studies, as experiences that are being tested in practice – that are currently trying to overcome the predicaments and shortfalls that we've just mentioned.

The Universidad Nómada believes there is an urgent need to identify the differentiating features and the differentials of political and institutional innovation that exist in specific experimentations. We've chosen to place the emphasis on two aspects that implicitly constitute the two transversal themes for this diverse compilation of texts, namely: (a) we give preference to metropolitan forms of political intervention, specifically looking at one of their most frequently recurring figures – social centers; by this, we don't mean to lay claim to social centers as fossilized forms or political artefacts with an essentialized identity, but to try and explore the extent to which the 'social center form' today points the way to processes of opening up and renewal (Kurnik and Beznec, 2008), producing, for example, innovative mechanisms for the enunciation of (and intervention in) the galaxy of the precariat; and at the same time, and partially intertwining with the above; (b) the constitution of self-education networks that are developing in – and perhaps result from? – the crisis of Europe's public university system.[4] Ultimately, 'Europe', not as a naturalized space for political intervention, but as a constituent process; the production of these mental prototypes and mechanisms of enunciation and intervention as an instituent process (Salvini, 2008).

Social Centers as 'Bodies Without Organs'

For a long time, and in many cases still today, squatted social centers (*Centros Sociales Okupados* in Spanish) have used the abbreviation CSO or CSOA (the 'a' stands for '*autogestionados*', or 'self-managed') as a differentiating element in the public sphere, as a kind of semiotic marker of the radical nature of their project. And inevitably, some of us who participated in them were bound to notice the virtuous coincidence between this label and the Spanish for Deleuze and Guattari's 'body without organs', 'Cuerpo sin Organos' or CsO, using it to try to imagine and put into practice the un-thought and un-spoken virtualities that we believe are present in the matrix of metropolitan social centers. The considerations found in the different articles in this transversal/transform dossier are heading in that same direction, that is, they point towards the ongoing reinvention of an institutional mechanism (a form of movement institution) that has already proven its validity and, in a certain sense, its irreversibility in terms of the politics of the subaltern subjects in the metropolis. But this doesn't mean that the irreversible validity arises from a stable, self-referential, identical 'social center form' that remains always the same as itself, but just the opposite, as set out in one of the collective texts included in this monograph (Carmona et al., 2008).

Perhaps we could speak of the need to counteract the solidification of the 'social center form' through the production of 'unsuitable social centers', that is, projects of political and subjective creation based on specific powers of different configurations of the (political, cultural and 'productive') make-up of the basins of metropolitan cooperation. Creations that wouldn't therefore try to seal themselves off as autarkic rather than autonomous islands, but to transform the existing context in accordance with the variable possibilities expressed by counter-powers that would then be capable of avoiding the dialectic of the antagonism between powers that tend towards equivalence.[5] This would thus open up new, constituent dimensions in terms of spatial, temporal, perceptive, cooperative, normative and value-based aspects.

Some twenty years have already gone by since squatters first made their appearance in the public sphere. From squatters to *okupas* to *centros sociales okupados*, there has undeniably been progress, evolution; but the experience hasn't emerged from its neoteny stage, so to speak. There are obviously numerous reasons for this, and they may be complex enough to deserve to be fully dealt with in this dossier. In any case, this complexity should not be simplified by labeling the factors that delay its growth as 'negative', and those that implement the model without further critical consideration of its present condition as 'positive'. The problem-factor of the (politics of) identity that has characterized the social center form, with its disturbing ambivalence, is proof of this: because identity politics can be blamed for many 'evils' and we can claim that this kind of politics has considerably contributed to the underdevelopment of the experiences and to the same errors being repeated; but if we don't take into account this aspect of identity (politics), it is difficult to explain why the great majority of relevant experiences arose in the first place and persist.

Metropolis and Identity

From the point of view of the production of subjectivity, the act of disobedience and direct re-appropriation of wealth ('fixed assets' – buildings, infrastructures, etc.) is and will probably remain fundamental in the evolution of the social center form (and of other things). We should keep this in mind when we confront a relatively recent issue that is generating endless tense disputes in the heart of the social movements: the negotiation of spaces – whether we're talking about negotiating the ongoing occupation of squatted social centers through dialogue, or about approaching public bodies for new spaces to be self-managed. Basically, how can disobedience and re-appropriation be reconciled with negotiation? Or, in other words: how is it possible to articulate the conflict/negotiation dialectic? The crucial problem is along these lines, and undoubtedly a substantial source of controversy.

There is a permanent niche of political impulses – which doesn't just affect the younger participants in social centers – that cannot do without a predetermined way of conceiving the act of disobedience and conflict as an element of political subjectivation and identity. The political function of social centers and identity, militancy and identity, and metropolitan commons and identity thus emerge as some of the permanent problematic nodes that end up deciding whether the experience is to make progress or be annulled. That is, what's at stake here is the possibility of producing a new type of institutionality of movement that can profit from the experience gained over two decades of social centers in Europe. In this sense, the last thing we need is a new 'argument' or a new 'program'. What we need is to explicitly question the way in which we confront the 'singularization' of collective existence in the productive, cooperative and relational medium of the metropolis; a singularization that always entails – that 'normally' implies – complex processes of difference/identity. If we think there is a need to re-start a cycle of creative experimentation in relation to the social center form, it is not because of a fetishistic attachment to novelty, but precisely because the forms of singularization that we experience in our bodies and in our own lives are currently going through a phase of transformation in our cities, and inevitably require us to respond through the practice of risk-taking forms of political re-composition.

One's 'immersion' in the metropolis of total mobilization can't be simply a willing act. The development of aspects of political entrepreneurship – as foreshadowed in the social centers' production of services, aspects that are bio(syndicalist) and cooperative, based on public self-education projects and so on (López, Martínez and Toret, 2008) – requires that we confront the dead-end streets of endemic, self-marginalized political experiences in the city. But it also implies the need to clarify what we could call the supplements of subjectivation that allow languages, value universes and collective territories to be re-founded as part of a device that can continue to be subversive, particularly on the level of forms of life. This means no longer aspiring to be subversive simply in terms of a dialectic of molar confrontation between subjects that are always pre-formed, channeling us towards a binary dynamic in the face of forces that have already been counted, with results that are already taken for granted.

Governance as an Adversary

Social centers' geometry of hostility in the productive metropolis becomes fixed in accordance with the establishment of government figures that try and combine the power of centralized command with social diffusion of (metropolitan and transnational) powers. The multicentric scheme of capitalist powers demonstrates the crisis of party-like, representative forms of integration. Governance has become its transitional mode:

> Thus when we speak about metropolitan governance we are alluding to a set of public practices that represent, in the face of the harmonization of irreducible and heterogeneous interests, the response to the inability of deriving decisions from an initial process of institutional legitimization. The weakening of traditional mechanisms of social regulation and the channeling of interests has in fact rendered subjectivities impervious to the practice of government. Governance, in a certain sense, constitutes the struggle to continually produce, through variable and flexible structures, subjectivities that are consonant with the 'administrationalization' of life, where the boundaries between public and private become transient and elusive. (Atelier Occupato ESC, 2008)

Governance is the device that opposes social centers, the counterpart with productions of consensus, obedience and exclusion that have to be dismantled, destabilized and sabotaged. The main objective of metropolitan governance consists of making the shared conditions of life productive in accordance with the concept of the city-company; it consists of organizing the total mobilization of its inhabitants and of linguistic, emotional and financial flows in political and institutional terms – a total mobilization that neutralizes the political and existential valences that emerge from cooperation and from communal metropolitan life; it consists of producing a 'government of difference' based on a constant inflation of statutes, segmentations, regulations and restrictions that allow the subordinate groups to be ordered hierarchically, isolated and divided. Social centers are one of the crucial operators of practical criticism of metropolitan governance (and are destined to become even more intensely so). The fight of the social centers against governance takes place in the field of practices of de-individualization; in the re-appropriation of spaces that can then be used to configure political situations that transform the conflict arising from placing a heterogeneous mix of population singularities up against the devices of urban income into a new motor for urban dynamics; in the production of new service relationships, such as those that try out a re-appropriation of the relationships involved in care provision, which can de-privatize and de-nationalize the processes of reproduction and valorization of life that remain confiscated by metropolitan biopower institutions; and in experimentation with ways of practicing and experiencing the time of the metropolis in the face of the total mobilization of frightened, anxious individuals.

Education, Self-education and Research in Monster Institutions

Ultimately, the medley of experiences that this dossier deals with reveals unequivocal traces of the monster institutions that are necessary today in order to bring about the inevitability of new manifestations of the 'frustrated virtualities' resulting from the long and unfinished sequence that followed the existential revolution of 1968: this takes us back to the beginning and closes a circular argument that considers present emergences by making the most of the virtualities of the immediate revolutionary past. Needless to say, the case studies shown here aren't exhaustive and don't inflate these virtualities. The Universidad Nómada is interested in tackling the possibility of constructing these new mental prototypes linked to the desired monstrosity, to the need to think and do another, different kind of politics based on education, self-education and research. We believe there are four basic circuits to be implemented, as follows:

(a) *A circuit of educational projects*, to be developed in order to allow the circulation of theoretical paradigms and intellectual tools suitable for producing these cognitive maps that can be used to (1) intervene in the public sphere by creating swarming points of reference and producing counter-hegemonic discourses; and, in addition, to (2) analyze existing power structures and dynamics, as well as potentials;

(b) *A circuit of co-research projects*, to be organized for the systematic study of social, economic, political and cultural life for the purpose of producing dynamic maps of social structures and dynamics that can be useful for guiding antagonist practices, redefining existing conflicts and struggles, and producing new forms of expression endowed with a new principle of social and epistemological intelligibility (Malo de Malina, 2004);

(c) *A publishing and media circuit*, to be designed with the aim of influencing the public sphere, areas of intellectual production and university teaching, for the purpose of creating intellectual-analytic laboratories and, consequently, new segments of reference and criticism of hegemonic forms of knowledge and ways of conceptualizing the social situation;

(d) *A circuit of foundations, institutes and research centers*, to be devised as an autonomous infrastructure for the production of knowledge, which would constitute an embryonic stage for forms of political organization by means of the accumulation of analysis and specific proposals. Its activities should link the analysis of regional and European conditions with the global structural dynamics of the accumulation of capital and of the recreation of the global geo-strategic options that are favorable to the social movements.

In some cases, the devices that make these tasks possible are already operating, and their manifestations can be found or intuited here and there, peppering the texts in the monograph we are extending with this short introduction. To finish off: we are talking about devices that are necessarily hybrid and monstrous:

hybrid, because right from the start they make it necessary to create networks out of resources and initiatives that are very different and contradictory in nature, that appear strange and even seemingly incongruent among themselves; these resources and initiatives mix together public and private resources, institutional relations with relations of movement, non-institutional and informal models for action with forms of representation that may be formal and representative, and struggles and forms of social existence that some would accuse of being non-political or contaminated or useless or absurd but take on a strategic aspect because they directly give a political and subjectivity-producing dimension to processes of allocation of resources and logistical elements that end up being crucial for bursting onto nationalized and/or privatized public spheres and transforming them;

monstrous, because they initially appear to be pre-political or simply non-political in form, but their acceleration and accumulation as described above must generate a density and a series of possibilities for intellectual creativity and collective political action that will contribute to inventing another politics;

another politics, that is, another way of translating the power of productive subjects into new forms of political behavior and, ultimately, into original paradigms for the organization of social life, for the dynamic structuring of the potential of that which is public and communal.

Notes

1. The original document (in Spanish) presenting the Universidad Nómada is online at: http://www.universidadnomada.net/spip.php?article139. And Raúl Sánchez Cedillo's essay in this volume has become something of a summary for the new phase of the Universidad Nómada.

2. Along these lines, see also Raunig (2008).

3. This is also what Paolo Virno (2004b) seems to be saying, using an accurate image, when he states that in recent years the global movement was like a huge battery that had been charged in a short, vertiginous process, but couldn't find where to connect itself and discharge its power, and that it specifically couldn't manage to connect with "those forms of struggle that are necessary in order to transform the situation of precarious, temporary and atypical work into political assets". In any case, in these notes for (self-)critical reflection, we continue to declare that the configuration process of the global movement already constitutes the inalienable genetic code of the cycle of struggles that is currently in course.

4. How can we avoid mentioning the centrality of 'the university' in the 1968 world revolution, how students discerned the paradox of an institution that is in crisis in terms of its historic model, but meanwhile plays an increasingly central role in capitalist modes of production and valorisation? See, among many other recent reflections, Roggero (2007) and Atelier Occupato ESC (2008). See also two Universidad Nómada texts by Montserrat Galcerán, '¿Tiene la universidad interés para el capital?' ('Are universities already of interest to capital?') (http://www.universidadnomada.net/spip.php?article242) and 'La crisis de la universidad' ('The crisis of the university') (http://www. universidadnomada.net/spip.php?article184), both n/d.

5. Thus the type of asymmetry between powers and counter-powers that characterizes the movements in the new cycle of struggles that we've called 'another geometry of hostility'. See Fernández-Savater (2006).

Bibliography

Adorno, T.W. (1975) *Negative Dialektik*. Frankfurt/Main: Suhrkamp.

Adorno, T.W. (1992) 'Commitment', in *Notes to Literature*, vol. 2, trans. S. Weber Nicholsen. New York: Columbia University Press.

Adorno, T.W.(1997) *Aesthetic Theory*, trans. R. Hullot-Kentor. Minneapolis: University of Minnesota.

Agamben, G. (1999) *Remnants of Auschwitz: The Witness and the Archive*, trans. Daniel Heller-Roazen. New York: Zone Books.

Agamben, G. (2005) *State of Exception*. Chicago: University of Chicago Press.

Anderson, B. (1983) *Imagined Communities*. London: Verso.

Appadurai, A. (2001) 'Grassroots globalization and the research imagination', in A. Appadurai (ed.), *Globalization*. Durham: Duke University Press.

Araeen, R. (1997) ,Westliche Kunst kontra Dritte Welt', in P. Weibel (ed.) *Inklusion: Exklusion. Versuch einer Kartografie der Kunst im Zeitalter von Postkolonialismus und globaler Migration*. Köln: DuMont.

Arendt, H. (1990) *On Revolution*. London: Penguin.

Atelier Occupato ESC (2008) 'The metropolis and the so-called crisis of politics: the experience of Esc', trans. N. Dines, *transversal*, online at: http://transform.eipcp.net/transversal/0508/esc/en.

Bataille, G. (1971) 'Musée', in *Oeuvres Complètes*, vol. 1. Paris: Gallimard.

Benjamin, W. (1969) *Illuminations: Essays and Reflections*, trans. H. Zohn. New York: Schocken.

Benjamin, W. (1978) *Reflections: Essays, Aphorisms, Autobiographical Writings*, trans. E. Jephcott. New York: Schocken.

Bennett, T. (1995) *The Birth of the Museum: History, Theory, Politics*. New York: Routledge.

Bhabha, H.K. (1992) 'A good judge of character: men, metaphors and the common culture', in T. Morrison (ed.) *Race-ing Justice, En-gendering Power: Essays on Anita Hill, Clarence Thomas, and the Construction of Social Reality*. New York: Pantheon.

Bismarck, B. (2006) 'Freedom I have none: Martha Rosler in der Galerie Christian Nagel', *Texte zur Kunst*, 62(June): 239-241.

Blanchot, M. (1969) *L'entretien infini*. Paris: Gallimard.

Böhmler, D. and P. Scheiffele (2005) 'Überlebenskunst in einer Kultur der Selbstverwertung', in F. Schultheis and C. Schulz (eds) *Gesellschaft mit beschränkter Haftung: Zumutungen und Leiden im deutschen Alltag*. Konstanz: UVK.

Boltanski, L. and E. Chiapello (2005a) *The New Spirit of Capitalism*, trans. G. Elliott. London: Verso.

Boltanski, L. and E. Chiapello (2005b) 'The Role of criticism in the dynamics of capitalism: Social critique vs. artistic critique', in M. Miller (ed.) *Worlds of Capitalism: Institutions, Governance, and Economic Change in the Era of Globalization*. London, New York.

Bosma, J. et al. (1999) *Readme! Filtered by Nettime: ASCII Culture and the Revenge of Knowledge*. New York: Autonomedia.

Bourdieu, P. (1993) *The Field of Cultural Production: Essays on Art and Literature*, trans. R. Johnson. Cambridge: Polity Press.

Bourdieu, P. (1996) *The Rules of Art: Genesis and Structure of the Literary Field*, trans. S. Emmanuel. Stanford: Stanford University Press.

Bourdieu, P. (2003) 'Einführung in die Soziologie des Kunstwerks', in J. Jurt (ed.) *Pierre Bourdieu*. Freiburg: Orange Press.

Brecht, B. (2001) *The Measures Taken and Other Lehrstücke*, trans. R. Mannheim et al. New York: Arcade.

Bröckling, U., S. Krasmann and T. Lemke (eds) (2000) *Gouvernementalität der Gegenwart: Studien zur Ökonomisierung des Sozialen*. Frankfurt/Main: Suhrkamp.

Broodthaers, M. (1987) 'To be bien pensant... or not to be. To be blind', trans. Paul Schmidt, *October*, 42(Fall): 35.

Bruckner, F. (1990) *Dramen*. Vienna and Cologne: Böhlau.

Bryan-Wilson, J. (2003) 'A curriculum of institutional critique', in J. Ekeberg (ed.) *New Institutionalism*. Oslo: OCA/verksted.

Buchloh, B. (1990) 'Conceptual art, 1962-1969: from the aesthetics of administration to the critique of institutions', *October*, 55(Winter): 60-82.

Buchmann, S. (2006) 'Kritik der Institution und/oder Institutionskritik? (Neu-)Betrachtung eines historischen Dilemmas', in *Bildpunkt: Zeitschrift der IG Bildende Kunst* (Autumn): 22-23.

Bürger, P. (1984) *Theory of the Avant-Garde*, trans. Michael Shaw. Minneapolis: University of Minnesota Press.

Butler, J. (2002) 'What is critique?' in D. Ingram (ed.) *The Political: Readings in Continental Philosophy*. London: Basil Blackwell, and online at http://eipcp.net/transversal/0806/butler/en.

Carmona, P. et al. (2008) 'Social centres: monsters and political machines for a new generation of movement institutions', *transversal*, online at: http://transform.eipcp.net/transversal/0508/carmonaetal/en.

Castel, R. (2005) *Die Stärkung des Sozialen: Leben im neuen Wohlfahrtsstaat*. Hamburg: Hamburger Edition.

Cixous, H. (1981) 'The laugh of the Medusa', in E. Marks and I. de Courtivron (eds) *New French Feminisms: An Anthology*. New York: Schocken.

Cohn, N. (1970) *The Pursuit of the Millennium*. Oxford: Oxford University Press.

Colectivo Situaciones (2003) *¡Que se vayan todos! Krise und Widerstand in Argentinien*. Berlin: Assoziation A.

Crimp, D. (1993) *On the Musuem's Ruins*. Cambridge, Massachusetts: MIT Press.

Dany, H-C. (1996) 'Was Park alles sein könnte: Ein Gespräch mit Christoph Schäfer und Cathy Skene', *Kritik*, 2(Dezember): 56.

De Martino, E. (1977) *La fine del mondo: Contributo all'analisi delle apocalissi culturali*. Turin: Einaudi.

Debord, G. (1994) *The Society of the Spectacle*, trans. D. Nicholson-Smith. New York: Zone.

Deleuze, G. (1988) *Foucault*, trans. S. Hand. Minneapolis: University of Minnesota.

Deleuze, G. (1992) 'Postscript on the societies of control', *October*, 59(Winter): 3-7.

Deleuze, G. (2004a) *Desert Islands and Other Texts, 1953-1974*, trans. M. Taormina. Los Angeles: Semiotext(e).

Deleuze, G. (2004b) *Difference and Repetition*, trans. P. Patton. London: Continuum.

Deleuze, G. and C. Parnet (2002) *Dialogues*, trans. H. Tomlinson and B. Habberjam. New York: Columbia University.

Deleuze, G. and F. Guattari (1984) 'May 68 did not take place', online at http://illogicaloperation.com/textz/deleuze_gilles_guattari_felix_may_68.htm.

Deleuze, G. and F. Guattari (1987) *A Thousand Plateaus: Capitalism and Schizophrenia*, trans. B. Massumi. Minneapolis: University of Minnesota Press.

Demirovic, A. (1997) *Demokratie und Herrschaft: Aspekte kritischer Gesellschaftstheorie*. Münster: Westfälisches Dampfboot.

Dinzelbacher, P. (1993) *Mittelalterliche Frauenmystik*. Paderborn: Schöningh.

Dinzelbacher, P. (1998) 'Die christliche Mystik und die Frauen: Zur Einführung', in W. Beutin and T. Bütow (eds.) *Europäische Mystik vom Hochmittelalter zum Barock: Eine Schlüsselepoche in der europäischen Mentalitäts-, Spiritualitäts- und Individuationsentwicklung*. Frankfurt/Main and Berlin: Peter Lang.

Duncan, C. (1995) *Civilizing Rituals: Inside Public Art Museums*. New York : Routledge.

Ekeberg, J. (ed.) (2003) *New Institutionalism*. Oslo: Office for Contemporary Art.

Enzensberger, U. (2004) 'Warum brennst du, Konsument?' in *Die Tageszeitung*, Berlin, 29 April, online at http://www.taz.de/pt/2004/09/25/a0315.1/text (21.07.2006).

Fernández-Savater, A. et al. (2006) 'Ingredientes de una onda global', *Desacuerdos* 2. Barcelona: Macbe, Unia and Arteleku.

Fiori, R. (1996) *Homo sacer: Dinamica politico-constituzionale di una sanzione giuridico-religiosa*. Napoli: Jovene Editore.

Foltin, R. (2004) *Und Wir Bewegen Uns Doch: Soziale Bewegungen in Österreich*. Vienna: Edition Grundrisse.

Foster, H., R. Krauss, B. Buchloh and Y-A. Bois (2004) *Art Since 1900: Modernism, Antimodernism, Postmodernism*. New York: Thames & Hudson.

Foucault, M. (1979) *Discipline and Punish: The Birth of the Prison*, trans. A. Sheridan. New York: Random House.

Foucault, M. (1980) *The History of Sexuality I: An Introduction*, trans. R. Hurley. New York: Vintage.

Foucault, M. (1985) *The Use of Pleasure*, trans. R. Hurley. New York: Vintage.

Foucault, M. (1991) 'Governmentality', in G. Burchell et al. (eds) *The Foucault Effect: Studies in Governmentality*. Chicago.

Foucault, M. (1997a) *The Politics of Truth,* ed. S. Lotringer and L. Hochroch. New York: Semiotext(e).

Foucault, M. (1997b) *Diskurs und Wahrheit*, trans. M. Köller. Berlin: Merve (1996), and online at http://foucault.info/documents/parrhesia/.

Foucault, M. (1999) *In Verteidigung der Gesellschaft: Vorlesungen am Collège de France (1975-76)*, trans. M. Ott. Frankfurt/Main: Suhrkamp.

Foucault, M. (2000) *Power*, ed. J. Faubion, trans. R. Hurley et al. New York: The New Press.

Foucault, M. (2003) *Dits et Ecrits: Schriften in vier Bänden*, vol. 3. Frankfurt/Main.

Foucault, M. (2004a) *Geschichte der Gouvernementalität I. Sicherheit, Territorium, Bevölkerung: Vorlesungen am Collège de France 1977-78*, trans. C. Brede-Konersmann and J. Schröder. Frankfurt/Main: Suhrkamp.

Foucault, M. (2004b) *Geschichte der Gouvernementalität II. Die Geburt der Biopolitik: Vorlesungen am Collège de France 1978-79*, trans. J. Schröder. Frankfurt/Main: Suhrkamp.

Foucault, M. (2005) 'Was ist Aufklärung?' trans. H. Gondek, in *Dits et Ecrits: Schriften in vier Bänden*, vol. 4. Frankfurt am Main.

Fourquet, F. (1981) 'La acumulation du pouvoir ou le désir d'État', online at: http://multitudes.samizdat.net/article2751.html.

Franke, A. (ed.) (2005) *B-Zone: Becoming Europe and Beyond.* Berlin: KW/Actar.

Fraser, A. (1985) 'In and out of place', *Art in America*, 73(6): 122-129.

Fraser, A. (2005) 'From the critique of institutions to an institution of critique', *Artforum*, 44(1): 278-283.

Freud, S. (1960) *Jokes and Their Relation to the Unconscious.* New York: Norton.

Freud, S. (2000) ,Vorlesungen zur Einführung in die Psychoanalyse', *Freud Studienausgabe*, Band 1. Frankfurt/Main: Fischer Verlag.

Fukuyama, F (1992) *The End of History and the Last Man.* New York: Avon Books.

Gallese, V. (2003) 'Neuroscienza delle relazioni sociali', in F. Ferretti (ed.) *La mente degli altri: Prospettive teoriche sull'autismo.* Rome: Editori Riuniti.

Gehlen, A. (1985) *L'uomo: La sua natura e il suo posto nel mondo.* Milan: Feltrinelli.

Gilcher-Holtey, I. (2003) *Die 68er Bewegung: Deutschland – Westeuropa – USA.* Munich: C.H. Beck.

Gnädinger, L. (1987) 'Margareta Porete, eine Begine', in M. Porete *Der Spiegel der einfachen Seelen*, trans. L. Gnädinger. Zürich: Artemis.

Godfrey, T. (2005) *Konzeptuelle Kunst.* Berlin: Phaidon.

Graw, I. (2005) 'Jenseits der Institutionskritik: ein Vortrag im Los Angeles County Museum of Art', *Texte zur Kunst*, 59(September): 40-53.

Gross, K. (1992) *The Dream of the Moving Statue.* Ithaca: Cornell University Press.

Guattari, F. (1964) 'La transversalidad', in *Psicoanálisis y transversalidad*, XXI. Buenos Aires.

Guattari, F. (1995) *Chaosmosis: An Ethico-Aesthetic Paradigm*, trans. J. Pefanis. Indianapolis: Indiana University Press.

Guattari, F. (2003) *Psychanalyse et transversalité: Essais d'analyse institutionnelle.* Paris: La Découverte.

Gürses, H. (2006) 'On the topography of critique', online at http://eipcp.net/transversal/0806/guerses/en.

Hall, S. (1997) 'The spectacle on the 'other'', in S. Hall (ed.) *Representation: Cultural Representations and Signifying Practices*. London: Sage.

Hamacher, W. (1994) 'Afformativ, Streik', in C. Hart Nibbrig (ed.) *Was heißt 'Darstellen'?* Frankfurt/Main: Suhrkamp.

Hardt, M. and A. Negri (2000) *Empire*. Cambridge, MA: Harvard University Press.

Hierlmeier, J. (2002) *Internationalismus: Eine Einführung in die Ideengeschichte des Internationalismus von Vietnam bis Genua*. Stuttgart: Schmetterling Verlag.

Höller, C. (2006) 'Tun, Sein, Sehen, Sagen: Über drei Neuerscheinungen von Jacques Rancière', *Texte zur Kunst*, 63(September): 180-183.

Holmes, B. (2001) 'L'extradisciplinaire', in H-U. Obrist and L. Bossé (eds) *Traversées*. Paris : Musée d'art moderne de la Ville de Paris.

Horkheimer, M. and T.W. Adorno (2002) *Dialectic of Enlightenment: Philosophical Fragments*, trans. E. Jephcott. Stanford: Stanford University Press.

Howard, K. (ed.) (1994) *The Metropolitan Museum of Art Guide*. New York: Metropolitan Musuem of Art.

Jacobs, R. (1997) *Which Way the Wind Blew: A Biography of the Weather Underground*. London: Verso.

Jantzen, G. (2001) 'Disrupting the sacred: religion and gender in the city', in J. Ruffing (ed.) *Mysticism & Social Transformation*. Syracuse: Syracuse University Press.

Kaller-Dietrich, M. and D. Mayer (undated) *Geschichte Lateinamerikas im 19. und 20. Jahrhundert: Ein historischer Überblick*, online at http://www.lateinamerika-studien.at/content/geschichtepolitik/geschichte/geschichte-titel.html.

Kant, I. (2000) *Political Writings*, trans. H.B. Nisbet. Cambridge: Cambridge University Press.

Kant, I. (n.d.) *Handschriftlicher Nachlaß*, Logik/, Refl. 2665. Akademie-Ausgabe, Vol. 16, 459, http://www.ikp.uni-bonn.de/kant/aa16/459.html

Kleines Postfordistisches Drama/kpD (2005a) 'Prekäre Subjektivierung: Interview', *Malmoe*, 7: 20.

Kleines Postfordistisches Drama/kpD (2005b) 'Prekarisierung von KulturproduzentInnen und das ausbleibende 'gute Leben'', *arranca!*, 32(Summer): 23-25.

Kofman, S. (1987) *Paroles suffoquées*. Paris: Galilée.

Kolbowski, S. (2005) 'Diary of a Buren spectator', *Texte zur Kunst*, 59(September): 138-143.

Kosseleck, R. (1976) *Kritik und Krise*. Frankfurt/Main: Suhrkamp.

Kress, S. (1991) *Bird Life: A Guide to the Behavior and Biology of Birds*. New York: St. Martin's Press.

Kurnik, A. and B. Beznec (2008) 'Rog: struggle in the City', *transversal*, online at: *http*://transform.eipcp.net/transversal/0508/kurnikbeznec/en.

Kuster, B. (2006) 'Die eigenwillige Freiwilligkeit der Prekarisierung', *Grundrisse, Zeitschrift für linke Theorie & Debatte*, 18: 12-15.

Lacan, J. (1978) *Écrits*, trans. A. Sheridan. New York: Norton.

Latour, B. and P. Weibel (eds) (2005) *Making Things Public: Atmospheres of Democracy*. Karlsruhe: ZKM.

Lawler, L. (2000) *An Arrangement of Pictures*. New York: Assouline.

Lazzarato, M. (2006a) 'The machine', online at: http://eipcp.net/transversal/1106/lazzarato/en.

Lazzarato, M. (2006b) *Por una política menor*. Madrid: Traficantes de Sueños.

Leicht, I. (1999) *Marguerite Porete – eine fromme Intellektuelle und die Inquisition*. Freiburg: Herder.

Lemke, T. (2004) 'Räume der Regierung: Kunst und Kritik der Menschenführung', in P. Gente (ed.) *Foucault und die Künste*. Frankfurt/Main: Suhrkamp.

Lemke, T., S. Krasmann and U. Bröckling (2000) 'Gouvernementalität, Neoliberalismus und Selbsttechnologien', in U. Bröckling, S. Krasmann and T. Lemke (eds) *Gouvernementalität der Gegenwart: Studien zur Ökonomisierung des Sozialen*. Frankfurt/Main: Suhrkamp.

Linker, K. (1986) 'Rites of exchange', *Artforum*, 25(November): 99-100.

Locke, J. (1823) *Two Treatises of Government*, from *The Works of John Locke. A New Edition*, vol. 5. London, online at

http://socserv2.mcmaster.ca/~econ/ugcm/3ll3/locke/government
.pdf.

López, S., X. Martínez and J. Toret (2008) 'Las Oficinas de Derechos
Sociales: Experiences of Political Enunciation and Organisation in
Times of Precarity', *transversal*, online at:
http://transform.eipcp.net/transversal/0508/lopezetal/en.

Lorenz, K. (2005) *L'aggressività*. Milan: il Saggiatore.

Lorey, I. (2006a) 'Als das Leben in die Politik eintrat. Die biopolitisch
gouvernementale Moderne, Foucault und Agamben', in M. Pieper et
al. (eds) *Empire und die biopolitische Wende*. Frankfurt/Main: Campus.

Lorey, I. (2006b) 'Der weiße Körper als feministischer Fetisch:
Konsequenzen aus der Ausblendung des deutschen Kolonialismus',
in M. Tißberger et al. (eds) *Weiß, Weißsein, Whiteness: Critical Studies on
Gender an Racism*. Frankfurt/Main: Peter Lang.

Lorey, I. (2007) 'The dream of the governable city: on plague, policey
and raison d'état', *transversal*, online at:
http://eipcp.net/transversal/1007/lorey/en

Macpherson, C. (1962) *Political Theory of Possessive Individualism: Hobbes to
Locke*. Oxford: Oxford University Press.

Malo de Molina, M. (2004) 'Nociones comunes', in *Nociones comunes:
Experiencias y ensayos entre investigación y militancia*. Madrid: Traficantes
de Sueños.

Marcuse, H. (1968) *Negations: Essays in Critical Theory*, trans. J. Shapiro.
Boston: Beacon Press.

Marler, P. and C. Evans (1995) 'Birdcalls: just emotional displays or
something more?' *Ibis*, 138(1): 26-33.

Marx, K. (1975) *Early Writings*, trans. R. Livingstone and G. Benton.
New York: Vintage.

Marx, K. (1999) *A Contribution to the Critique of Political Economy*, online at
http://www.marxists.org/archive/marx/works/1859/critique-pol-
economy/index.htm.

Marx, K. and F. Engels (1998) *The Communist Manifesto: A Modern
Edition*. London: Verso.

McRobbie, A. (2001): "Everyone is creative': artists as new economy
pioneers?' online at
http://www.opendemocracy.net/arts/article_652.jsp (10/18/2005).

Mecheril, P. (2003) *Prekäre Verhältnisse: Über natio-ethno-kulturelle Mehrfachzugehörigkeit.* Münster: Waxmann.

Merleau-Ponty, M. (2003) *L'institution, La passivité: Notes de cours au Collège de France* (1954/55). Paris: Belin.

Metz, C. (1999) 'Photography and fetish', in C. Squiers (ed.) *Overexposed: Essays on Contemporary Photography.* New York: New Press.

Meyer, J. (1993) 'Whatever happened to institutional critique?' in P. Weibel (ed.) *Kontext Kunst.* Köln: DuMont.

Mommsen, T. (1971) *Römisches Staatsrecht.* Darmstadt: Wiss. Buchgesellschaft.

Moreno, H. (2005) *Le désastre argentin: Péronisme, politique et violence sociale (1930–2001).* Paris: Editions Syllepse.

Mulvey, L. (1989) *Visual and Other Pleasures.* Indianapolis: Indiana University Press.

Negri, A. (1980) *Politica di classe: Le cinque campagne.* Milan: Macchina Libri Edizioni.

Negri, A. (1999) *Insurgencies: Constituent Power and the Modern State.* Minneapolis: University of Minnesota Press.

Negri, A. (2003) 'Constituent Republic', in W. Bonefeld (ed.) *Revolutionary Writing: Common Sense Essays in Post-Political Politics.* New York: Autonomedia.

Negri, A. (2007) 'Critique of the italian edition of the book *19 and 20. Notes for the new social protagonism* by Colectivo Situaciones', online at: www.generation-online.org/t/sitcol.htm

Negri, A., M. Lazzarato and P. Virno (1998) *Umherschweifende Produzenten: Immaterielle Arbeit und Subversion.* Berlin: ID.

Nixon, M. (2005) *Fantastic Reality: Louise Bourgeois and a Story of Modern Art.* Cambridge, Massachusetts: MIT Press.

Nochlin, L. (1971) 'Why have there been no great women artists?' *Art News,* 69(January).

Nottebohn, F. (2005) 'Hitting the right note', *Nature,* 435(May)- 146.

Nowotny, S. (2003a) ''Kultur' und Machtanalyse', in S. Nowotny and M. Staudigl (eds) *Grenzen des Kulturkonzepts: Meta-Genealogien.* Vienna: Turia + Kant.

Nowotny, S. (2003b) 'The condition of becoming public', *transversal*, online at: http://eipcp.net/transversal/1203/nowotny/en

Nowotny, S. (2005) 'Polizierte Betrachtung: Zur Funktion und Funktionsgeschichte von Ausstellungstexten', in B. Jaschke, C. Martinz-Turek and N. Sternfeld (eds) *Wer spricht? Authorität und Authorschaft in Ausstellungen*. Vienna: Turia + Kant.

O'Doherty, B. (1986) *Inside the White Cube: The Ideology of the Gallery Space*. Berkeley: University of California Press.

Ott, C. (1997) 'Lust, Geschlecht und Generativität: Zum Zusammenhang von gesellschaftlicher Organisation von Sexualität und Geschlechterhierarchie', in I. Dölling and B. Krais (eds) *Ein alltägliches Spiel: Geschlechterkonstruktionen in der sozialen Praxis*. Frankfurt/Main: Suhrkamp.

Panagiotidis, E. (2005) 'DenkerInnenzelle X: Prekarisierung, Mobilität, Exodus', *arranca!*, 32(Summer): 12-14.

Panagiotidis, E. and V. Tsianos (2004) 'Reflexive Prekarisierung: Eine Introspektion aus dem Alltag von Projektlinken', *Fantômas*, 6(Winter): 18-19.

Pechriggl, A. (2007) 'Destituting, instituting, constituting… and the De/Formative Power of Affective Investment', *transversal*, online at: http://eipcp.net/transversal/0507/pechriggl/en.

Pelzer, B. (2004) 'Interpositions: the work of Louise Lawler', in *Louise Lawler and Others*. Basel: Hatje Cantz and Kunstmuseum Basel.

Pieper, M. and E. Gutiérrez Rodríguez(eds) (2003) *Gouvernementalität: Ein sozialwissenschaftliches Konzept im Anschluss an Foucault*. Frankfurt/Main: Campus.

Piper, A. (2001) 'Power relations within existing art institutions', in C. Kravagna, Kunsthaus Bregenz (eds) *The Museum as Arena: Artists on Institutional Critique*. Cologne: König.

Pühl, K. (2003) 'Der Bericht der Hartz-Kommission und die 'Unternehmerin ihrer selbst': Geschlechterverhältnisse, Gouvernementalität und Neoliberalismus', in M. Pieper and E. Gutiérrez Rodríguez (eds) *Gouvernementalität. Ein sozialwissenschaftliches Konzept im Anschluss an Foucault*. Frankfurt/Main: Campus.

Querrien, A. (2002) *Cerfi, 1965-1987*. Online at: http://www.criticalsecret.com.

Rambach, A. and M. Rambach (2001) *Les intellos précaires*. Paris.

Rancière, J. (2000) 'Konsens, Dissens, Gewalt', in M. Dabag, A. Kapust and B. Waldenfels (eds) *Gewalt: Strukturen, Formen, Repräsentationen*. Munich: Fink.

Rancière, J. (2002) *Das Unvernehmen: Politik und Philosophie*. Frankfurt/Main: Suhrkamp.

Rancière, J. (2006) 'Die Politik der Kunst und ihre Paradoxien', in Rancière, J., *Die Aufteilung des Sinnlichen: Die Politik der Kunst und ihre Paradoxien*, ed. Maria Muhle. Berlin: b_books/Polypen.

Rancière, J. (2006) *The Politics of Aesthetics: The Distribution of the Sensible*, trans. G. Rockhill. New York: Continuum.

Rancière, J. (2007) 'Entsorgung der Demokratie', *springerin*, 3.

Raunig, G. (2004) 'The double criticism of *parrhesia*: answering the question 'What is a progressive (art) institution?'', *transversal*, online at http://eipcp.net/transversal/0504/raunig/en.

Raunig, G. (2005) 'Ein Bolivarianischer Prozess für Europa!' online at: http://eipcp.net/policies/dpie/raunig1/de.

Raunig, G. (2007) *Art and Revolution: Transversal Activism in the Long Twentieth Century*, trans. Aileen Derieg. Los Angeles: Semiotext(e).

Raunig, G. (2008) 'On the breach', online at: ttp://transform.eipcp.net/correspondence/1209407525.

Roggero, G. (2007) 'The autonomy of the living knowledge in the metropolis-university', *transversal*, online at: http://transform.eipcp.net/transversal/0707/roggero/en.

Rosler, M. (1999) 'Drinnen, Drumherum und nachträgliche Gedanken (zur Dokumentarfotografie)', in S. Breitwieser (ed.) *Martha Rosler: Positionen in der Lebenswelt*. Vienna: Generali Foundation.

Rossiter, N. (2006) *Organized Networks: Media Theory, Creative Labour, New Institutions*. Rotterdam.

Rossiter, N. (2007) 'Can Organized Networks Make Money for Designers?' online at http://summit.kein.org/node/309.

Rousseau, J.J. (1966) *Émile, ou de l'éducation*, ed. M. Launay. Paris: Garnier Flammarion.

Salvini, F. (2008) 'The moons of Jupiter: networked institutions in the productive transformations of Europe', *transversal*, online at: http://transform.eipcp.net/transversal/0508/salvini/en.

Sarasin, P. (2001) *Reizbare Maschinen. Eine Geschichte des Körpers 1765-1914*. Frankfurt/Main: Suhrkamp.

Saussure, F. (2002) *Cours de linguistique générale*. Paris: Gallimard.

Schäfer, C. (2001) 'Der Garten des bescheidenen Politikers', in *Kulturrisse*, 2: 28-30.

Schmitt, C. (1996) *The Concept of the Political*, trans. G. Schwab. Chicago: University of Chicago Press.

Schor, N. (1987) *Reading in Detail: Aesthetics and the Feminine*. London: Methuen.

Situationist International (1958) 'Definitions', trans. K. Knabb, online at: http://www.cddc.vt.edu/sionline/si/definitions.html.

Situationist International (1960) 'The theory of moments and the construction of situations', trans. P. Hammond, online at: http://www.cddc.vt.edu/sionline/si/moments.html.

Situationist International (2002) 'Editorial notes: the avant-garde of presence', trans. J. Shepley, in T. McDonough (eds.) *Guy Debord and the Situationist International*. Cambridge, Massachusetts: MIT Press.

Smithson, R. (1996) 'Cultural confinement', in *Robert Smithson: The Collected Writings*, ed. J. Flam. Berkeley: University of California Press.

Smithson, R. (2001) 'Cultural confinement', in C. Kravagna and Kunsthaus Bregenz (eds.) *The Museum as Arena: Artists on Institutional Critique*. Cologne: König.

Stirner, M. (1927) *Der Einzige und sein Eigentum*. Leipzig: Zenith.

Stirner, M. (2001) *The Ego and Ist Own*, trans. S. Byington et al., online at: http://www.lsr-projekt.de/poly/enee.html#secondii2.

Stolle, G. (1736) *Anleitung zur Historie der Gelahrtheit, denen zum besten, so den Freyen Künsten und der Philosophie obliegen*. Jena: Meyer.

Ungern-Sternberg, J. (2001) 'Secessio', in H. Cancik (ed.) *Der Neue Pauly: Enzyklopädie der Antike*, vol. 11. Stuttgart: Metzger.

Vaneigem, R. (1993) *La résistance au christianisme: les hérésie des origines au XVIIIe siècle*. Paris: Fayard.

Vercauteren, D. (2007) *Micropolitique des groupes* (in collaboration with T Müller and O. Crabbé). Forcalquier: HB Editions.

Virno, P. (2004a) *A Grammar of the Multitude: For an Analysis of Contemporary Forms of Life*, trans. I. Bertoletti, J. Cascaito and A. Casson. Los Angeles: Semiotext(e).

Virno, P. (2004b) 'Un movimento performativo', *transversal*, online at: http://eipcp.net/transversal/0704/virno/it.

Virno, P. (2005) *Grammatik der Multitude*, trans. Klaus Neundlinger. Vienna: Turia + Kant.

Wallenstein, S. (2006) 'Institutional Desires', in N. Möntmann (ed.) *Art and Its Institutions*. London: Black Dog Publishing.

Walzer, M. (1986) *Exodus and Revolution*. New York: Basic Books.

Weizman, E. (2007) 'Walking through walls', *transversal*, online at http://transform.eipcp.net/transversal/0507.

Wieacker, F. (1988) *Römische Rechtsgeschichte: 1. Absch. Handbuch der Altertumswissenschaft*. Munich: Beck'sche Verlagsbuchhandlung.

Woolf, V. (1938) *Three Guineas*. London: Harcourt.

Zahner, N. (2006) Die neuen Regeln der Kunst: Andy Warhol und der Umbau des Kunstbetriebs im 20. Jahrhundert. Frankfurt/Main: Campus Verlag.

The Transform Project issues of *transversal*

do you remember institutional critique?

01/2006, http://eipcp.net/transversal/0106

brumaria: 'Art. Radical Political Imagination'
Boris Buden: 'Criticism without Crisis: Crisis without Criticism'
Rosalyn Deutsche: 'Louise Lawler's Rude Museum'
Brian Holmes: 'Extradisciplinary Investigations: Towards a New Critique of Institutions'
Jens Kastner: 'Artistic Internationalism and Institutional Critique'
Nina Möntmann: 'The Enterprise of the Art Institution in Late Capitalism'
Stefan Nowotny: 'Anti-Canonization: The Differential Knowledge of Institutional Critique'
Gerald Raunig: 'Instituent Practices: Fleeing, Instituting, Transforming'
Simon Sheikh: 'Notes on Institutional Critique'
Hito Steyerl: 'The Institution of Critique'
Stephen Zepke: 'Towards an Ecology of Institutional Critique'

militant research

04/2006, http://eipcp.net/transversal/0406

Colectivo Situaciones: 'On the Researcher-Militant'
Antonella Corsani: 'Knowledge production and new forms of political action'
Alice Creischer/Andreas Siekmann: 'Steps for Fleeing from Work to Action'
Marcelo Expósito: 'Differences and Antagonims'
Kleines postfordistisches Drama: 'The Precarization of Cultural Producers and the Missing 'Good Life''
Robert Foltin: 'Resistance and Organization in Post-Fordism'
Marta Malo de Molina: 'Common notions, part 1: workers-inquiry, co-research, consciousness-raising'
Antonio Negri: 'Logic and Theory of Inquiry'
Raniero Panzieri: 'Socialist use of workers' inquiry'

Javier Toret / Nicolás Sguiglia: 'Cartography and war machine'

critique

08/2006, http://eipcp.net/transversal/0806

Judith Butler: 'What is Critique? An Essay on Foucault's Virtue'
Alex Demirovic: 'On the Re-Formation of Critical Knowledge'
Marina Garcés: 'To Embody Critique'
Hakan Gürses: 'On the Topography of Critique'
Isabell Lorey: 'Critique and Category: On the limitations of political practice through recent theorems of intersectionality, interdependence and critical whiteness studies'
Artemy Magun: 'Torn between Objectivity and Utopia'
Gene Ray: 'Toward a Critical Art Theory'
David Riff: 'Criticality of Truth'
Irit Rogoff: 'From Criticism to Critique to Criticality / 'Smuggling' - An Embodied Criticality'
Loïc Wacquant: 'Critical Thought as Solvent of Doxa'

machines and subjectivation

11/2006, http://eipcp.net/transversal/1106

Katja Diefenbach: 'The Spectral Form of Value: Ghost-Things and Relations of Forces'
Brian Holmes: 'The Flexible Personality: For a New Cultural Critique'
Maurizio Lazzarato: 'The Machine'
Isabell Lorey: 'Governmentality and Self-Precarization: On the Normalization of Cultural Producers'
Gerald Raunig: 'A Few Fragments on Machines'
Gerald Raunig: 'Bicycles'
Suely Rolnik: 'The Geopolitics of Pimping'
Simon Sheikh: 'Domination, Competition and Exploitation: An Introduction to the Socialization of Capital (and How It Fails Us)'
Vassilis Tsianos/Dimitris Papadopoulos: 'Precarity: A Savage Journey to the Heart of Embodied Capitalism'

creativity hypes

02/2007, http://eipcp.net/transversal/0207

Brigitta Kuster/Vassilis Tsianos: 'Experiences Without Me or the Uncanny Grin of Precarity'
Maurizio Lazzarato: 'The Misfortunes of the 'Artistic Critique' and of Cultural Employment'
Esther Leslie: 'Add Value to Contents: the Valorization of Culture Today'

Isabell Lorey: 'Virtuosos of Freedom: On the implosion of political virtuosity and productive labor'
Angela McRobbie: 'The Los Angelization of London'
Stefan Nowotny: 'Immanent Effects: Notes on Cre-activity'
Marion von Osten: 'Unpredictable Outcomes/Unpredictable Outcasts'
Gerald Raunig: 'Creative Industries as Mass Deception'
Paolo Virno: 'Wit and Innovation'

progressive institutions

04/2007, http://eipcp.net/transversal/0407

Boris Buden: 'What is the eipcp? An Attempt at Interpretation'
Branka Ćurčić: 'Autonomous Spaces of Deregulation and Critique: Is a Cooperation with Neoliberal Art Institutions Possible?'
Marcelo Expósito: 'Inside and Outside the Art Institution: Self-Valorization and Montage in Contemporary Art'
Nina Möntmann: 'The Rise and Fall of New Institutionalism: Perspectives on a Possible Future'
Paolo Virno: 'Anthropology and Theory of Institutions'

extradisciplinaire

05/2007, http://eipcp.net/transversal/0507

Brian Holmes: 'The Speculative Performance: Art's Financial Futures'
Stefan Nowotny: 'The Double Meaning of Destitution'
Alice Pechriggl: 'Destituting, Instituting, Constituting ... and the De/Formative Power of Affective Investment'
Claire Pentecost: 'When Art Becomes Life: Artist-Researchers and Biotechnology'
Gerald Raunig: 'Instituent Practices, No. 2. Institutional Critique, Constituent Power, and the Persistence of Instituting'
Suely Rolnik: 'The Body's Contagious Memory: Lygia Clark's Return to the Museum'
Eyal Weizman: 'Walking Through Walls'

instituent practices

07/2007, http://eipcp.net/transversal/0707

Cátedra experimental sobre producción de subjetividad: 'From Knowledge of Self-Management to the Self-Management of Knowledge'
Aileen Derieg: 'Tech Women Crashing Computers and Preconceptions'
Frank John, Efthimia Panagiotidis, Vassilis Tsianos (PRECLAB Hamburg): 'The Fear at Eleven Meters: On the Attempt to Realize a Different Society'

Jens Kastner: "'... Without Becoming Hypnotized in this Questioning Process': Conceptualizing Autonomy, Localizing Instituting?'
Maurizio Lazzarato: 'The Political Form of Coordination'
Marta Malo de Molina: 'Common Notions, Part 2: Institutional Analysis, Participatory Action-Research, Militant Research'
Rodrigo Nunes: 'Pessimism of the Intellect, Optimism of the General Intellect? Some Remarks on Organisation'
Gerald Raunig: *eventum et medium*: Event and orgiastic representation in media activism'
Gigi Roggero: 'The Autonomy of the Living Knowledge in the Metropolis-University'
Raúl Sánchez Cedillo: 'Towards New Political Creations: Movements, Institutions, New Militancy'

art and police

10/2007, http://eipcp.net/transversal/1007

Franco Berardi aka Bifo: 'Pathologies of Hyper-Expression'
John Jordan: 'Notes Whilst Walking on 'How to Break the Heart of Empire''
Brigitta Kuster: 'Sous les yeux vigilants / Under the Watchful Eyes: On the international colonial exhibition in Paris 1931'
Isabell Lorey: 'The Dream of the Governable City: On Plague, Policey and Raison d'état'
Gerald Raunig: 'Instituting and Distributing: On the Relationship Between Politics and Police Following Rancière as a Development of the Problem of Distribution with Deleuze'
Hito Steyerl: 'The Empire of Senses: Police as art and the crisis of representation'
Tiziana Terranova: 'Failure to comply: Bioart, security and the market'

the post-yugoslavian condition of institutional critique

02/2008, http://eipcp.net/transversal/0208

Damir Arsenijević: 'Against Opportunistic Criticism'
Sezgin Boynik: 'The Principle of Secrecy and the Difficulty of Institutional Critique in Kosovo'
Ljubomir Bratić: 'On the Question of the Transformation of the Elite in Eastern Europe'
Boris Buden: 'The post-Yugoslavian Condition of Institutional Critique: An Introduction. On Critique as Countercultural Translation'
Ana Dević: 'To criticize, charge for services rendered, and be thanked'
Dušan Grlja/Jelena Vesić, Prelom kolektiv: 'The Neoliberal Institution of Culture and the Critique of Culturalization'
Marina Gržinić: 'Euro-Slovenian Necrocapitalism'

Leonardo Kovačević/Vesna Vuković: 'The Landscape of Post-transformation Institutions in Zagreb and their Political Impact'
Suzana Milevska: 'Internalisation of the Discourse of Institutional Critique and its Unhappy Consciousness'
Stevan Vuković: 'Pessimism of the Intellect, Optimism of the Will: Institutional Critique in Serbia and its Lack of Organic References'

monster institutions

05/2008, http://eipcp.net/transversal/0508

Universidad Nómada: 'Mental Prototypes and Monster Institutions: Some Notes by Way of an Introduction'
Atelier Occupato ESC (Rome): 'The Metropolis and the So-Called Crisis of Politics: The Experience of Esc'
Pablo Carmona, Tomás Herreros, Raúl Sánchez Cedillo, Nicolás Sguiglia: 'Social Centres: Monsters and Political Machines for a New Generation of Movement Institutions'
Erika Doucette, Marty Huber: 'Queer-Feminist Occupations'
Andrej Kurnik, Barbara Beznec: Rog: 'Struggle in the City'
Stefen Nowotny, Gerlad Raunig: 'On Police Ghosts and Multidisciplinary Monsters'
Silvia López, Xavier Martínez, Javier Toret: 'Oficinas de Derechos Sociales: Experiences of Political Enunciation and Organisation in Times of Precarity'
Francesco Salvini: 'The Moons of Jupiter: Networked Institutions in the Productive Transformations of Europe'

the art of critique

08/2008, http://eipcp.net/transversal/0808

Alexander Bikbov/Dmitry Vilensky: 'On Practice and Critique'
Alex Demirovic: 'Critique and Truth: For a new mode of critique'
Marina Garcés: 'What Are We Capable Of? From Consciousness to Embodiment in Critical Thought Today'
Hakan Gürses: 'Is an 'atopical critique' possible?'
Maurizio Lazzarato: 'From Knowledge to belief, from Critique to the Production of Subjectivity'
Isabell Lorey: 'Attempt to Think the Plebeian: Exodus and Constituting as Critique'
Chantal Mouffe: 'Critique as Counter-Hegemonic Intervention'
Patricia Purtschert: 'The Refusal to Be Governed Like This: On the relationship between anger and critcism'
Gerald Raunig: 'What is Critique? Suspension and Re-Composition in Textual and Social Machines'

Karl Reitter: 'Critique as a Way of Overcoming Quixotism: On the development of critique in Marx'
Ulf Wuggenig: 'Paradoxical Critique'